Study Guide to Accompany

COST ACCOUNTING

TRADITIONS AND INNOVATIONS
Second Edition

JESSE T. BARFIELD
LOYOLA UNIVERSITY – NEW ORLEANS

CECILY A. RAIBORN
LOYOLA UNIVERSITY – NEW ORLEANS

MICHAEL R. KINNEY
TEXAS A&M UNIVERSITY

PREPARED BY
LOU RAMSAY
CLEMSON UNIVERSITY

WEST PUBLISHING COMPANY
MINNEAPOLIS/ST. PAUL NEW YORK LOS ANGELES SAN FRANCISCO

WEST'S COMMITMENT TO THE ENVIRONMENT

In 1906, West Publishing Company began recycling materials left over from the production of books. This began a tradition of efficient and responsible use of resources. Today, up to 95% of our legal books and 70% of our college texts and school texts are printed on recycled, acid-free stock. West also recycles nearly 22 million pounds of scrap paper annually—the equivalent of 181,717 trees. Since the 1960s, West has devised ways to capture and recycle waste inks, solvents, oils, and vapors created in the printing process. We also recycle plastics of all kinds, wood, glass, corrugated cardboard, and batteries, and have eliminated the use of Styrofoam book packaging. We at West are proud of the longevity and the scope of our commitment to the environment.

Production, Prepress, Printing and Binding by West Publishing Company.

COPYRIGHT © 1994 by WEST PUBLISHING CO.
                                  610 Opperman Drive
                                  P.O. Box 64526
                                  St. Paul, MN 55164–0526

All rights reserved
Printed in the United States of America
01 00 99 98 97 96 95 94   8 7 6 5 4 3 2 1 0

ISBN 0–314–03508–7

TABLE OF CONTENTS

Chapter	Page
CHAPTER 1: Cost and Management Accounting Defined	7
CHAPTER 2: Cost Terminology and Cost Flows	15
CHAPTER 3: Considering Quality in an Organization	27
CHAPTER 4: Developing Predetermined Overhead Rates	35
CHAPTER 5: Activity-Based Cost Systems for Management	47
CHAPTER 6: Additional Overhead Allocation Concepts and Issues	57
CHAPTER 7: Job Order Costing	69
CHAPTER 8: Process Costing: Weighted Average, Fifo and Standard	81
CHAPTER 9: Special Production Issues: Spoiled/Defective Units and Acretion	95
CHAPTER 10: Cost Allocation for Joint Products and By-Products	107
CHAPTER 11: General Concepts of Standard Costing: Material and Labor Standards	117
CHAPTER 12: Standard Costing for Overhead	131
CHAPTER 13: Absorption and Variable Costing	145
CHAPTER 14: Cost-Volume-Profit Analysis	155
CHAPTER 15: Relevant Costing	167
CHAPTER 16: The Master Budget	185
CHAPTER 17: Cost Control for Discretionary Costs	195
CHAPTER 18: Control of Inventory and Production	205
CHAPTER 19: Capital Asset Selection and Capital Budgeting	219
CHAPTER 20: Advanced Capital Bdugeting Techniques	229
CHAPTER 21: Transfer Pricing for Products	241
CHAPTER 22: Measuring Organizational Performance	253
CHAPTER 23: Rewarding Performance	263

CHAPTER 1

THE CONTEMPORARY ENVIRONMENT OF COST AND MANAGEMENT ACCOUNTING

CHAPTER OVERVIEW

The business environment has changed from the development of a global economy. U.S. firms must compete with companies of other countries where wage rates may be considerably lower than here (see EXHIBIT 1-2). The new emphasis on product quality and high wage costs is forcing firms to automation (see EXHIBIT 1-1). Labor directly involved in production is being reduced while computer-aided-design (CAD) and computer-aided-manufacturing (CAM) is evolving in the work place. This increase in machine intensity in manufacturing provides more flexibility in the system (also called **flexible manufacturing systems, or FMSs**), but also increases manufacturing overhead costs while direct labor costs decrease. To be more competitive in the global economy, the U.S., Canada, and Mexico are seeking a trade agreement (called **NAFTA**) to open up markets among these countries while making it more difficult for countries outside the trading block to trade in the block or set up manufacturing operations in the trading zone (see the NEWS NOTE on p.5).

This chapter introduces the subjects of cost and management accounting. Some basic concepts and relationships are presented and demonstrated, such as how cost, management, and financial accounting relate. An examination of Exhibit 1-5 gives a broad overview of the objectives of management accounting. These objectives are broad and many are covered in more depth throughout the text.

Chapter 1 also discusses how cost accounting impacts on the management functions of planning, controlling, and decision making. The major sections of the text correspond to these management functions; however, some topics can be viewed as being included in more than one function. For example, a budget is a necessary planning instrument, but it is also important as a control instrument for after-the-fact comparisons.

Ethics in all areas of accounting is needed and is of particular importance in the area of management accounting. The National Association of Accountants (NAA) has determined that a code of ethics (Exhibit 1-6) is a necessity to give management accountants a set of standards by which to judge their conduct. There are ethical implications in almost every decision and some potential ethical-choice decisions are included for your consideration in the end of chapter materials.

Professional recognition is available to accountants through numerous certifications. Two of these, the CMA and the CPA are discussed and compared in Chapter 1.

Concluding the chapter, the appendix presents some concepts relating to organizational structure (through the illustration of an **organization chart** in EXHIBIT 1-12)and accounting positions. Variations of this exist using matrix structures with functional departments and project teams.

CHAPTER STUDY GUIDE

I. As discussed in the chapter, cost accounting can be viewed as the overlap between financial and management accounting. Cost accounting provides information for external uses/users (financial) and internal uses/users (management) accounting.

Chapter 1: Cost and Management Accounting Defined

    A. External users include (present and potential) creditors, stockholders, and regulatory agencies. Information is provided to these external users through financial statements. Internal users include managers in the organization.

        1. These managers need information for timely planning, controlling, and decision making purposes.

        2. Financial accounting must abide by generally accepted accounting principles, while management accounting does not. Financial accounting is quite standardized while management accounting must be very flexible.

    See EXHIBIT 1-4 for more comparisons.

II. Cost accounting traces the flow of inputs to the outputs of organizations. This information is maintained in the same accounts as is financial accounting information.

    A. Cost accounting is a component of the larger field of management accounting and uses both quantitative and qualitative data.

        1. Quantitative data allow managers to look at the "numbers" and their impact on alternatives.

        2. Qualitative data provide facts to managers about alternative courses of action.

III. Management accounting has dual purposes. First, it must provide information to managers for planning, controlling, and decision making purposes. Second, it must provide information to determine the cost values for financial statements.

    A. Mandatory guidelines for financial accounting have been established by the Financial Accounting Standards Board.

    B. Designated enforceable standards do not exist for cost/management accounting, except for the Cost Accounting Standards Board (CASB) standards that must be followed by companies bidding on contracts for the federal government.

IV. The code of ethics adopted by the Institute of Management Accountants (formerly called the National Association of Accountants) combines ethics into management accounting is evidenced by (Exhibit 1-10).

    A. This code furnishes guidelines for conduct and was deemed necessary because of certain illegal or immoral acts committed by various business entities in the recent past. Passage of the Foreign Corrupt Practices Act and the RICO Act provide indications of legal recognition of the importance of ethical behavior in business.

    B. One of the provisions of the Foreign Corrupt Practices Act makes it illegal for an entity to make "questionable" foreign payments. The RICO Act was passed in 1970 to help entities protect themselves against organized crime.

    See EXHIBIT 1-11 for a way to resolve an ethical conflict.

V. Accountants obtain professional recognition through a variety of certifications. The CMA, CPA and CIA are three certifications available in the field of accounting. The basic difference between the three is the licensing aspect.

    A. The CMA and CIA certificates are professional titles, while the CPA is both a professional title and the support for licensing by states. Passing a rigorous national exam and meeting specified experience requirements designated by the state licensing bodies are required by all accounting certifications.

Chapter 1: Cost and Management Accounting Defined

SELF TEST

TRUE/FALSE

1. T F

   Management accounting focuses on external users of data while financial accounting focuses on internal users.

2. T F

   Financial accounting is required to follow generally accepted accounting principles and management accounting is not.

3. T F

   Data for financial accounting and management accounting comes from the same set of accounts.

4. T F

   Cost accounting is a process of determining the cost of a project or product.

5. T F

   In planning, managers exert their influence over operations.

6. T F

   Controlling refers to creating the goals and objectives for a business and developing a strategy for achieving them in a systematic manner.

7. T F

   The process of converting raw materials, labor and supplies into a finished product creates the need for cost accounting.

8. T F

   The Certificate of Management accounting is a specialized designation for Certified Public Accountants.

9. T F

   Integrity means "a strict or firm adherence to a code of moral values".

MULTIPLE CHOICE

1. Which of the following is **not** a responsibility of management accounting?

   a. planning strategies
   b. controlling operations
   c. developing computer programs
   d. evaluating performance

2. Which of the following is **not** a definition of cost?

   a. the consequence of a finished product or service
   b. the cash or cash equivalent value required to reach an objective
   c. the dollar value placed on a finished item
   d. the initial funds required to purchase goods or services from **external** sources that are needed to provide finished goods or services

Chapter 1: Cost and Management Accounting Defined

3. Which of the following are the correct usages for accounting information?

	Management Accounting	Financial Accounting
a.	internal	internal
b.	external	internal
c.	internal	external
d.	external	external

4. Overhead does **not** include

   a. cost of electricity
   b. production equipment maintenance
   c. direct materials
   d. depreciation

5. In the NAA Code of Ethics, standards were established for all of the following areas **except**

   a. disclosure.
   b. competence.
   c. integrity.
   d. objectivity.

6. Financial accounting focuses on external information needs of an organization. Who of the following is not a user of external information?

   a. creditors
   b. regulatory agencies
   c. stockholders
   d. cost accountants

7. The basic management functions do **not** include

   a. controlling.
   b. decision making.
   c. planning.
   d. allocating.

8. Which of the following is information as opposed to data?

   a. a list of movie titles
   b. a course registration book
   c. a column of monetary figures
   d. a scantron sheet with multiple choice answers and the word "key" filled in

9. Which of the following is **not** a part of the CMA exam?

   a. accounting theory
   b. economics and finance
   c. internal reporting
   d. decision analysis

10. Legally binding cost accounting standards have been established by

    a. the National Association of Accountants.
    b. the Cost Accounting Standards Board.
    c. the Financial Accounting Standards Board.
    d. both a and b.

11. Legally binding financial accounting standards have been established by

    a. the National Association of Accountants.
    b. the Cost Accounting Standards Board.
    c. the Financial Accounting Standards Board.
    d. both a and b.

Chapter 1: Cost and Management Accounting Defined

12. The common body of knowledge for management accountants

    a. focuses primarily on accounting principles and functions.
    b. is the same regardless of an individual's career level or functional area of responsibility.
    c. may change as business conditions change.
    d. may be obtained either from on-the-job training or classroom courses.

13. Using a hammer to kill a fly is

	Effective	Efficient
a.	yes	no
b.	yes	yes
c.	no	yes
d.	no	no

14. (Appendix) Line employees are those individuals who

    a. are responsible for providing advice to others.
    b. are responsible for achieving the organization's goals.
    c. work in assembly operations in the production plant.
    d. hold supervisory positions in a business organization.

15. (Appendix) An organization chart illustrates all of the following **except**

    a. functions.
    b. positions.
    c. divisions.
    d. informal channels of communication.

16. Which of the subsequent activities is not normally a duty of the controller?

    a. Operational reporting and interpreting
    b. Insurance coverage
    c. Preparing tax returns
    d. Establishing internal control procedures to safeguard the company's assets

17. Which of the following is not a aspect of managerial accounting?

    a. Managerial reports are future oriented
    b. It is subject to regulatory reporting standards
    c. It creates reports primarily for internal users
    d. There are no established record-keeping requirements

18. Differences and similarities exist between managerial accounting and financial accounting. Which of the following statements is true?

    a. Financial accounting reports are prepared primarily for the firm's managers.
    b. Managerial accounting standards are subject to GAAP.
    c. Managerial accounting reports are prepared primarily for the firm's managers.
    d. Financial reporting is not under the jurisdiction of regulatory agencies.

19. Financial accounting:

    a. is constrained by regulatory bodies such as the SEC.
    b. has its primary importance on the future.
    c. provides data primarily for internal uses by managers.
    d. draws heavily from other disciplines.

20. Financial and managerial accounting are comparable in that both:

    a. are mandatory.
    b. rely on the accounting information system.
    c. emphasize the relevance and flexibility of data.
    d. emphasize the organization as a whole.

21. A company's controller is qualified to set policy in accounting and financial reporting matters because the controller:

    a. occupies a staff position.
    b. occupies a position at the top of the organization chart.
    c. occupies a line position.
    d. is delegated this authority by top management.

22. The manager in charge of the accounting department in an organization is commonly known as the:

    a. Vice President of Finance.
    b. Internal Auditor.
    c. Controller.
    d. Treasurer.

23. An organization chart does not display:

    a. staff and line positions.
    b. areas of responsibility for each manager.
    c. formal lines of authority between managers.
    d. informal lines of communication.

24. In which of the following ways is managerial accounting like to financial accounting?

    a. Both are governed by generally accepted accounting principles.
    b. Both deal with economic events.
    c. Both concentrate on historical costs.
    d. Both classify reported information in the same way.

25. Which of the following would be deemed a line function?

    a. production
    b. maintenance
    c. public relations
    d. administrative services

26. The management accountant is expected to

    a. determine product unit costs.
    b. prepare reports to examine and support management decisions.
    c. develop cost budgets and cost controls for management.
    d. prepare reports to furnish background for management decisions.
    e. all of the above.

QUESTIONS AND PROBLEMS

1. Discuss the differences between management accounting and financial accounting.

2. Why has ethics become an important aspect of the business world? What are the two laws that have an impact on businesses? Discuss these laws briefly.

Chapter 1: Cost and Management Accounting Defined

3. Discuss the importance of the CMA certificate. How are the CMA and CPA different?

4. How does cost accounting relate to management accounting? To financial accounting? What information does cost accounting provide to managers?

Communication Projects

AECC or the Accounting Education Change Commission acknowledges the need in college education for more active learning by students. Methods used in active learning put students more actively involved in their learning process through communication between themselves and people outside their class. Throughout this study guide, suggested cooperative learning problems are presented to encourage an expansion of your communication skills while increasing your awareness of managerial accounting.

In class, write a short 100-150 word understanding of what you think managerial accounting is all about. Give your paper to a student next to you so that he may interpret what you said and whether he agrees or disagrees with your comments.

The purpose of this exercise is break the ice with your classmates and enhance your ability to communicate in writing what you are thinking.

SELF TEST SOLUTIONS

TRUE/FALSE

1. F	3. T	5. F	7. T	9. T
2. T	4. T	6. F	8. F	

MULTIPLE CHOICE

1. C	6. D	11. C	16. B	21. D	26. E
2. A	7. D	12. B	17. B	22. C	
3. C	8. C	13. A	18. C	23. D	
4. C	9. A	14. C	19. A	24. B	
5. A	10. B	15. A	20. B	25. A	

QUESTIONS AND PROBLEMS

1. One difference between management and financial accounting is that management accounting is needed for internal purposes while financial is needed for external purposes. Management accounting does not have to adhere to generally accepted accounting principles while financial accounting must strictly abide by these standards. Management accounting is future and segment oriented while financial accounting is historical in nature and has a corporate wide orientation. Management accounting uses a significant number of estimates while financial accounting uses information that is verifiable in nature.

2. Ethics has become important in the business world because of misbehavior by some corporate entities (bribes, kick backs, coverups, and insider trading). **Two laws that relate to ethics that have had an impact on businesses are the** Foreign Corrupt Practices Act and the Racketeer Influenced and Corrupt Organizations Act. The FCPA makes it illegal for an entity to make "questionable" payments in a foreign country. A "questionable" payment would be one that raises doubt about its legality and appropriateness. RICO is aimed at helping entities protect and defend themselves against organized

crime. It has been used to prosecute numerous widely varying activities because of its "umbrella" scope.

3. The CMA certificate is a professional designation; it is not a basis for licensing. The CPA certificate, however, has both characteristics. CMAs are found in private business rather than in public accounting. The CMA is an indication of proficiency in management accounting as well as other areas of business. CPAs work both in public accounting and private business. The CPA is an indication of proficiency in all areas of accounting and business law. CPAs in public practice are licensed to perform audit engagements; CPAs working in industry are not considered independent and cannot provide audits to the companies for which they work.

4. Cost accounting can be viewed as the overlap between management and financial accounting. Two separate sets of accounts are not needed since the data for both can be gathered from the financial accounting set of accounts. Cost accounting provides information relating to the determination of product cost. It also helps to establish standards of materials, labor, overhead and provides information for pricing of the finished product. Cost accounting also enables the accountant compute and isolate variances/deviations from set standards.

5. The three stages of production are raw materials (work not started), work in process and finished goods. The accounts used are as follows: work not started is shown in the Raw Materials and, possibly, Supplies account; the Work in Process account includes direct labor, direct materials, and overhead; and Finished Goods includes the cost of goods available for sale by the company.

CHAPTER 2
COST TERMINOLOGY AND COST FLOWS

CHAPTER OVERVIEW

This chapter introduces many cost terms and their classifications (Exhibit 2-1). It is necessary to be able to distinguish among these costs in order to evaluate management performance and properly cost products or services that are produced. Awareness with these terms is crucial for understanding and communicating cost and management accounting data to management.

The terms of EXHIBIT 2-1 are used throughout the text. Their definitions are crucial to understanding all other chapter information. For example, cost accounting focuses on determination of product cost. This term is compared to period cost in merchandising, manufacturing and service companies (see Exhibit 2-5 for more specific items). Activity changes effect how costs modify (cost behavior) and this is also discussed (see EXHIBITs 2-3 and 2-4). Understanding of such behavior is essential for management planning, controlling, and performance evaluation activities.

Additionally, the chapter presents (in Exhibit 2-11), the journal entries for product cost flows. These entries will be used in Chapters 7 and 8 which illustrate two different costing systems. Finally, the chapter explains and illustrates the Schedules of Cost of Goods Manufactured and Cost of Goods Sold. Manufacturers use the Cost of Goods Manufactured Schedule as a supporting document for the cost of goods sold calculation in income statement preparation.

CHAPTER STUDY GUIDE

1. There are a variety of cost terms and classifications; Exhibit 2-1 summarizes these classifications and some of costs included in each. To properly discuss cost behavior a few definitions are necessary.

    a. A variable cost varies in total, but remains constant on a per unit basis (direct material). It is felt that variable costs are are supposed to positiveiy correlated with an activitly called a **cost driver**.

    b. A fixed cost remains constant in total, but varies on a per unit basis (rent).

    c. To obtain proper utilization and analysis of cost behavior, a time frame and range of activity must be specified. This range of activity is called the relevant range (Exhibit 2-2) and refers to a range of activity in which costs (both fixed and variable) behave in accordance with the way they are defined. To see the graphical presentation of cost behavior, see EXHIBIT 2-3 for variable and fixed costs.

    d. A cost that includes both fixed and variable components is called a **mixed cost (see EXHIBIT 2-4)**. Further discussion of the separation of mixed costs into their fixed and variable components is discussed in Chapter 4.

Chapter 2: Cost Terminology and Cost Flows

        i. Treatment of fixed and variable costs in financial reporting is shown in EXHIBIT 2-6. Notice that product costs are inventoriable while nonproduct costs are period costs and expensed as incurred.

2. An meaningful distinction must be made between product costs and period costs.

    a. A product cost (inventoriable cost) is any cost incurred in making or acquiring a product.

        i. Product costs are viewed as attaching to products as items are purchased or manufactured; these costs are inventoried until the products are sold. When sold, product costs are released from inventory as an expense (cost of goods sold) and matched with revenue.

    b. A period cost is one that relates to a specific time period. Period costs (selling and administrative expenses) are matched with revenues on a time period basis. Period costs are not included as part of the cost of either purchased or manufactured goods.

        i. Unlike product costs which are assets which have future value, theoretically period costs have no future value and expensed when incurred.

    c. Raw or direct materials are converted or processed into a final product or finished good in a conversion area. Period costs are spent in non-production areas such as the sales office. The outputs of the conversion process are shown in EXHIBIT 2-7. Whether the firm is manufacturer or service company, a product or service is prepared.

        i. A further distinction is made between a manufacturing and retail company. The inputs and outputs of these two types of companies is shown in EXHIBIT 2-8.

        ii. Manufacturing firms process materials through different stages of production. See EXHIBIT 2-9 for more discussion of this.

        iii. The APPENDIX shows the differences between income statements and schedules of a retailer and manufacturer.

3. The distinction between direct and indirect costs is a factor that affects product costing and management decisions. A direct cost can be easily traced to a product or another defined item (cost object). An indirect cost is one that cannot be easily traced to a particular product.

    a. It maybe burdensome to classify a cost as to whether it is direct or indirect. This difficulty is frequently due to the nature of the item being classified. For example, power to run a fabricating machine to cut out metal for a car fender is a product cost. Its not convenient to trace the cost of electricity directly to the product (an automobile). This cost is an indirect product cost and part of overhead rather than a direct material.

4. Product costs consist of three elements: direct materials, direct labor and overhead. Direct materials and direct labor are easily traced and categorized, while overhead most frequently must be allocated. This allocation process is discussed in more detail in Chapters 4, 5 and 6.

5. Two other terms relating to product costs are prime cost and conversion cost. Prime cost consists of both the cost of direct materials used plus direct labor cost incurred. Conversion cost is equal to the cost of direct labor plus the cost of overhead. Prime cost and conversion cost have direct labor cost in common (Exhibit 2-10) and cannot be added together to determine product cost.

6. The final section of Chapter 2 presents the schedules of cost of goods manufactured and cost of goods sold (Exhibit 2-12). Notice that in Exhibit

Chapter 2: Cost Terminology and Cost Flows

2-12 the line item "Cost of Goods Manufactured" is the element that connects the two schedules and ties them together. Cost of goods manufactured represents the cost of goods completed and transferred to Finished Goods Inventory during the period.

SELF TEST

TRUE/FALSE

1. **(T)** F

    Prime cost consists of direct materials and direct labor.

2. **(T)** F

    Conversion cost consists of direct labor and overhead.

3. **(T)** F

    The difference between a product cost and a period cost is that a product cost is traced to the product, whereas a period cost relates to a specific time frame.

4. **(T)** F

    A cost that remains constant in total but varies on a per unit basis with changes in activity is called a fixed cost.

5. T **(F)**

    A cost that varies in total, but remains constant on a per unit basis is called a relevant cost.

6. T **(F)**

    A mixed cost fluctuates in direct proportion to changes in activity.

7. T **(F)**

    Cost drivers do not have a direct cause-effect relationship to a cost.

8. T **(F)**

    Period costs are also called inventoriable costs.

9. **(T)** F

    Product costs include direct materials, direct labor and overhead.

10. T **(F)**

    Expired costs are shown on the balance sheet.

11. T **(F)**

    Unexpired product costs are shown on the income statement.

12. **(T)** F

    The process of converting raw materials, labor and supplies into a finished product creates the need for cost accounting.

Chapter 2: Cost Terminology and Cost Flows

MULTIPLE CHOICE

1. Cost classifications are used to define costs in terms of their relationships to certain categories. Which of the following categories is **not** used to define costs?

    a. a reaction to changes in activity
    b. financial statement classification
    c. impact on decision making
    d. impact on production

2. A cost that remains constant in total but varies on a per unit basis with changes in activity is called a/an

    a. expected cost.
    b. fixed cost.
    c. variable cost.
    d. mixed cost.

3. A cost that varies in total, but remains constant on a per unit basis with changes in activity is called a/an

    a. mixed cost.
    b. fixed cost.
    c. variable cost.
    d. expected cost.

4. An example of a fixed cost is

    a. raw materials.
    b. hourly wages.
    c. sales commissions.
    d. supervisors' salaries.

5. An example of a variable cost is

    a. sales commissions.
    b. supervisors' salaries.
    c. straight line depreciation.
    d. insurance.

6. Which of the following is **not** an example of a mixed cost?

    a. electricity used during the accounting period
    b. water used during the period
    c. maintenance expense during the period
    d. hourly wages for the period

7. Which of the following statements is false?

    a. A predictor is an activity measure that, when changed, is accompanied by consistent, observable changes in another item.
    b. Cost drivers are factors that have a direct cause-effect relationship to a cost.
    c. The balance sheet is a statement of expired costs.
    d. The income statement is a statement of expired costs.

The following information relates to questions 8-11.
The ABC Co. manufactures roll top desks and the product is considered the cost object.

8. What is the proper classification of the supervisor's salary?

	Product	Period
a.	yes	yes
b.	no	yes
c.	no	no
d.	**yes**	**no**

Chapter 2: Cost Terminology and Cost Flows

9. What is the proper classification of the supervisor's salary?

	Direct	Product
a.	no	yes
b.	no	no
c.	yes	yes
d.	yes	no

10. What is the proper classification of the cost accountant's salary?

	Product	Period
a.	yes	yes
b.	no	yes
c.	no	no
d.	yes	no

11. What is the proper classification of the carpenters' wages?

	Direct	Product
a.	no	no
b.	no	yes
c.	yes	yes
d.	yes	no

The following data relate to questions 14-18.

Inventories	Beginning	Ending
Work in Process	$ 8,000	$12,000
Raw Materials	5,500	7,000
Finished Goods	11,200	13,700

Additional data is as follows: purchases of raw materials $23,000; 150 direct labor hours @ $10.50; and overhead incurred $19,500

12. What is the value of raw materials used?
    a. $21,500
    b. $28,500
    c. $35,500
    d. $24,500

13. Prime cost equals _____.
    a. $21,075
    b. $30,075
    c. $23,075
    d. $41,000

14. Conversion cost equals _____.
    a. $30,075
    b. $21,075
    c. $41,000
    d. $23,075

15. Cost of Goods Manufactured is _____.
    a. $50,575
    b. $38,575
    c. $54,575
    d. $46,575

16. If Cost of Goods Manufactured were $50,000, Cost of Goods Sold would be _____?
    a. $47,500
    b. $52,500
    c. $74,900
    d. $84,875

Chapter 2: Cost Terminology and Cost Flows

17. If the beginning balance of Raw Materials is $14,400, the ending balance of Raw Materials is $10,000, and raw materials used is $53,200 what is the value of raw materials purchased during the period?

    a. $63,200
    b. $73,200
    c. $48,800
    d. $57,600

18. Which of the following is the journal entry to record the transfer of items completed during a period?

    a. Debit Cost of Goods Sold, credit Finished Goods
    b. Debit Work in Process, credit Finished Goods
    c. Debit Finished Goods, credit Work in Process
    d. Debit Finished Goods, credit Raw Materials

19. Which of the following is the journal entry to record depreciation on factory equipment?

    a. Debit Depreciation Expense, credit Accumulated depreciation.
    b. Debit Overhead, credit Accumulated Depreciation.
    c. Debit Overhead, credit Equipment.
    d. Debit Equipment, credit Overhead.

20. Prime cost and conversion cost have which of the following in common?

    a. direct materials
    b. overhead
    c. direct labor
    d. direct materials and direct labor

21. Total manufacturing costs for the period are $560,000, raw materials used are $215,000, and overhead is $93,000. How many direct labor hours were worked, if our employees are paid $12.50 per hour?

    a. 24,640 DLH
    b. 17,200 DLH
    c. 21,000 DLH
    d. 20,160 DLH

22. Cost of goods manufactured equals $1,250,000, the beginning balance of Finished Goods is $373,000 and Cost of Goods Sold is $1,000,000. What is the ending balance in Finished Goods?

    a. $ 623,000
    b. $ 123,000
    c. $1,500,000
    d. $ 573,000

23. (Appendix) The income statements of a merchandising firm and a manufacturing firm are similar in that both contain a cost of goods sold section. Which of the following is true regarding these statements?

    a. The income statement of a merchandising firm does not contain the line item "Gross Margin on Sales".
    b. The income statement of a manufacturing firm references a supporting schedule for Cost of Goods Manufactured.
    c. The income statement of a manufacturer does not contain the line item "Gross Margin on Sales".
    d. Both income statements are identical.

24. The process of _____ causes the need for cost accounting.

    a. conversion
    b. selling
    c. manufacturing
    d. allocation

Chapter 2: Cost Terminology and Cost Flows

25. The process of conversion

    a. does not exist in retail or service firms.
    b. creates the need for cost accounting.
    c. can be conveniently ignored in a company such as General Motors.
    d. indicates the movement of period costs through the three basic stages of production.

26. Which of the following is **true** concerning the difference between a retailing company and a manufacturing company?

    a. A retail company does not have a production center.
    b. A manufacturing company does not have a production center.
    c. Both have production centers.
    d. Neither one has a production center.

27. A manufacturer accounts for which of the following?

    a. raw materials, work in process, and finished goods
    b. finished goods and cost of goods sold only
    c. raw materials and work in process only
    d. cost of goods sold and raw materials only

28. The conversion process can be thought of as existing in which of the following stages?

	Work in Process	Raw Materials	Finished Goods
a.	no	no	no
b.	yes	no	no
c.	yes	yes	yes
d.	no	yes	yes

QUESTIONS AND PROBLEMS

1. What is a relevant cost? What other terms could be used for relevant cost?

2. What are the formulas for computing Cost of Goods Manufactured and Cost of Goods Sold?

3. What are the three components of product cost? Why may it be difficult to categorize costs into one of these components?

4. What is prime cost? What is conversion cost? What do they have in common?

5. In accumulating product costs, a periodic or perpetual inventory system can be used. What is the difference in product cost flow between the two?

Chapter 2: Cost Terminology and Cost Flows

6. Compute prime cost and conversion cost given the following data:

   Raw Materials (May 1) $12,000
   Raw materials purchases $7,500
   Raw Materials (May 31) $3,300
   Direct Labor (17,500 direct labor hours @ $11.50)
   Depreciation on factory equipment $1,700
   Depreciation on office equipment $1,500
   Insurance-Factory $2,100
   Supplies Used-Factory $350
   Office supplies used $720
   Indirect material used $710
   Indirect labor $440

7. Use the data in #6 above and prepare a Schedule of Cost of Goods Manufactured (in good form). Assume the beginning balance of Work in Process is $43,000 and the ending balance of Work in Process is $51,700.

8. Compute Total Manufacturing Costs for the month of September given the data below.

	Beginning	Ending
Raw Materials	$ 4,500	$ 6,100

   Purchases of raw materials were $27,300. There were 21,300 direct labor hours worked at an hourly rate of $14. Overhead costs totaled $33,500.

9. Assume Total Manufacturing Costs are $360,000 and the following data are available. Compute Cost of Goods Sold.

	Beginning	Ending
Work in Process	$11,700	$14,400
Finished Goods	3,900	7,800

10. Compute the dollar value of Raw Materials purchased for the month of December, given the following data.

	Beginning	Ending
Raw Materials	$11,000	$14,300
Work in Process	9,500	21,100

    Raw materials used cost $87,200.

11. What are the stages of production and what accounts are related to each of these stages?

Chapter 2: Cost Terminology and Cost Flows

COMMUNICATION PROJECT

The instructor will give a lecture today on cost and managerial accounting terminology today. You are encouraged to listen closely because a short quiz will be given at the end of the class period regarding topics lectured on in class.

The purpose of this exercise is to improve your ability to listen effectively. The quiz will accurately capture the content of the information given. You will be questioned on the content of this regular classroom lecture.

SELF TEST SOLUTIONS

TRUE/FALSE

1. T
2. T
3. T
4. T
5. F
6. F
7. F
8. F
9. T
10. F
11. F
12. F

MULTIPLE CHOICE

1. D
2. B
3. C
4. D
5. A
6. D
7. C
8. D
9. A
10. B
11. C
12. A
13. C
14. B
15. B
16. A
17. C
18. C
19. B
20. C
21. D
22. A
23. B
24. A
25. B
26. A
27. A
28. B

QUESTIONS AND PROBLEMS

1. A relevant cost is one that is associated with a specific decision or problem. It is a cost that has a bearing on future alternatives; it must be differential to the decision that must be made which means it must have an impact on the decision. A differential cost is also called an out-of-pocket cost.

2. The formula for computing Cost of Goods Manufactured begins as follows: Beginning Work in Process plus Raw Materials Used plus Direct Labor plus Overhead. This summation equals Total Costs in Process. Total Costs in Process minus Ending Work in Process equals Cost of Goods Manufactured. Cost of Goods Sold equals Beginning Finished Goods plus Cost of Goods Manufactured minus Ending Finished Goods.

3. The three components of product cost are raw materials used, direct labor and overhead. It usually is not difficult to categorize direct materials or direct labor because these costs should be physically and conveniently easily traced to the product being manufactured. Initially, one might think that a particular cost is direct materials or direct labor, but in fact the cost is considered overhead. This categorization arises from the difficulty of tracing such costs to the cost object, such as the cost of glue to affix labels or overtime premiums.

4. Prime cost consists of direct labor and direct materials and conversion cost consists of direct labor and overhead. Prime cost and conversion cost have direct labor in common.

5. A business can accumulate product costs in either a periodic or perpetual inventory system. The difference between the two systems is as follows: in a perpetual system all product costs flow through Work in Process to Finished Goods to Cost of Goods Sold. The perpetual system provides constant information for preparation of financial statements. A perpetual system is **more expensive to maintain. The expense of maintaining a perpetual system** has decreased in the past few years with the usage of computers. A periodic inventory system uses special accounts such as Purchases, Purchase Discounts, Purchase Returns and Allowances to accumulate costs. This system does not provide constant information for financial statement preparation. Nor does it provide good control information.

6.
Raw Materials (Jan. 1)	$12,000	
Raw materials purchased	7,500	
Raw materials available	19,500	
Raw Materials (Jan. 31)	<3,300>	
Raw materials used	$16,200	

Direct labor hours $201,250
(17,500 @ $11.50)

Prime Cost = $16,200 + $201,250 = $217,450

Overhead :
Depreciation-Factory	$1,700
Insurance-Factory	2,100
Cleaning supplies used (Factory)	350
Indirect materials	710
Indirect labor	440
TOTAL OVERHEAD	$5,300

Conversion Cost = $201,250 + $5,300 = $206,550

7.
XYZ COMPANY
SCHEDULE OF COST OF GOODS MANUFACTURED
JUNE 30, 1990

Work in Process (June 1)	$ 43,000
Raw Mat. (June 1)	$ 12,000
Raw mat (purch)	7,500
	19,500
Raw Mat (June 30)	< 3,300>
Raw Mat Used	16,200
Direct Labor (17,500 DLH @ $11.50)	201,250
Overhead: (see above list)	5,300
TOTAL MANUFACTURING COSTS	222,750
TOTAL COSTS IN PROCESS	265,750
Work in Process (June 30)	<51,700>
COST OF GOODS MANUFACTURED	**$ 214,050**

8.
Raw Mat. (July 1)	$ 4,500
Raw mat. (purch)	27,300
	31,800
Raw Mat. (July 31)	< 6,100>
Raw Mat. Used	25,700
Direct Labor (21,300 DLH @ $14)	298,200
Overhead	33,500
TOTAL MANUFACTURING COSTS	$357,400

9.
TOTAL MANUFACTURING COSTS (from # 8 above)	$360,000
Work in Process (July 1)	11,700
Work in Process (July 31)	<14,400>
COST OF GOODS MANUFACTURED	$357,300
Finished Goods (July 1)	$ 3,900
CGM	357,300
	361,200
Finished Goods (July 31)	< 7,800>
COST OF GOODS SOLD	$353,400

10.
Raw Materials Used	$ 87,200
Raw Materials (Feb. 28)	14,300
	$101,500
Raw Materials (Feb. 1)	< 11,000>
Raw Materials Purchased	$ 90,500

11. The three stages of production are raw materials (work not started), work in process and finished goods. The accounts used are as follows: work not started is shown in the Raw Materials and, possibly, Supplies account; the Work in Process account includes direct labor, direct materials, and overhead; and Finished Goods includes the cost of goods available for sale by the company.

CHAPTER 3
CONSIDERING QUALITY IN AN ORGANIZATION

CHAPTER OVERVIEW

Chapter 3 considers quality in the manufacturing and service industries. The chapter looks at products/services made or provided in the United States in particular. Choice in products and services is perceived important to the consumer. Consumers know that quality, price, service and lead time are variables available to them. Quality is perceived by the supplier to be paramount. Chapter 3 discusses issues on total quality management (or TQM), quality costs, quality standards, and quality culture.

Quality is defined as the "pride of workmanship" or "conformance to requirements". Characteristics of product quality are shown in EXHIBIT 3-2.

CHAPTER STUDY GUIDE

1. Quality is based on factors of the user, not of the provider. Traditionally, it has been based on provider specifications (**quality assurance**). Companies have used control charts to identify when the number of units produced that are defective exceed an acceptable level (see EXHIBIT 3-1).

    a. Firms are moving away from this policy towards **total quality control** by the use of **statistical process control** which shows when defects in the production process are truly errors.

    b. The emphasis on quality stems from the following factors: 1) increased competition, 2) increased consumer interest in product safety, and 3) an increase in litigation regarding product safety.

    c. From the provider's point of view, activities required to produce the product (**value-added activities**) increase the product's value. Activities that do not add value to the product (**non-value-added activities**) should be eliminated where possible.

        i. Examples of non-value-added activities include reworking goods that do not meet specification, quality inspection, and scrap.

    d. The costs of quality may be 15-25% of sales but increasing good quality can reduce these costs to 2-3% of sales which drastically increases profits. Quality may be broken down into two categories: design and conformance.

        i. Quality of design is the degree of excellence set by the product's design specifications. Design quality offers little chance to reduce costs without reducing the design quality.

        ii. Quality of conformance is the degree of excellence shown by how well the product meets its specifications. Through conformance quality, costs can be significantly reduced and market share of the product increased.

Chapter 3: Considering Quality in an Organization

    e.   The characteristics of product quality are listed in EXHIBIT 3-2. The level of quality is a function of price. Customers often measure a product's quality based on their perception of ideal quality.

        i.   Comparing a product against the best product's quality is called **benchmarking** (see EXHIBIT 3-4).

        ii.   **Results benchmarking** compares a firm's specifications against a competitors' specifications (see the NEWS NOTE on p.12).

2. The four categories of quality costs are: prevention, appraisal, internal failure and external failure. The definitions are as follows.

    a.   Prevention costs: Those costs incurred to prevent defects in the products or services being produced.

    b.   Appraisal costs: Cost incurred to determine whether the products are conforming to their requirements.

    c.   Internal failure costs: Costs incurred because the product doesn't conform to the specifications and must be reworked.

    d.   External failure costs: Costs incurred after the product is delivered to the customer because the product doesn't meet specifications.

    e.   See EXHIBIT 3-6 for the types of quality costs and their components. The first two types of costs are called compliance costs and the latter two are noncompliance costs.

3. **Total Quality Management** (or **TQM**)-organization-wide participation in implementing a continuous improvement process.

    a.   Managers must be given information on the quality process so they can plan, control and evaluate performance.

        i.   Historically, emphasis has been placed on unnecessary errors after they occur and tolerating them unless they exceed an acceptable error level (see EXHIBIT 3-1).

    b.   In TQM, companies try to prevent errors from occurring and use a continuous improvement system to improve on what they make or provide. Including employees in the TQM process is encouraged by recommending they make suggestions for process improvements. Employees are made to feel a part of the organization. TQM focuses on the relationship between the production process and customer expectations.

        i.   Customers want quality , value and (most importantly), good service. As quality increases, noncompliance costs decrease while compliance costs increase (see EXHIBIT 3-7). As quality improves, total costs decline also.

        ii.   Pareto analysis can be used to identify where to concentrate quality prevention efforts by classifying external failure costs by product and product component.

        iii.   New quality accounts may be needed to identify quality costs in a TQM company *see EXHIBIT 3-9) to show these costs in a quality cost report (see EXHIBIT 3-10).

4. **Malcolm Baldridge Quality Award**-recognition of quality products/services of a firm measured in 7 categories (see Exhibit 3-12).

    a.   **ISO 9000** quality standards-firms seeking international recognition of quality must meet the 5 standards shown in EXHIBIT 3-13. Firms that want to sell their products in Europe must conform to ISO 9000 standards.

Chapter 3: Considering Quality in an Organization

5. Organizational commitment to quality-TQM implores management to seek a quality that exceeds customer expectations. Employees are directed toward the TQM approach with encouragement, training, and job enrichment. Employees seek zero defects in their products or services.

SELF TEST

TRUE/FALSE

1. T F

    Recent changes in the business environment have fostered changes in cost accounting methods.

2. T F

    Global competition has decreased the demand for customer service.

3. T F

    The present American economy is comprised mostly of service industries rather than manufacturing industries.

4. T F

    The two most important current performance objectivies of U.S. businesses are profit and volume.

5. T F

    One difference between traditional standard cost analysis and the new performance measures is the focus of the latter on trends over time rather than meeting specific standards.

6. T F

    In using a statistical control chart, observation points plotted between the upper and lower limits will be due to random or chance occurrences and would not typically result in management review.

7. T F

    The use of statistical quality control charts is acceptable in a company that has adopted TQM.

8. T F

    Benchmarking of the product which focuses on the product's specifications to see if the specs are met is called process benchmarking.

9. T F

    A quality audit is the review of the financial records to if the prcedures are being followed to record the data.

MULTIPLE CHOICE

1. Which of the following does not characterize the "new age" of American business?

    a. high wage rates
    b. high machine intensity
    c. restricted product variety
    d. deregulated markets

Chapter 3: Considering Quality in an Organization

2. Which of the following is not a consumer-based demand of American business?

    a. reasonable prices
    b. integrity
    c. product variety
    d. increased profitability

3. Which of the following parts of the production process are value-adding?

    a. inspection time
    b. transfer time
    c. idle time
    d. none of the above

4. Non-value-added activities can be attributed to

    a. physical factors.
    b. system factors.
    c. people factors.
    d. all of the above.

5. Good performance indicators can be

    a. qualitative.
    b. quantitative but nonfinancial.
    c. quantitative and financial.
    d. all of the above.

6. A greater concern in American industry for quality products and customer service is mostly attributable to

    a. increased machine intensity of production systems.
    b. the pressure of foreign competition.
    c. the availability of new cost accounting techniques.
    d. new production technologies.

7. There are many reasons why traditional standards may be inappropriate in an automated environment. Which of the following is not one of these reasons?

    a. Traditional variances tend to focus on price while ignoring quality factors.
    b. Traditional quantity variances are either minimal or cease to exist.
    c. Costs tend to be more variable in behavior, resulting in less need for standards.
    d. Direct labor is less significant, resulting in the labor variances being of little value to management.

8. An example of a prevention cost is:

    a. researching customer needs
    b. quality audits during production
    c. reinspection
    d. repair costs

9. Costs incurred because products or services fail to meet requirements after delivery to customers are called:

    a. external failure costs
    b. internal failure costs
    c. appraisal costs
    d. prevention costs

10. Costs incurred to determine whether products and services are conforming to requirements are called:

    a. external failure costs
    b. internal failure costs
    c. appraisal costs
    d. prevention costs

Chapter 3: Considering Quality in an Organization

11. Quality training programs are:

    a. prevention costs
    b. appraisal costs
    c. internal failure costs
    d. external failure costs

12. In-process inspection is a(n):

    a. prevention cost
    b. appraisal cost
    c. internal failure cost
    d. external failure cost

13. Product recalls are:

    a. prevention costs
    b. appraisal costs
    c. internal failure costs
    d. external failure costs

14. In the "new era" of manufacturing, good performance indicators are

    a. production-based.
    b. sales-based.
    c. cost-based.
    d. consumer-based.

15. In the ranking of product quality, which of the following standards results in the highest quality:

    a. Industry standards
    b. military standards
    c. ISO 9000
    d. Deming prize

16. To earn the Malcolm Baldrige Quality Award, which of the following categoies does not have to show excellence in:

    a. Customer satisfaction
    b. quality assurance of the product
    c. human resource utilitzation
    d. personnel productivity increase

17. Total Failure Cost is not a function of the which of the following quality costs:

    a. prevention cost
    b. rework cost
    c. costs of processing customer returns
    d. profits lost by selling units as defects

QUESTIONS AND PROBLEMS

1. How has global competition affected the focus of American managers?

2. What is the graphically relaionship between costs of compliance and costs of noncompliance.

Chapter 3: Considering Quality in an Organization

3. At the opening of the year, Forefront Company began a quality improvement program. The program was successful in reducing scrap and rework costs. To help evaluate the effect of the quality improvement program, the subsequent data was collected for the current and preceding year.

	Preceding Year	Current Year
Sales	$15,000,000	$15,000,000
Quality training	60,000	90,000
Materials inspection	150,000	120,000
Rework	800,000	600,000
Waste	900,000	800,000
Product inspection	250,000	300,000
Product warranty	1,000,000	900,000

Required:
Classify each of the preceding costs into one of the following four categories:

Prevention	Appraisal	Internal Failure	External Failure
----------	--------	----------------	----------------
----------	--------	----------------	----------------
----------	--------	----------------	----------------
----------	--------	----------------	----------------

Communication Projects

Source: **West Tape 2**, Segment 3.

Your professor will show you a video on Federal Express, a company that delivers packages all over the U.S.. The demand for that type of product/service is growing rapidly "hub and spoke concept". They maintain a computerized tracking system that tracks packages and manages inventories. Federal Express received the first Malcolm Baldridge National Quality Award for a service company.

1. How can Federal Express help manage another company's inventory?

2. What is the Baldridge award? Why do you think it was developed?

3. What is a non-value-added activity? Why wouyld companies seek to eliminate non-value-added activities?

Having completed this exercise by answering these questions, you will acquire an ability to accurately capture information given and identify the intent of the information being present in a video format.
This is an important attribute in the business world because more presentations are being shown in the video form.

SELF TEST SOLUTIONS

TRUE/FALSE

1. T   4. F   7. F
2. F   5. T   8. F
3. F   6. F   9. F

MULTIPLE CHOICE

1. C   4. D   7. C   10. C   13. D   16. D
2. D   5. D   8. A   11. A   14. D   17. A
3. D   6. B   9. A   12. A   15. D

Chapter 3: Considering Quality in an Organization

QUESTIONS AND PROBLEMS

1. Global competition has increased managerial awareness of customer service and product quality. High-quality products from Europe and Japan have forced American managers to become more competitive in providing quality products and more attentive to consumer value.

2. Compliance costs consist of prevention costs and appraisal costs. Noncompliance costs consist of internal and external failure costs. An inverse relationship exists between these two quality cost categories. As failure costs increase, prevention costs per unit of defects decrease.

3.

Prevention	Appraisal	Internal Failure	External Failure	
Quality Training	Material Inspection	Product Inspection	Product Warranty	Rework
				Waste
----------	----------	----------	--------	----------

CHAPTER 4
DEVELOPING PREDETERMINED OVERHEAD RATES

CHAPTER OVERVIEW

Chapter 4 discusses the following major topics: a) the calculating of predetermined overhead rates; b) separating mixed costs; c) applying flexible budgets to setting predetermined overhead rates; d) using predetermined overhead rates; e) separating overhead into variable and fixed components and their rates; f) applying overhead to production and its disposition at year end; g) alternative capacity measures used for predetermining fixed overhead rate; h) introducing activity based costing(ABC); and i) determining correlation analysis and how it applies to regression analysis.

CHAPTER STUDY GUIDE

I. In Chapter 4 overhead was allocated through the determination of a predetermined overhead application rate(POHR). The formula for POHR is:

POHR = <u>Budgeted overhead costs</u>
         Budgeted level of volume or activity

The base in the denominator, called an activity base, should be correlated with overhead costs incurred. Traditionally this base(called cost driver in Chapter 5) has been a volume based activity, such as direct labor hours or direct labor cost. However, the chapter's News Note points out flaws with this base, and other bases are now being used(this will be discussed further in the chapter on ABC, Chapter 5).

II. Other chapter sections include the separation of overhead into fixed and variable components. They behave differently in respect to changes in activity. Fixed costs remain constant while variable costs change directly in proportion to these activity changes. The activity used to calculate the POHR is the capacity measure or activity level used in the denominator of the equation above. The activity levels that might be used are: a) theoretical capacity where all factors are operating in a perfect manner; b) practical capacity that is achieved during normal working conditions; c) normal capacity which is a long-term average level of activity; and d) expected annual capacity which anticipates operating level for the coming year.

III. POHR can be broken down into the predetermined overhead rates for fixed and variable overhead, PFOHR and PVOHR. This can be done since PFOHR is a function of activity level. It will vary depending upon which activity level is chosen. Once the POHR is determined, it is used to apply overhead to production by multiplying the POHR by the activity level for the period. This gives applied overhead.

IV. At the end of the annual period, the actual overhead costs (which have been debited to the overhead account) and the applied overhead costs(which have been credited to overhead or to a separate applied overhead account) must be closed. The difference between these two accounts, or the balance in the overhead account, is called underapplied or overapplied overhead. If the amount is immaterial, it may be closed to cost of goods sold. Otherwise, it may be allocated to Work in Process, Finished Goods, and Cost of Goods Sold(EXHIBIT 4-13).

Chapter 4: Developing Predetermined Overhead Rates

V. In order to separate out mixed costs into their variable and fixed components, the cost behavior of the category is determined. The two methods for determining cost behavior discussed are the high-low method and the regression analysis method.

   A. The high-low method generates a line by taking the difference between the high and low activity points and dividing them into the corresponding costs at these two points. This gives the variable cost rate. Next, the variable cost rate multiplied by the activity level at either point is subtracted from the total cost from either point. This determines the fixed cost. The POHR is found using the following formula:

   $$PVOHR = \frac{OH_h - OH_l}{Activity_h - Activity_l}$$

   PFOHR = TC(at either h or l) - PVOHR * Activity(at either h or l).

   Although the high-low method is easy to use, it has some shortcomings. The cost equation for the straight line, y = a + bx, is found from only two observations. They may not be representative of all the points observed. Secondly, the validity of the equation can not be statistically measured so its reliability is questionable.

   B. To overcome the shortcomings of the high-low method, the use of regression analysis is more precise than the high-low method. This is executed by using all the observed values in the following formulas:

   $$b = \frac{\sum xy - n(\bar{x})(\bar{y})}{\sum x^2 - n*\bar{x}^2}$$

   $$a = \bar{y} - b*\bar{x}$$

   with:
   $\bar{x}$ = mean of the independent variable
   $\bar{y}$ = mean of the dependent variable
   n = number of observations

   The independent variable could be a cost driver like labor hours and the dependent variable could represent something like overhead cost. See the example given in Chapter 4's Demonstration Problem.

VI. The advantages of the regression method include:

   A. the use of all observed values

      1. if an observed value is clearly out of the ordinary, it should omitted in the calculation because it is an outlier;
      2. a statistical measure of goodness of fit (correlation, R^2, is possible);
      3. more than one activity base can be used (this requires the use of multiple regression which is covered in detail in a statistics class on regression) which increases the goodness of fit for the equation.

Chapter 4: Developing Predetermined Overhead Rates

VII. Causality or correlation(R^2) must be determined between the independent and dependent variable. Correlation is determined by seeing if the independent variable drives the dependent variable. This is calculated by the following formula:

$$r = \frac{\Sigma[(x - \bar{x})(y - \bar{y})]}{\sqrt{\Sigma[(x-\bar{x})^2 \Sigma(y-\bar{y})^2]}}$$

Normally, a high correlation value is sought with the range between -1 and +1 with perfect correlation at +1.

The standard error of the estimate(S_e) measures the dispersion between the predicted and actual data values. It measures the dispersion of actual observations from the estimated values from the regression line. In your regression line calculations, seek variables and coefficients yielding values for Se around 2 or less. Increasing values of Se make the regression line less precise.

SELF TEST

TRUE/FALSE

1. **T** F

   The formula for computing a predetermined overhead rate is total estimated overhead cost divided by a selected measure of volume/activity.

2. T **F**

   Variable overhead includes indirect material, indirect labor, and all mixed costs.

3. **T** F

   Cost estimates for computing predetermined overhead rates should not take into consideration inflation.

4. **T** F

   Homogeneity means having identical distribution functions or values.

5. **T** F

   Mixed costs change in proportion to changes in activity.

6. **T** F

   Managerial accountants normally assume that cost behavior can be reflected satisfactorily by a single independent variable in a linear relationship.

7. T **F**

   The full cost of a product includes only those costs that are directly traceable to the product.

8. **T** F

   A reasonable base to use in establishing a predetermined overhead rate in a service company is direct labor hours or direct labor cost.

Chapter 4: Developing Predetermined Overhead Rates

9. **T** F

   An appropriate base to use in establishing a predetermined overhead rate in an automated plant is machine hours.

10. **T** F

    A company determines its overhead rate in the beginning of the year of usage.

11. **T** F

    The high-low method chooses actual observations of total cost at two levels of activity and calculates the change in both at the two levels.

12. T **F**

    A good candidate for an independent variable will be artificially correlated with the dependent variable.

13. T **F**

    The variable to be predicted is referred to as the independent variable in the forecasting model.

14. **T** F

    A perfect correlation between two variables is indicated by a coefficient of correlation measure = 1.

15. **T** F

    A weakness of the high-low method is that it is susceptible to influence by outliers.

16. T **F**

    In the model: Y = a + bX; b is the intercept term.

17. **T** F

    The high-low method assumes that the dependent and independent variables are linearly-related.

18. T **F**

    A major advantage of the scattergraph approach over the high-low method is that it requires less subjective evaluation on the part of the analyst.

19. **T** F

    The major advantage of the least squares approach over the scattergraph approach is that it has a formal rule for determining a unique line slope.

20. **T** F

    The magnitude of the coefficients of a prediction model are a measure of the strength of the relationship between the independent and dependent variables.

21. **T** F

    The scattergraph approach to estimating the prediction model's coefficients utilizes more information than the high-low method.

22. **T** F

    The regression method of cost estimation is theoretically similar to the scattergraph method.

Chapter 4: Developing Predetermined Overhead Rates

23. **T** F

    The actual and applied overhead accounts are normally closed at the end of each fiscal year instead of at the end of the month.

24. An activity base used to develop a flexible budget is often called a cost driver.

25. A flexible budget is a summary of expected costs for a range of activity level and is geared to changes in the level of productive output.

26. **T** F

    The number of purchase orders, the number of employees, and the number of products sold are examples of activities that act as cost drivers in a manufacturing setting.

27. T **F**

    The use of volume-based cost drivers to assign costs tends to over cost low volume products.

MULTIPLE CHOICE

1. Normal costing uses all of the following except:

    a. Actual direct labor
    b. Actual direct materials
    c. Actual manufacturing overhead
    d. Applied manufacturing overhead

2. In order to compute a predetermined overhead rate, you must:

    a. Estimate the allocation base and the total variable costs
    b. Know the amount of direct and indirect materials and labor that will be used in the next period
    c. Estimate the total manufacturing overhead to be incurred
    d. Arbitrarily assign certain costs to the work in process account

3. In the model Y = a + bX; X is the

    a. slope coefficient.
    b. intercept coefficient.
    c. independent variable.
    d. dependent variable.

4. In the model Y = a + bX; b is the

    a. slope coefficient.
    b. intercept coefficient.
    c. independent variable.
    d. dependent variable.

5. With the high low method, the analyst estimates the coefficients of the prediction model from the highest and lowest values of

    a. the independent variable.
    b. the dependent variable.
    c. the centroids.
    d. error terms.

6. The basic difference between multiple regression and simple regression is

    a. in the number of independent variables.
    b. in the number of dependent variables.
    c. in the number of intercept parameters.
    d. in the number of random errors.

Chapter 4: Developing Predetermined Overhead Rates

7. Bogus correlation may exist between variables that

    a. are causally related.
    b. are logically related.
    c. are not causally or logically related.
    d. are dependent in fact.

8. The coefficient of determination is equal to

    a. the square root of the coefficient of correlation.
    b. the ratio of total variance to unexplained variance.
    c. the ratio of explained variance to unexplained variance.
    d. the ratio of explained variance to total variance.

9. Which of the following is **not** a reason to use a predetermined overhead rate?

    a. It allows overhead to be assigned to the goods produced or services rendered during the period rather than at the end.
    b. It compensates for fluctuations in actual overhead cost that have nothing to do with activity levels.
    c. It overcomes the problem of fluctuations in activity levels that have no impact on actual fixed costs.
    d. It allows an adjustment to Cost of Goods Sold to be made at year-end to correct an inaccurate account balance.

10. Which of the following is **true** of a normal costing system?

    a. It uses a predetermined overhead rate to assign overhead to Work in Process.
    b. It uses all actual costs such as direct materials, direct labor, and actual overhead.
    c. It uses all applied costs rather than actual costs.
    d. All of the above statements are true.

11. The formula for computing a predetermined overhead rate is

    a. total fixed costs divided by selected measure of volume/activity.
    b. total estimated overhead costs divided by actual overhead.
    c. total estimated overhead costs divided by selected measure of volume/activity.
    d. actual overhead divided by selected measure of volume/activity.

12. When actual overhead exceeds applied overhead,

    a. overhead is overapplied.
    b. too much was spent on overhead.
    c. overhead is underapplied.
    d. Overhead Control has a credit balance.

13. The Kerr Co. applies overhead at the rate of 150% of direct labor cost. Kerr Co. incurred $265,000 of direct labor cost during the year; Kerrs' actual overhead amounted to $393,000. Kerrs' Overhead account is?

    a. $128,000 overapplied.
    b. $ 4,500 underapplied.
    c. $ 4,500 overapplied.
    d. $128,000 underapplied.

14. To apply overhead to production which journal entry is made?

    a. Debit Work in Process, credit Overhead Control
    b. Debit Overhead Control, credit Work in Process
    c. Debit Overhead Control, credit Finished Goods
    d. Debit Finished Goods, credit Overhead Control

Chapter 4: Developing Predetermined Overhead Rates

15. If the coefficient of correlation between two variables = -1, then the variables

    a. are perfectly correlated.
    b. are completely independent.
    c. have a weak, negative relationship to each other.
    d. have a strong, positive correlation.

16. Assume that you have developed a model based on direct labor hours to predict the periodic cost of labor benefits. The model is: Y = $3,000,000 - $8X. Why would you have very little confidence in this model?

    a. The intercept is too high.
    b. Direct labor hours and the cost of labor benefits are not causally related.
    c. The magnitude of the slope coefficient indicates that there is a low correlation between the independent and dependent variables.
    d. Logically, the slope coefficient should be positive.

17. Using units of production as the independent variable (X) to predict the cost of factory rent, you have developed the following model: Rent = $100,000 + $0X. Based on this information you might conclude that

    a. rent is a strictly variable cost.
    b. rent is a strictly fixed cost.
    c. rent is a mixed cost.
    d. rent expense and unit volume have a strong positive correlation.

18. Which of the following models assume that a linear relationship exists between the independent and dependent variables?

    a. high-low method
    b. scattergraph method
    c. simple regression
    d. all of the above

19. An item that has a cause and effect relationship with the incurrence of a variable cost is called:

    a. Direct costing
    b. An activity base
    c. Direct cost
    d. Indirect cost

20. Which of the following methods uses the most information in estimating the parameters of the prediction model?

    a. simple regression
    b. scattergraph
    c. semiaverages
    d. multiple regression

21. The estimated absolute maximum potential activity of an entity at all times is known as _____ capacity.

    a. normal
    b. expected
    c. practical
    d. theoretical

22. Consideration of operating capacity is important because

    a. cost patterns will probable change if additional capacity is added.
    b. operating capacity provides information about the upper limit of all costs.
    c. operating capacity is rarely achieved and is usually ignored.
    d. operating capacity provides information on the efficiency of operations.

Chapter 4: Developing Predetermined Overhead Rates

23. The use of volume-based cost drivers to assign costs tends to:

    a. over cost low volume products.
    b. over cost high volume products.
    c. under cost all products.
    d. over cost special orders.
    e. equally cost all products based on activity volume.

24. An everyday example of a mixed cost would be:

    a. Apartment rent
    b. Telephone bill
    c. Electric Bill
    d. Housing mortgage payment

25. The formula: Y - bX yields

    a. the regression estimate.
    b. the regression residual.
    c. the regression intercept term.
    d. none of the above.

The data below should be used for questions 26-27.

The following data was taken from the records of the Anthony Co. for 1991:

    Actual overhead $145,000
    Applied overhead   185,000
    Work in Process   110,000
    Finished Goods   180,000
    Cost of Goods Sold   450,000

26. Manufacturing overhead is

    a. overapplied by $40,000.
    b. underapplied by $40,000.
    c. overapplied by $5,000.
    d. underapplied by $5,000.

27. What amount of under- or overapplied overhead should be prorated to Work in Process (to the nearest dollar)?

    a. $ 743
    b. $5,946
    c. $9,730
    d. $5,405

28. The closing of underapplied overhead will cause

    a. Cost of Goods Sold to decrease.
    b. Cost of Goods Sold to increase.
    c. Raw Materials to increase.
    d. Work in Process to decrease.

29. In a least squares regression, the sum of the differences between the fitted lines and the observed data points is equal to

    a. the prediction error.
    b. zero.
    c. the standard error of the the estimate.
    d. coefficient of correlation.

QUESTIONS AND PROBLEMS

1. What is the major strength of the scattergraph method relative to the high-low method?

Chapter 4: Developing Predetermined Overhead Rates

2. List and define the four capacity measures. Which ones are **not** used in determining a predetermined overhead rates?

3. What is the major advantage in using simple regression rather than the scattergraph approach?

4. What does the coefficient of correlation measure and how is it related to forecasting?

BELOW IS THE DATA ON THE STUDY HOURS AND MATH TEST SCORES FROM THE EARLIER EXAMPLE IN THE CHAPTER. USE THIS INFORMATION TO ANSWER THE NEXT 6 QUESTIONS:

OBSERVATION #	STUDY HOURS	MATH SCORE
1.	2	50
2.	5	75
3.	6	70
4.	8	80
5.	12	90
6.	15	95

5. What ranges of the independent variable would require the analyst to extrapolate from this data to predict a math score?

6. Prepare a scattergraph plot and estimate the parameters of the prediction model from the scattergraph.

7. What are the predictive model's parameters based on the simple regression approach?

8. Compute the coefficient of correlation between the two variables.

9. Using the high-low method, compute the prediction function in math based on study time.

Chapter 4: Developing Predetermined Overhead Rates

10. Why are predetermined overhead rates used? What is the formula for determining the overhead rate?

11. How does underapplied overhead occur? How does overapplied overhead occur? What factors have an impact on these occurrences?

12. The following data relates to the Fuzzy Flow Co. for 1993:

Depr. on factory equipment	$ 3,300
Depr. on office equipment	5,600
Insurance on factory	1,250
Insurance on office	2,730
Indirect material	4,750
Indirect labor	11,900
Direct labor	43,000
Direct material	62,500

    Fuzzy Flow applies overhead at the rate of 45% of direct labor. Compute applied overhead and determine if overhead is under- or overapplied.

13. Use the data from #12 above and assume that, Work in Process is $27,350, Finished Goods is $56,700, and Cost of Goods Sold is $83,100. Prepare the journal entry to close overhead assuming that the amount is immaterial. Prepare the journal entry to close overhead assuming that the amount is material.

Communication Projects

1. With a partner, present the strenghts of the regression method over the high-low method for cost behavior determination. Next, your partner should repeat what he heard you say about the regression method vs. the high-low method. Next, your partner should discuss the weaknesses of the scattergraph method when compared to the regression method. You then should reiterate what he said.

    This project should enhance your ability to verbalize to a colleague a topic you should have learned about. Secondly, you should develop listening skills for your work environment.

SELF TEST SOLUTIONS

TRUE/FALSE

1. F	5. F	9. F	13. F	17. T	21. T	25. T
2. F	6. T	10. T	14. T	18. F	22. T	26. T
3. T	7. F	11. T	15. T	19. T	23. T	27. F
4. T	8. T	12. F	16. F	20. T	24. T	

MULTIPLE CHOICE

1. C	6. A	11. C	16. D	21. D	26. A
2. C	7. C	12. C	17. B	22. A	27. B
3. C	8. D	13. C	18. D	23. B	28. B
4. A	9. D	14. A	19. B	24. B	29. C
5. A	10. A	15. A	20. D	25. C	

Chapter 4: Developing Predetermined Overhead Rates 39

QUESTIONS AND PROBLEMS

1. The major strength of the scattergraph method is that it considers all of the available data on the variables. The high-low method only considers the high and low data points which means you could use outliers to distort your estimated cost function

2. Theoretical capacity (or ideal capacity)- the estimated absolute maximum potential activity of an entity. This capacity disregards things as breakdowns of machines and plant operations stopped because of holidays.

    Practical capacity is the level of activity that could be achieved during normal working hours. This level of activity could be achieved but often is not probable.

    Normal capacity is the long-run average activity of the firm. This capacity considers cyclical and seasonal fluctuations.

    Expected capacity is a short-run concept representing the anticipated level which the company expects to achieve in the coming year.

    Theoretical capacity disregards realities such as machinery breakdowns and reduced or stopped plant operations on holidays. Because of these unrealistic assumptions, this method is unacceptable basis for overhead application. Also, practical capacity is not used because it is typically not achievable and because the IRS issued temporary regulations under the 1986 Tax Act that prohibit its use in accounting for inventory.

3. There are really several advantages. From a theoretical perspective, the simple regression yields a unique and precise solution to estimation of the parameters. Alternatively, the scattergraph estimates to the parameters of the prediction model are not unique and they are determined by a process that is highly subjective. From a practical perspective, the simple regression estimates can be generated by a computer with probably less human effort than the scattergraph estimates require.

4. The coefficient of correlation, r, measures the strength of the relationship between two variables. This measure can be used as a criterion to select independent variables and to assess a model's potential for forecasting.

5. The student would be extrapolating if he was considering committing less than 2 hours to the study effort or more than 15 hours to the study effort.

6. No suggested parameter estimates are unique because of the subjective parameter estimation process, but your scattergraph parameter estimates should be fairly close to the estimates in 6. above and 8. below.

7. The simple regression parameter estimates that follow were generated by a computer package, and your estimates may differ slightly due to rounding error: Y = 51.40 + 3.16X

    The coefficients in this function are based on the following equations:
    $$b = \frac{\Sigma xy - n(\bar{x})(\bar{y})}{\Sigma x^2 - n\bar{x}^2}$$

    $$a = \bar{y} - b\bar{x}$$

8. The coefficient of correlation is approximately .9412, which indicates a very high level of correlation between the two variables.

The c value above is derived from the following equation:

9. You must calculate the variable performance rate first:

    $$PVOHR = \frac{OH_h - OH_l}{Activity_h - Activity_l}$$

    PFOHR = TC(at either h or l) - PVOHR * Activity(at

Chapter 4: Developing Predetermined Overhead Rates

The high activity is 15 hours and the low activity is 2 hours.

$$b = \frac{95 \text{ pt} - 50 \text{ pt}}{15 \text{ hr} - 2 \text{ hr}}$$
$$= 3.4615 \text{ pt/hr}$$

$$a = 95 - 3.4615 \times 15 = 51.9225 = 52$$

Math Score = $52 + 3.4615 \times SH$

10. Predetermined overhead rates are used for several reasons. First, these rates allow overhead to be assigned to items produced while they are in production instead of waiting until production is finished. Second, the use of predetermined rates allows managers to perform their duties in a timely manner and these rates also have an impact on the evaluation of managers. Third, overhead rates can compensate for fluctuations in actual overhead costs that have nothing to do with activity levels. Finally, these rates can overcome the problem of fluctuations in levels that have no impact on actual fixed overhead costs.

    The formula for determining a predetermined overhead rate is:

    $$\text{Predetermined OH rate} = \frac{\text{total estimated OH costs}}{\text{selected measure of volume/activity}}$$

11. Underapplied overhead occurs when actual overhead costs are greater than overhead applied to production. Overapplied overhead occurs when actual overhead costs are greater than applied overhead. Some factors that have an impact on under or overapplied overhead are as follows:

    a. If actual variable unit cost is higher or lower than the estimated variable unit cost, under- or overapplied overhead will occur.
    b. If actual fixed overhead and estimated fixed overhead are different, then under or overapplied overhead will result.
    c. If the actual activity level is different from the expected activity level, then under- or overapplied overhead will result.

12.
       Actual overhead $21,200*
       Applied overhead   19,350
       ($43,000 x 45%) $ 1,850 under-applied

   *($3,300, $1,250, $4,750, and $11,900)

13.
       Cost of Goods Sold   1,850
           Overhead Control   1,850

       Work in Process   303*
       Finished Goods   627*
       Cost of Goods Sold   920*
           Overhead   1,850

*(rounded)

CHAPTER 5
ACTIVITY-BASED COST SYSTEMS FOR MANAGEMENT

CHAPTER OVERVIEW

Technological alterations have diminished the managerial usefulness of "traditional" accounting information. Product design and production modernization compel parallel alterations in accounting routines. This chapter discusses several of the latest developments in accounting techniques and procedures that are evolving in response to technological changes in service and product markets.

Two of the most meaningful changes to affect many industries are an expansion in machine intensity and an increase in global markets. The increase in machine technology has been compensated for by a decrease in direct labor use. Direct labor relevance in product costing and as an overhead allocation base has lessened. Global market growth has compelled firms to be more sensitive to consumer needs in order that they stay competitive. Managers are interested in recognizing which organizational activities generate value to the consumer.

Many of the accounting and control techniques discussed in Chapter 5 are responses to the new global competition and increase in machine intensity. Other techniques have been developed in response to other recent changes in industry.

CHAPTER STUDY GUIDE

1. Production in the 1980's forced practitioners to recognize that many traditional accounting procedures were made obsolete due to the technological changes taking place in many industries. Having recognized this, changes in accounting and other control techniques were taking place.

2. Annual reporting is the bedrock of accounting conventions. They are required by governmental and regulatory agencies such as the SEC, FASB, and the IRS. The focus on annual or periodic accounting information is not always appropriate for high-quality managerial decisions. Managers have investigated other ways to use accounting information which covers a more genuine period of time in the life of the organization called product life cycle.

    a. Product life cycle costing helps in the area of cost control. Considering cost control over a product's life makes managers recognize the important role of product design in determining a product's profitability. Considering alternative ways to produce the product before production actually begins can significantly control future period costs. The 5 stages of the product life cycle are presented in Exhibit 5-2. Distinguish which costs are the focus of each stage in the life cycle.
    b. In product life cycle planning, the focus is on profitability over the entire life of the product and a comparison of the target costs to projected actual costs becomes an important basis for deciding which potential products to produce.
    c. The target cost is the projected sales price less a desired profit.

Chapter 5: Activity-Based Cost Systems for Management

        i. Target cost is important as a managerial focus.

        Note: The target cost is based on a projected sales price.

    d. Computation of the projected sales price requires management to consider which product features are valued by consumers. Knowing which elements of a new product are valued by consumers (and which are not) gives management a basis for improving the efficiency of production.

        i. Those activities and product features that do not add consumer value should be minimized through the design of: the product, the production technology, and the distribution technology.

    e. The text places production activities in one of four categories: production time, inspection time, transfer time, or idle time. Of these activities, only production time creates value for the consumer. The other activities add costs to the products but not consumer value.

    f. A ratio of production time to the total time consumed in the manufacturing process is a measure of the efficiency of the manufacturing process. This ratio is called manufacturing cycle efficiency (**MCE**). Perfect efficiency would be indicated by a ratio of 1.

3. To determine which activities add value to the product and which activities do not, managers must understand the connection of each organizational activity to each product. This association can be specified by determining why each activity exists and what "drives" the cost of an activity.

    a. The interest with consumer value and the managerial emphasis on activities rather than transactions ed to the development of activity-based costing(ABC). Activity-based costing relates and assigns organizational costs to organizational activities. Thus, costs are accumulated by activities or cost pools.

    b. Costs put in the pools are charged to units of product based on the activity used by each product. ABC relates a cost to its cause or driver.

    c. Cost drivers are identified to explain why an activity exists and how the activity relates to a product. Cost drivers identify activities that generate cost. They are an ideal justification for allocating costs to activities and products. [Exhibit 5-12 graphically demonstrates the relationships between costs, activities, cost drivers, and products(cost objects).]

        i. Since cost drivers are identified, better cost control is achieved through a focus on controlling the level of the cost-driver activity.

    d. Cost drivers may be placed in one of four types of categories: unit costs(e.g. direct materials); batch costs(e.g. set-ups); product costs(e.g. product development); and organizational or facility costs(e.g. plant manager's salary).

    e. ABC may be an appropriate substitute for the traditional volume-based cost driver approach. This may be suitable when significant changes have occurred in the production process. Significant automation is one such change. Large drops in labor costs may be justification for change. An increasing variety of products may necessitate change. Increased competition may also be reason for change. Changes in management strategy may require a change in the costing system for overhead.

    f. Advantages gained from ABC include improved product cost information and improving the performance measurement process by focusing on controlling the activities that drive the costs. ABC disadvantages include more costs to implement the system. Management must be

Chapter 5: Activity-Based Cost Systems for Management

committed to implementing this new system. ABC doesn't conform completely with GAAP and may be limited to internal use only.

g. ABC II is an expansion of ABC and may be of use to companies.

4. The theory of constraints is a procedure that may be used to improve production flow and the design of production facilities. These methods help managers eliminate production activities that do not add consumer value.

   a. The theory of constraints helps managers focus on bottlenecks (factors that limit production capacity) in the production process. Bottlenecks concentrate managerial attention because any improvement in them will improve the efficiency of the entire production process. Efforts are made to reduce bottlenecks and quality control inspections should occur before a bottleneck.

5. Chapter 5 gives an introduction into the future aim of cost and production control techniques. The relationship between Chapters 4 and 5 emphasizes the harmony between value-added discussed in this chapter and the general philosophy of JIT. JIT is concerned with reducing inventory and improving quality which is tied in with enriching product flow and designing the production activities.

SELF TEST

TRUE/FALSE

1. T F

   Recent changes in the business environment have fostered changes in cost accounting methods.

2. T F

   Global competition has decreased the demand for customer service.

3. T F

   Recent changes in the manufacturing environment include an increase in the utilization of machines.

4. T F

   The present American economy is comprised mostly of service industries rather than manufacturing industries.

5. T F

   A firm will produce a product if the product's target costs are less than its forecasted costs.

6. T F

   The greatest opportunity to control product costs is in the maturity stage of the product life cycle.

7. T F

   Variable costs should be allocated to costs based on volume related cost drivers.

8. T F

   Activity-based costing encourages the use of nonfinancial measures of activity.

Chapter 5: Activity-Based Cost Systems for Management

9. T F

   The two most important current performance objectives of U.S businesses are profit and volume.

10. T F

    Quality inspection points should be placed just downstream of major production bottlenecks.

MULTIPLE CHOICE

1. Which of the following does not characterize the "new age" of American business?

   a. high wage rates
   b. high machine intensity
   c. restricted product variety
   d. deregulated markets

2. Which of the following is not a consumer-based demand of American business?
   a. reasonable prices
   b. integrity
   c. product variety
   d. increased profitability

3. Heavy R&D expenditures are likely to be incurred in which of the following stages of product development?

   a. decline
   b. development
   c. growth
   d. maturity

4. Which of the following accounting techniques has allowed managers to reduce their dependence on annual accounting data?

   a. product life cycle costing
   b. activity-based costing
   c. critical path analysis
   d. theory of constraints

5. Which of the following parts of the production process are value-adding?

   a. inspection time
   b. transfer time
   c. idle time
   d. none of the above

6. The lead time is equal to

   a. the production time.
   b. the non-value-added time.
   c. the production time + the non-value-added time.
   d. production time + idle time.

7. The manufacturing cycle efficiency is equal to

   a. production time/non-value-added time.
   b. idle time/production time.
   c. value-added time/non-value-added time.
   d. production time/lead time.

8. Non-value-added activities can be attributed to

   a. physical factors.
   b. system factors.
   c. people factors.
   d. all of the above.

Chapter 5: Activity-Based Cost Systems for Management

9. Activity-based costing focuses on

    a. transactions.
    b. cost drivers.
    c. critical paths.
    d. resource constraints.

10. Activity-based costing will be most beneficial to firms that

    a. have very low overhead costs.
    b. have high machine intensity.
    c. have a very narrow product line.
    d. have high labor intensity.

11. A benefit of activity-based costing is that cost-reduction efforts can be focused on specific

    a. departments.
    b. transactions.
    c. cost drivers.
    d. products.

12. To eliminate non-value-adding activities, performance measures should be

    a. externally focused.
    b. based on traditional standards.
    c. based on historical performance.
    d. based on profitability.

13. The theory of constraints requires managers to concentrate on

    a. bottlenecks.
    b. cost drivers.
    c. transactions.
    d. product life cycles.

14. Target cost is equal to

    a. the forecasted sales price minus a profit.
    b. the forecasted cost.
    c. standard cost.
    d. the cost of "customer-valued" activities.

15. A cost-driver that is unaffected by volume would be used to allocate

    a. variable costs.
    b. fixed costs.
    c. period costs.
    d. product costs.

16. A firm's manufacturing cycle efficiency = .20; this indicates

    a. efficiency is optimal.
    b. non-value-adding activities = 20% of all activities.
    c. the time spent on non-value-adding activities is four times as great as the time spent on value-adding activities.
    d. the critical path is much longer than other paths.

17. Good performance indicators can be

    a. qualitative.
    b. quantitative but nonfinancial.
    c. quantitative and financial.
    d. all of the above.

Chapter 5: Activity-Based Cost Systems for Management

18. A greater concern in American industry for quality products and customer service is mostly attributable to

    a. increased machine intensity of production systems.
    b. the pressure of foreign competition.
    c. the availability of new cost accounting techniques.
    d. new production technologies.

19. In the product life cycle, high advertising costs may create operating losses in the

    a. development stage.
    b. introduction stage.
    c. the growth stage.
    d. the maturity stage.

20. If the projected cost of a product exceeds its target cost, managers would strive to

    a. eliminate non-value-added activities.
    b. reduce development costs.
    c. increase the sales price.
    d. reduce advertising costs.

21. In activity-based costing, cost drivers are used to

    a. allocate costs to activities.
    b. allocate costs from activities to products.
    c. allocate costs to activities and from activities to products.
    d. allocate variable costs only.

22. In activity-based costing, costs are first collected into cost pools for each

    a. product.
    b. production process.
    c. activity.
    d. department.

23. Delays in a production environment are caused by

    a. constraints.
    b. the critical path.
    c. the lead time.
    d. long production runs.

24. Which of the following would be the least appropriate cost driver for allocating overhead in a highly automated manufacturer of specialty valves:

    a. machine hours.
    b. power consumption.
    c. direct labor hours.
    d. machine setups.

25. More accurate product costing information is produced by assigning costs using:

    a. a volume-based, plant-wide rate
    b. volume-based, departmental rates
    c. activity-based pool rates
    d. all of the above produce accurate product costing information

26. The use of volume-based cost drivers to assign costs tends to:

    a. overcost low volume products
    b. overcost high volume products
    c. undercost all products
    d. overcost all products

Chapter 5: Activity-Based Cost Systems for Management   47

27. The term "cost driver" refers to

   a. a causal or beneficial relationship that can be used for the allocation of indirect costs.
   b. the attempt to control expenditures at a reasonable level.
   c. the person who gathers and transfers cost data to the management accountant.
   d. any activity that causes costs to be incurred.

28. The numbers of vendors, products, and engineering change orders are examples of

   a. potential cost drivers.
   b. beneficial relationships.
   c. unavoidable overhead costs.
   d. inputs to processing time.

29. The use of flexible manufacturing systems and production work cells

   a. is advantageous in all manufacturing situations.
   b. results in the merging of direct labor with factory overhead, and thus the accounting problem becomes one of accounting for conversion costs.
   c. results in the merging of direct labor and factory overhead, and thus there is increased accounting emphasis on tracking direct labor cost.
   d. All of the above

30. The JIT environment has caused a reassessment of product costing techniques. Which of the following statements is true with respect to this reassessment?

   a. Traditional cost allocations based on direct labor are being questioned and criticized.
   b. The federal government, through the SEC, is responsible for the reassessment.
   c. The problem is caused by the replacement of machine hours with labor hours.
   d. None of the above

QUESTIONS AND PROBLEMS

1. How has global competition affected the focus of American managers?

2. At what stage of the product life cycle do managers have the greatest capability to influence production costs?

3. Why does activity-based costing offer greater opportunities than traditional accounting approaches to reduce costs?

Chapter 5: Activity-Based Cost Systems for Management

4. How has technological innovation affected the types of costs that a manufacturing firm incurs?

5. Why have new cost accounting techniques evolved in recent years?

6. How has the product life cycle approach improved traditional accounting approaches to production and cost control?

Question 7 refers to the following: Tiger Company produces two items, Standard and Super. Data for last year's production are as follows:

	Model	
	Regular	Special
Direct material cost per unit	$35	$40
Direct labor cost per unit	$30	$50
Direct labor hours per unit	6 hrs.	10 hrs.
Units produced	3,000	7,000

The company's overhead costs of $154,000 can be traced to three major activities as follows:

	Traceable Costs	Number of Events or Transactions		
		Total	Regular	Special
Machine setups required	$ 50,000	1,250	500	750
Power consumption in Hs	60,000	90,000	30,000	60,000
Shipments made	44,000	800	300	500
	$ 154,000			

7. If Tiger uses activity-based costing, the total cost per unit of producing the Regular and Special items (round to the nearest penny) are what?

Chapter 5: Activity-Based Cost Systems for Management

COMMUNICATION PROJECT

In your group, one of your members should verbally explain why activity based costing(ABC) has stimulated interest in U.S. industries. Another member of the group explain the steps to be followed in using ABC. A third member of the group explain the shortcomings of using ABC.

SELF TEST SOLUTIONS

TRUE/FALSE

1. T	3. T	5. F	7. T	9. F
2. F	4. T	6. F	8. T	10. F

MULTIPLE CHOICE

1. C	6. C	11. C	16. C	21. C	26. B
2. D	7. D	12. A	17. D	22. C	27. D
3. B	8. D	13. A	18. B	23. A	28. A
4. A	9. B	14. A	19. B	24. C	29. C
5. D	10. B	15. B	20. A	25. C	30. A

QUESTIONS AND PROBLEMS

1. Global competition has increased managerial awareness of customer service and product quality. High-quality products from Europe and Japan have forced American managers to become more competitive in providing quality products and more attentive to consumer value.

2. The authors suggest that about 90% of product cost is determined in the development stage. Hence, this stage is the most appropriate stage for considering alternative product design and production design features to reduce and control costs.

3. Activity-based costing has greater potential to reduce costs than traditional accounting techniques. Such potential stems from the fact that activity-based costing focuses on cost drivers (not costs) which are the activities that actually create costs. Thus, as non-value-adding activities are eliminated, costs are reduced.

4. Technological innovation has increased the level of machine costs and decreased the level of direct labor costs. Technology has also increased product variety and hence the related costs of switching from the production of one product to another.

5. New accounting techniques have evolved in recent years because managers need different information today than they needed in prior years to make quality decisions. The need for different accounting procedures stems from the increased managerial focus on product quality and customer service, and the need for extensive planning in the product design stage because of the subsequent extensive investment in fixed, machine-intensive production technology.

6. Product life cycle planning has improved the quality of managerial decisions by bringing the managerial focus to pre-production planning, and elimination of activities that do not create value for the consumer. Efficient production is achieved through reductions in time and resources committed to non-value-adding activities.

7. Activity based costing (or ABC) assigns overhead based on the amount of overhead consumed by each product with costs first assigned to cost pools and then determining the cost driver for each pool.

Cost pools	Traceable Costs	Cost Driver	Cost per Driver Unit
Setup costs	$ 50,000	1,250 su	$40 / su
Power costs	60,000	90,000 H	$ .667 H
Shipping costs	44,000	800 ship.	$55 per ship.

	Regular	Special
Setups @ $40/su	$20,000	$30,000
Power @ $.667/H	20,000	40,000
Shipping @ $55/ship.	16,500	27,500
Total overhead	56,500	97,500
Divide by units produced	3,000	7,000
OH $ per unit	$ 18.833	$ 13.929
DM	35	40
DL	30	50
Total cost per unit	$ 83.833	$ 103.929

CHAPTER 6

ADDITIONAL OVERHEAD ALLOCATION CONCEPTS AND ISSUES

CHAPTER OVERVIEW

In Chapter 4 overhead was allocated through the calculation of a predetermined overhead application rate. Chapter 6 shows how cost pools can be used to allocate overhead (Exhibit 6-2). Cost pools are installed to give a more practical allocation procedure. Cost pools are collected through a common element, such as being incurred for the same purpose or at the same organizational level.

Chapter 6 reviews different methods of allocating service department costs to revenue producing departments so that these costs can be included as part of overhead and, therefore, part of product cost. There are three basic methods of allocating service department costs: the direct method, the step method, and the algebraic method. The text also discusses some reasons for and against this allocation process (Exhibit 6-3). The direct method allocates service department costs directly to the revenue-producing divisions (Exhibits 6-9 and 6-10). The step method (or "benefits provided" ranking method) allocates service department costs to both revenue-producing and non-revenue-producing divisions and is illustrated in Exhibit 6-11. The algebraic method (reciprocal or matrix approach) is the third method which analyzes interdepartmental relationships (Exhibits 6-12 and 6-13) and allocates costs between service departments and revenue departments at the same time.

The appendix discusses the Uniform Capitalization Rules of the Tax Reform Act of 1986. These rules require entities to capitalize, for tax purposes, certain period costs as product costs.

CHAPTER STUDY GUIDE

1. The chapter discusses what cost allocation is and three reasons why indirect costs are allocated. Cost allocation is the methodical apportionment of costs to cost objects. This may be done over several periods(e.g. depreciation) or in a single period(e.g. overhead).

    a. The reasons for the indirect cost allocations are as follows:

        i.   to determine a full product cost;
        ii. to motivate managers; and
        iii. to provide information for decision making.

    b. To make this allocation process more credible, cost pools can be used. A cost pool is a collection of dollar amounts that are incurred for the same purpose or at the same organizational level.

        i. For a cost pool to be helpful, there must be some likeness among the costs. Each cost pool may then be allocated to cost objects using separate cost drivers that are correlated to the incurence of the costs in the pool.

2. The chapter then deals with allocation of costs from non-revenue-producing departments (service and administrative) to revenue-producing departments.

Chapter 6: Additional Overhead Allocation Concepts and Issues

    a.   A service department (such as the Data Processing Department) provides a functional task(s) to other internal units.

    b.   An administrative department (such as the Personnel Department) provides management activities that will benefit the entire organization. "Service departments" include both types of organizational areas. Exhibit 6-3 discusses why such allocations are needed by organizations. Chapter 6 covers three basic methods of allocating service department costs: the direct method, the step method, and the algebraic method.

3.   The direct method distributes service department costs directly to revenue-producing units; a specific basis (such as the number of people in a department) is used for each service department allocation.

4.   The step method distributes costs to both non revenue-producing divisions and revenue-producing departments in a stair step fashion.

    a.   First determine the relationships between the departments so they can be ranked in order of the amount of service provided to other departments, from most to least.

    b.   A specific basis for each department is used to allocate costs from a department to other departments. Once costs are allocated out of a department, they cannot flow back in. This is done until all costs are distributed from the service departments to the revenue departments.

5.   The algebraic method sets up simultaneous equations to represent functional relationships between the departments. Costs can then flow to and from a department.

    a.   Ideally, this provides the most realistic service department allocations and, with the increase in computer spreadsheet usage, is no longer the complex task it was in the past.

    b.   This method does, however, create some "fictional" costs in the reallocation process; these costs are disregarded in the final allocation system. Exhibits 6-9 through 6-13 illustrate the various service department allocation methods.

6.   Lastly, the appendix discusses the Uniform Capitalization Rules (unicap rules) that require organizations to capitalize some period costs that had previously been accounted for as product costs.

    a.   Exhibit 6-16 illustrates the costs that are required to be included and excluded from product cost. These rules have also been referred to as **super-full absorption costing**.

SELF TEST

TRUE/FALSE

1.   T F

Cost allocation is the assignment of direct costs to one or more cost objects using some reasonable basis.

2.   T F

The term allocation means the systematic assignment of something to a recipient set of categories.

3.   T F

A cost pool is a collection of accounts that are used for the same purpose within the organization.

Chapter 6: Additional Overhead Allocation Concepts and Issues

4. T F

    A service department provides functional tasks for other external units.

5. T F

    An administrative department performs management activities that benefit the entire organization.

6. T F

    The three objectives of cost allocation are full cost, managerial motivation, and decision making.

7. T F

    The full cost of a product includes only those costs that are directly traceable to the product.

8. T F

    The two criteria used most often to decide on allocation bases are benefits received and fairness.

9. T F

    The direct method assigns service department costs directly to revenue-producing areas with no other intermediate cost pools or allocations.

10. T F

    The step method assigns indirect service department costs before considering interrelationships of the cost objects.

11. T F

    The algebraic method considers all interrelationships of the departments and reflects these in simultaneous equations.

12. T F

    The step method assigns costs in a "benefits-provided" ranking order.

13. T F

    The direct method of assigning indirect service department costs is also referred to as the "reciprocal" method.

MULTIPLE CHOICE

1. Which of the following methods of assigning indirect service department costs recognizes, on a partial basis, the reciprocal relationships among the departments?

    a. the step method
    b. the direct method
    c. the indirect method
    d. the algebraic method

2. The _____ method is also referred to as the reciprocal method.

    a. the step method
    b. the direct method
    c. the indirect method
    d. the algebraic method

Chapter 6: Additional Overhead Allocation Concepts and Issues

3. The _____ method uses a "benefits-provided" ranking.

    a. the step method
    b. the direct method
    c. the indirect method
    d. the algebraic method

4. The _____ method assigns service department costs to revenue-producing departments without flows into any other service departments.

    a. the step method
    b. the direct method
    c. the indirect method
    d. the algebraic method

5. Which of the following is **not** a basic method of allocating service department costs?

    a. the step method
    b. the direct method
    c. the indirect method
    d. the algebraic method

6. Regardless of the method chosen to allocate service department costs, the method should be

    a. easy to use and reasonable.
    b. systematic and reasonable.
    c. systematic and rational.
    d. a, b, and c

7. What is the most important goal of a product cost system?

    a. To estimate the short-run costs of producing each product.
    b. To estimate the short-run costs of producing proto-types.
    c. To estimate the long-run costs of producing proto-types.
    d. To estimate the long-run costs of producing each product.

8. Why do organizations incur costs?

	To Generate Revenue	To Incur Losses
a.	no	no
b.	yes	yes
c.	no	yes
d.	yes	no

9. Service departments provide functional tasks for which of the following?

	Internal Units	External Units
a.	no	no
b.	yes	yes
c.	no	yes
d.	yes	no

10. An administrative department typically performs management activities that benefit which of the following?

	Entire Business	Parts of the Business
a.	no	no
b.	yes	yes
c.	no	yes
d.	yes	no

Chapter 6: Additional Overhead Allocation Concepts and Issues

11. Which of the following would be classified as a service department?

	Central Supply	Central Purchasing	Central Repair
a.	yes	yes	yes
b.	yes	yes	no
c.	no	yes	yes
d.	no	no	no

12. Which of the following are considered objectives of cost allocation?

	Full Cost	Management Motivation	Decision Making
a.	no	no	no
b.	no	no	yes
c.	yes	yes	yes
d.	yes	yes	no

13. Which of the following is **not** an objective for computing full cost?

    a. To provide for cost recovery.
    b. To accurately indicate usage of services.
    c. To instill a consideration of support costs in production managers.
    d. To reflect production's "fair share" of costs.

14. Which of the following is **not** a management motivation objective of service department cost allocation?

    a. To provide relevant information in determining corporate wide profits generated by alternative actions.
    b. To encourage the usage of certain services.
    c. To encourage production managers to help service departments control costs.
    d. To reflect usage of services on a fair and equitable basis.

15. The two criteria that are used most often to decide on allocation bases are

    a. benefits received and fairness.
    b. benefits received and causal relationships.
    c. causal relationships and fairness.
    d. fairness and ability-to-bear.

Use the following data for questions 16-22

The Murphy Co. has 2 service departments: Personnel and Administration. The company also has 3 divisions: A, B, and C. Personnel costs are allocated based on the number of employees, while Administration costs are allocated based on value of assets employed.

	Direct Costs	Number of Employees	Value of Assets Employed
A	$450,000	20	$1,000,000
B	300,000	10	850,000
C	800,000	50	2,150,000
Pers.	200,000	5	350,000
Admin.	500,000	12	300,000

16. Using the direct method, what amount of Personnel costs is allocated to A (to the nearest dollar)?

    a. $47,000
    b. $50,000
    c. $41,237
    d. $43,478

Chapter 6: Additional Overhead Allocation Concepts and Issues

17. Using the direct method, what amount of Administration costs is allocated to B (to the nearest dollar)?

    a. $106,250
    b. $ 91,398
    c. $ 98,837
    d. $ 97,701

18. Using the direct method, what amount of Personnel costs is allocated to B (to the nearest dollar)?

    a. $ 50,000
    b. $ 25,000
    c. $125,000
    d. $ 66,667

19. Using the direct method, what amount of Personnel costs is allocated to C (to the nearest dollar)?

    a. $120,000
    b. $117,647
    c. $125,000
    d. $103,093

20. Assume that Administration provides more service to the other areas than does Personnel. What cost is allocated to A from Personnel using the step method (to the nearest dollar)?

    a. $50,000
    b. $60,058
    c. $40,230
    d. $55,000

21. Assume that Administration provides more service to the other areas than does Personnel. What is the Administration cost allocated to B using the step method (to the nearest dollar)?

    a. $ 97,701
    b. $114,943
    c. $247,126
    d. $ 40,230

22. Assume that Administration provides more service to the other areas than does Personnel. What is the ratio to allocate Administration costs to C using the step method?

    a. $5000,000/$4,350,000 x $500,000
    b. $2,150,000/$4,000,000 x $500,000
    c. $2,150,000/$4,650,000 x $500,000
    d. $2,150,000/$4,350,000 x $500,000

The FJZ Co. has 3 service departments and 2 production departments. The chart below presents the data needed for numbers 23-25.

Dept.	S1	S2	S3	P1	P2
S1	--	.1	.1	.1	.7
S2	.2	--	.1	.4	.3
S3	.1	.1	--	.4	.4

Costs have accumulated for S1, S2, and S3 as follows:
$60,000, $50,000 and $70,000 respectively.

23. Using the algebraic method, what is the interdepartmental formula for S1?

    a. S1=$60,000 + .1S2 + .1S3
    b. S1=$60,000 + .1S2 + .1S3 + .1P1 +.1P2
    c. S1=$180,000 + .1S2 + .1S3
    d. S1=$120,000 + .1S2 + .1S3 + .1P1 +.1P2

Chapter 6: Additional Overhead Allocation Concepts and Issues

24. Using the algebraic method, what is the interdepartmental formula for S2?

    a. S2= $50,000 + .4P1 + .3P2
    b. S2= $50,000 + .2S1 + .1S3
    c. S2= $180,000 + .2S1 + .1S3
    d. S2= $50,000 + .2S1 + .1S3 + .4P1 + .3P2

25. Using the algebraic method, what is the formula representing interdepartmental usage of services for S3?

    a. S3= $180,000 + .1S1 + .1S2 + .4P1 + .4P2
    b. S3= $70,000 + .1S1 + .1S2 + .4P1 + .4P2
    c. S3= $70,000 + .4P1 + .4P2
    d. S3= $180,000 + .1S1 + .1S2

26. Which allocation method, direct or step, would be classified as the most difficult and which would be classified as the most accurate?

	Most difficult	Most accurate
a.	Direct	Direct
b.	Direct	Step
c.	Step	Direct
d.	Step	Step

27. Which of the following would be classified as an operating department?

    a. The buildings and grounds department of a hospital.
    b. The cost accounting department in a manufacturing company.
    c. The tax department in a public accounting firm.
    d. The custodial department in a medical clinic.

28. Which of the following would be classified as a service department?

    a. The maternity department in a hospital.
    b. The employee training department of a computer manufacturer.
    c. The academic marketing department of a university.
    d. The jewelry department of a department store.

29. The step method of allocating service department costs:

    a. can't be used when a company has more than two service departments.
    b. ignores some interdepartmental services.
    c. is a less accurate method of allocation than the direct method.
    d. is a simpler allocation method than the direct method.

30. Which of the following allocation methods partially recognize services that service departments provide to each other?

    a. direct method
    b. step method
    c. reciprocal method
    d. all of the above methods partially recognize reciprocal services

31. Which of the following allocation methods fully recognizes services that service departments provide to each other?

    a. direct method
    b. step method
    c. reciprocal method
    d. all of the above methods fully recognize reciprocal services

32. Which of the following allocation methods does not recognize any services that service departments provide to each other?

    a. direct methods
    b. step method
    c. reciprocal method
    d. none of the above methods recognize reciprocal services

58   Chapter 6:   Additional Overhead Allocation Concepts and Issues

33. Service departments:

   a. are responsible for manufacturing the products sold to customers
   b. work directly on the products of the firm
   c. provide services directly to customers
   d. provide support services to the producing departments

34. The major objectives of allocations are:

   a. to motivate managers
   b. to compute product line profitability
   c. to value inventory
   d. all of the above

35. A possible causal factor to use when allocating cafeteria costs would be:

   a. number of square feet
   b. number of direct labor hours
   c. number of employees
   d. none of the above

36. Proper cost allocation procedures are necessary for management accountants to

   a. determine product or service unit costs.
   b. prepare budgets and cost controls for management.
   c. prepare reports to aid and support management decisions.
   d. all of the above

QUESTIONS AND PROBLEMS

1. Define service departments and administrative departments. Give examples of each.

2. Discuss the reasons for and against the full cost objective of allocating service department costs.

3. In determining an allocation base an accountant must consider four criteria. What are these criteria?

4. What are the three basic allocation methods for service department costs? Briefly discuss each.

Chapter 6: Additional Overhead Allocation Concepts and Issues

5. (Appendix) What are the unicap rules? Briefly discuss these rules.

Use the data below to answer questions 6-7.

The Dawn Co. has three service departments: Personnel, Administration and Data Processing. Dawn also has two production departments A and B. Personnel costs are allocated based on employees; Administration costs are allocated based on value of assets employed; and Data Processing costs are allocated based on hours of usage.

	Direct Costs	Employees	Assets Used	Hours Used
Pers.	$550,000	6	$200,000	1,000
Admin.	$230,000	20	$650,000	1,800
Data Proc.	$800,000	4	$900,000	2,100
A	$150,000	10	$100,000	800
B	$300,000	15	$300,000	1,200

6. Using the direct method, what amount of Personnel costs is allocated to A?

7. Using the direct method, what amount of Personnel costs is allocated to B?

COMMUNICATION PROBLEMS

Within your class work group, do the following problem. Your groups solution will be the basis for this assignment. Your results will be a basis for the grade. However, a bonus will be given for group scores higher than the class average based on a sliding scale. You are encouraged to work together for the betterment of the group. This process stimulates positive interdependence in a "I win-you win" environment. You learn to work together gaining from each group members' strenghts.

The Dawn Co. has three service departments: Personnel, Administration and Data Processing. Dawn also has two production departments A and B. Personnel costs are allocated based on employees; Administration costs are allocated based on value of assets employed; and Data Processing costs are allocated based on hours of usage.

	Direct Costs	Employees	Assets Used	Hours Used
Pers.	$550,000	6	$200,000	1,000
Admin.	$230,000	20	$650,000	1,800
Data Proc.	$800,000	4	$900,000	2,100
A	$150,000	10	$100,000	800
B	$300,000	15	$300,000	1,200

Chapter 6: Additional Overhead Allocation Concepts and Issues

Assume that the service departments provide service in the order listed. How much overhead (Pers., Admin., and Data Proc.) is allocated to A and B using the step method? Show your work.

SELF TEST SOLUTIONS

TRUE/FALSE

1. F	6. T	11. T
2. T	7. F	12. T
3. F	8. F	13. F
4. F	9. T	
5. T	10. F	

MULTIPLE CHOICE

1. A	7. D	13. B	19. C	25. D	31. A
2. D	8. D	14. A	20. B	26. D	32. A
3. A	9. D	15. B	21. A	27. C	33. A
4. B	10. D	16. B	22. D	28. B	34. A
5. C	11. A	17. A	23. A	29. B	35. A
6. B	12. C	18. B	24. C	30. A	36. D

QUESTIONS AND PROBLEMS

1. A service department provides functional tasks to other internal units. Service departments include central purchasing, central supply, central warehousing, and central computer services. An administrative department performs management duties that typically benefit the entire business. Administrative departments include personnel and organization headquarters.

2. The computation of full cost is one objective of allocating service department costs. Some reasons for the full cost objective include the following: it provides for cost recovery; it reflects production's fair share of costs; it meets regulations in some pricing situations; and it helps implant consideration of support costs in production managers. Some reasons against the full cost objective include the following: it provides costs that are beyond the control of the production manager; it provides arbitrary costs that are not useful in making decisions; and it confuses the issues of pricing and costing.

3. The four criteria that must be reflected in an allocation base are: (1) the benefits received by the departments that generate revenue; (2) causal relationships that exist between costs incurred and the departments generating revenue; (3) fairness or equity in the allocations between or among the revenue-generating departments; and (4) the ability of the departments generating revenue to bear the allocated costs.

4. The three methods used for service department cost allocation are (1) the direct method, (2) the step method, and (3) the algebraic method. The direct method assigns service department costs directly to the departments that generate the revenue. The step method assigns costs using a benefits provided ranking after taking into consideration the relationships that exist between the cost objects. The algebraic method assigns costs based on relationships between the departments and reflects these in simultaneous equations.

Chapter 6: Additional Overhead Allocation Concepts and Issues

5. The Uniform Capitalization Rules (also referred to as the unicap rules) require businesses to capitalize certain period costs as product costs. The rationalization for this is that these costs are incident to production or acquisition of products.

6. 10/25 x $550,000 = $220,000 Pers. Costs to A

7. 15/25 x $550,000 = $330,000 Pers. Costs to B

CHAPTER 7
JOB ORDER COSTING

CHAPTER OVERVIEW

Chapter 7 addresses two main topics: methods of valuation and job order costing. Chapters 7 and 8 cover the two basic costs systems (job order costing and process costing, respectively). The following definitions are necessary to study these two chapters. Job order costing is a cost system used by entities that produce diverse products or services, while process costing is used by entities that produce identical products.

The chapter discusses three basic methods of valuation: actual, normal, and standard costing. An entity must have both a cost system and a method of valuation. Exhibit 7-1 summarizes these two cost systems and three valuation methods. Chapter 7 covers job order costing using a normal cost system. The Appendix discusses job order costing using a standard cost system. Standard costing is covered in more depth in Chapters 11 and 12.

CHAPTER STUDY GUIDE

1. Chapter 7 begins with an overview of job order and process cost systems. A job order cost system is used by businesses that produce small quantities of items for special requests from customer. Entities that might utilize this type of cost system include an auto repair shop, a jeweler who makes special order items, and a dentist office.

    a. A process cost system is used by entities producing large quantities of products that are similar in nature. Manufacturers of canned food goods, auto parts, and soda might utilize this type of cost system.

2. The valuation methods discussed in Chapter 7 include actual, normal, and standard costing.

    a. An actual costing method uses the actual costs of direct materials, direct labor, and overhead in the determination of Work in Process inventory.

    b. A normal costing system uses actual direct materials, direct labor costs, and a predetermined overhead rate instead of actual overhead.

        i. Chapter 4 discussed the use and computation of predetermined overhead rates. These rates are calculated by dividing estimated or budgeted overhead by a specific activity level or volume.

    c. Standard costing requires that standards be developed for direct materials and/or direct labor. Standards for direct materials and direct labor may be developed for quantities and/or costs. In a standard cost system, overhead is applied to Work in Process based on a predetermined rate and the units produced. Exhibit 7-1 summarizes the cost systems and methods of valuation.

    d. A business entity must use both a cost system (either job order or process) and a method of valuation for its products or services.

Chapter 7: Job Order Costing

3. A job order cost system is used when an entity produces diverse items. The term "job" refers to each individual item or cost object. In a job order cost system, each job is accounted for separately.

   a. The records for each job in process are maintained in a subsidiary ledger (composed of job cost records) for Work in Process (Exhibit 7-2). Most job order systems use normal costing to determine the cost of the job.

4. In a job order or cost system, there are three stages of work: (1) agreed upon but not started (2) work in process and (3) finished jobs. The system uses a variety of source documents such as job cost records, material requisition forms and employee time sheets (Exhibits 7-3 through 7-6).

   a. A job cost sheet records virtually all of the financial data about a particular job.

   b. A material requisition form indicates the types and quantities of materials that are being sent to production.

   c. An employee time sheet indicates for each employee the amount of time spent on each job.

      i. The time may be recorded manually by the employee or electronically by a computer, which maintains the time spent on each job, along with materials issued for the job.

5. Journal entries must be prepared to record the purchase of raw materials, the transfer of raw material costs to Work in Process, incurring labor charges, the actual overhead, the application of overhead to Work in Process, and the transfer of goods completed to Finished Goods. Costs are traced to each particular job and are posted to the related job cost record. These costs can then be compared to estimates (assuming the job cost record has budgeted costs shown on it).

   a. As with time sheets, manual recording of journal entries may be done electronically by a computer.

6. Actual costs are not used in inventory accounts in a standard costing system. The standards or "norms" that were set in advance of actual production or provision of service are recorded in the various inventory accounts.

   a. At appropriate points in time, actual and standard costs are compared for control purposes to determine the efficiency of the production process. Any differences that exist between the actual and standard costs are recorded as variances. Variances are covered in more detail in Chapters 9 and 10.

   b. Since each job in a job order cost system is unique, it may be feasible to develop standards only for materials, labor costs, or quantities, rather than standards for all production factors. See the APPENDIX for more detail about standard costs in a job order system.

7. High-tech environments and product costing are the last topics discussed in Chapter 7. JIT (or "just in time"), a relatively new concept in manufacturing, is mentioned. JIT means inventory is produced when it is needed or in time to be sold or used.

8. The theory of constraints is discussed in the Appendix. In a firm, bottlenecks exist that may cause a system to operate at a lower level of performance. Repetitive manufacturing, an evolving processing system, produces homogeneous goods in large volumes similar to a process system.

   a. The major differences between the two are that the goods in a repetitive system are made in discrete units, rather than in a continuous process, and that process time is short, rather than long.

Chapter 7: Job Order Costing

SELF TEST

TRUE/FALSE

1. T **F**

    Heterogeneous products are produced in a process costing system.

2. **T** F

    Homogeneous products are produced in a process costing system.

3. **T** F

    A job order cost system is characterized by the production of unique or one-of-a-kind items.

4. **T** F

    A process cost system is characterized by the production of mass quantities of like products.

5. T **F**

    A process cost system is appropriate for service firms.

6. **T** F

    Actual costing uses actual costs for direct materials, direct labor, and a predetermined overhead rate for applying overhead to production.

7. **T** F

    Normal costing uses actual costs for direct materials, direct labor, and a predetermined overhead rate for applying overhead to production.

8. **T** F

    Standard costing uses norms only for direct labor and direct material quantities.

9. T **F**

    Product costing is concerned only with the measurement of costs and the identification of costs.

10. T **F**

    A job order system does **not** require the use of a subsidiary ledger for Work in Process inventory.

11. **T** F

    The job cost sheet is a source document that provides almost all financial information about a job.

12. **T** F

    An employee time sheet indicates the amount of time and the particular job(s) on which an employee worked.

13. T **F**

    A variance is the difference between actual cost and historical cost.

14. **T** F

    A major difference in using job order costing for a service firm and for a manufacturing firm is that a service firm will use less direct material.

Chapter 7: Job Order Costing

15. T (F)

    Job order costing is not useful to managers for planning or decision making purposes.

16. (T) F

    A job order costing system is primarily used when the production process is single jobs or batches.

17. (T) F

    A key control element to a job order costing system is a source document.

18. T (F)

    The purchase requisition is the document that authorizes a vendor to ship the desired merchandise.

19. T (F)

    If an employee is paid overtime wages while working on a job, the overtime premium is always charged to the job through the manufacturing overhead account.

20. T (F)

    The use of predetermined overhead rates eliminates the need to accumulate actual manufacturing overhead costs during a period.

21. (T) F

    A job cost sheet is used to accumulate costs chargeable to a job.

MULTIPLE CHOICE

1. Which of the following is **not** a basic method of valuation?

    a. actual costing
    b. standard costing
    c. normal costing
    (d.) assigned costing

2. Which of the following characteristics does **not** relate to a job order cost system?

    (a.) large quantities
    b. small quantities
    c. distinct items
    d. identifiable items

3. Which of the following is correct for job order and process costing?

	Job Order	Process Costing
a.	heterogeneous	heterogeneous
b.	homogeneous	heterogeneous
(c.)	heterogeneous	homogeneous
d.	homogeneous	homogeneous

4. Which of the following is most likely to utilize a job order cost system?

    a. Brewery
    (b.) Shipbuilder
    c. Oil refinery
    d. Chemical company

Chapter 7: Job Order Costing

5. The combination of actual direct labor, actual direct materials, and predetermined overhead is called

    a. standard costing.
    b. actual costing.
    c. normal costing.
    d. opportunity costing.

6. The use of actual direct labor, direct material, and overhead costs is called

    a. standard costing.
    b. actual costing.
    c. normal costing.
    d. abnormal costing.

7. Standard costing requires that "norms" be used for

	Direct Material	Direct Labor	Overhead
a.	yes	yes	no
b.	yes	no	yes
c.	**yes**	**yes**	**yes**
d.	no	no	yes

8. In regard to costs, product costing is concerned with which of the following?

	Identification	Measurement	Assignment
a.	**yes**	**yes**	**yes**
b.	yes	no	no
c.	no	no	yes
d.	no	yes	no

9. Job cost records are used for which of the following cost systems?

	Job Order	Process Costing
a.	yes	yes
b.	**yes**	**no**
c.	no	no
d.	no	yes

10. Which of the following is most likely to utilize a process cost system?

    a. Construction company
    b. Printer
    c. Yacht builder
    d. Sugar refinery

11. A material requisition form shows which of the following?

	Types of Materials	Quantities of Materials
a.	yes	no
b.	no	yes
c.	**yes**	**yes**
d.	no	no

12. Which of the following is the correct journal entry for the requisition of direct material for production?   Dr WIP / Cr DM

    a. Debit Raw Materials, credit Accounts Payable
    b. Debit Work in Process, credit Accounts Payable
    c. Debit Overhead, credit Work in Process
    d. Debit Work in Process, credit Raw Materials

Chapter 7: Job Order Costing

13. Which of the following is the correct journal entry for the requisition of indirect material for production?

    a. Debit Overhead, credit Raw Materials
    b. Debit Raw Materials, credit Accounts Payable
    c. Debit Overhead, credit Accounts Payable
    d. Debit Raw Materials, credit Work in Process

Use the following information for questions 14-19.

The North Co. (which just began operations) has the following data available from its job order cost system. The company began work on three jobs this period: #101, #102, and #103. The balance in the Raw Materials account is $90,000. Direct materials are requisitioned at the following percentages: 20%, 30%, and 35%. respectively. The remainder of the Raw Materials is utilized as indirect material. Direct labor hours (DLH) are as follows: #101-350 DLH, #102-200 DLH, and #103-300 DLH. All of the employees are paid at the rate of $10 per DLH. North Co. has indirect labor in the amount of $1,500 and applies overhead at 150% of direct labor cost.

14. What amount of direct materials is assigned to Job 101?

    a. $18,000
    b. $27,000
    c. $31,500
    d. $76,500

15. What amount of direct labor is allocated to Job 103?

    a. $10,300
    b. $3,000
    c. $8,500
    d. $3,500

16. What amount of overhead is allocated to Job 102?

    a. $ 450
    b. $3,000
    c. $2,250
    d. $1,275

17. What is the total balance in Work In Process?

    a. $104,250
    b. $90,750
    c. $97,750
    d. $109,875

18. What amount of indirect materials is allocated to overhead?

    a. $ 1,500
    b. $ 3,000
    c. $13,500
    d. $13,000

19. What is the balance in the overhead account?

    a. $ 5,625
    b. $ 2,250
    c. $27,750
    d. $15,000

20. The difference between actual cost and the standard established is called a

    a. variance.
    b. norm.
    c. benchmark.
    d. fluctuation.

Chapter 7: Job Order Costing

21. Repetitive manufacturing produces which of the following types of products?

	Discrete Units	Continuous Flows
a.	yes	yes
b.	yes	no
c.	no	no
d.	no	yes

22. A repetitive manufacturing system involves which of the following?

	Large Volume	Heterogeneous
a.	no	no
b.	yes	yes
c.	yes	no
d.	no	yes

23. A JIT inventory system is defined as an inventory system in which items are manufactured

    a. as quickly as possible.
    b. in a regular manner.
    c. as the need arise.
    d. to keep machinery and labor fully utilized.

24. The theory of constraints holds that, in an organization, there are bottlenecks that

    a. keep a system from achieving higher performance.
    b. will not allow the use of a job order system.
    c. will not allow the use of a standard costing system.
    d. keep the flow of production at a rate conducive to direct labor abilities.

25. When a service is completed, it is typically recorded in which of the following accounts?

	Cost of Goods Sold	Finished Goods
a.	yes	yes
b.	no	yes
c.	no	no
d.	yes	no

26. In job order costing, what journal entry should be made for the replacement to the storekeeper of direct materials previously issued to the factory for use on a particular job?

    a. Debit materials and credit factory overhead
    b. Debit materials and credit work in process
    c. Debit purchase returns and credit work in process
    d. Debit work in process and credit materials

27. American utilizes a job order cost system and applies factory overhead to production orders on the basis of direct labor cost. The overhead rates for July are 200 percent for department A and 50 percent for department B. Job 123 started and completed during July was charged with the following costs:

	Department A	Department B
Direct Materials	$25,000	$ 5,000
Direct Labor		$30,000
Factory Overhead	$40,000	

    The total manufacturing cost associated with Job 123 should be:

    a. $135,000
    b. $180,000
    c. $195,000
    d. $240,000

Chapter 7: Job Order Costing

28. Work in Process is a control account sustained by detailed cost data contained in the:

    a. job cost sheets.
    b. Manufacturing Overhead account.
    c. Finished Goods inventory account.
    d. time tickets and purchase requisitions issued during the accounting period.

29. A correct journal entry (without numbers) to record the issuance of raw materials into production would be:

    a. Finished Goods
           Raw Materials
    b. Raw Materials
           Work in Process
    c. Work in Process
           Raw Materials
    d. Raw Materials
           Finished Goods

30. In a job-order cost system, the application of manufacturing overhead typically would be recorded as an increase in:

    a. Cost of goods sold.
    b. Work in process inventory.
    c. Manufacturing overhead.
    d. Finished goods inventory.

31. The cost elements incurred when producing a product include all of the following costs excluding:

    a. direct materials
    b. direct labor
    c. selling and administrative
    d. manufacturing overhead

QUESTIONS AND PROBLEMS

1. Discuss the characteristics of job order and process costing systems.

2. Discuss the three valuation methods.

3. What type of information appears on a job cost record?

Chapter 7: Job Order Costing

4. Briefly discuss repetitive manufacturing. Contrast it to job order and process costing.

5. Prepare the necessary journal entries for each of the following:

   a. Raw materials were requisitioned for production $36,000.

   b. Direct labor was incurred and paid $13,500.

   c. Overhead is applied at the rate of 170% of direct labor.

   d. Indirect labor and indirect materials were $2,500 and $1,700 respectively (used and paid for).

   e. Items costing $56,500 were completed and transferred to finished goods.

   f. Goods costing $43,200 were sold for $76,000 on account.

Use the following information for questions 6-9.

   The Ruff Co. has the following information available for use in its job order costing system. Raw materials were requisitioned for production as follows: job #5--$21,000; job #6--$17,600; and job #7--$15,600. Direct labor is $12,600; $5,500; and $11,300 respectively. Overhead is applied to jobs at the rate of 125% of direct labor. Indirect labor and indirect materials are $3,200 and $4,400, respectively. Other overhead costs totaled $23,980.

6. Compute the total value of job #5.

7. Compute the total value of job #6.

72 Chapter 7: Job Order Costing

8. Compute the total value of job #7.

9. What is the balance in the overhead account? Is overhead under or overapplied?

COMMUNICATION PROBLEM

With your group, go to a local business entity, such as a doctor, dentist, lawyer, CPA or auto repair shop and ask the in-house accountant if they follow a job order cost type system. Write down the procedures they follow to keep track of costs incurred by the job. Subsequently, rewrite this in a synopsis form and present this to your class for your group. Ask for questions from the class and have someone else in the group answer the question.

SELF TEST SOLUTIONS

TRUE/FALSE

1. F	6. F	11. T	16. T	21. T
2. T	7. T	12. T	17. T	
3. T	8. F	13. F	18. F	
4. T	9. F	14. T	19. T	
5. F	10. F	15. F	20. F	

MULTIPLE CHOICE

1. D	6. B	11. C	16. B	21. B	26. B	31. C
2. A	7. D	12. D	17. C	22. C	27. A	
3. C	8. A	13. A	18. C	23. C	28. A	
4. B	9. B	14. A	19. B	24. A	29. C	
5. C	10. B	15. B	20. A	25. D	30. B	

1. In a job order costing system, small quantities of distinct items are produced. A job order cost system makes use of job cost records in which all the financial data for the job can be found.

    In a process costing system, large quantities of homogeneous goods are produced. Costs are accumulated in "cost centers" rather than by job.

2. The three methods of valuation are actual, normal, and standard costing. In an actual cost system, the entity uses the actual cost of direct material, direct labor, and overhead to cost products.

    In a normal costing system, actual costs for direct material and direct labor are used for product costing but a predetermined overhead rate is used to apply overhead to production.

    In a standard costing system, "norms" are established for direct material and/or direct labor quantities and/or costs and are used in the inventory accounts. Overhead is applied using a predetermined overhead rate. Any differences between actual cost and standard cost is considered a variance.

3. A job cost record contains the following data: name of the customer, description of the job to be performed, contract price, budgeted amounts for direct materials, direct labor and overhead.

4. A repetitive manufacturing system produces large volumes of discrete homogeneous units of products rather than continuous flows. Job order costing is not conducive to repetitive manufacturing because job order is

best for small quantities or special orders by customer specification. Repetitive manufacturing differs from process costing in that process costing is best employed for continuous flows of products while repetitive produces discrete units of products rather than a continuous flow.

5. a. WIP   36,000
           RM   36,000
    b. WIP   13,500
           Cash   13,500
    c. WIP   22,950
           OH   22,950
    d. OH   4,200
           Cash   4,200
    e. FG   56,500
           WIP   56,500
    f. CGS   43,200
           FG   43,200
        A/R   76,000
           Sales   76,000

6. Job #5 = (DM) $21,000 + (DL) $12,600 + (OH) $15,750 = $49,350

7. Job #6 = (DM) $17,600 + (DL) $5,500 + (OH) $6,875 = $29,975

8. Job #7 = (DM) $15,600 + (DL) $11,300 + (OH) $14,125 = $41,025

9. $7,600 + $23,980 − $36,750 = $5,170 overapplied

CHAPTER 8

PROCESS COSTING

CHAPTER OVERVIEW

Chapter 8 reviews process costing which is used in firms that produce large quantities of identical products such as canned food items or replacement parts. Job order is used in companies producing limited quantities of diverse or unlike products.

Within a process costing system, there are 2 alternative methods (weighted average and FIFO) of computing equivalent units of production (EUP) and assigning costs. The difference between the two methods is the treatment of beginning Work in Process. In a process costing system, there are 6 basic steps to determine the assignment of costs to the units produced during the period. These steps are shown in Exhibit 8-4. APPENDIX 2 illustrates a process costing system that uses standard rather than actual costs.

CHAPTER STUDY GUIDE

1. Process costing is the second type of cost system that was mentioned in Chapter 7. Process costing accumulates costs by cost components (direct material, direct labor, and overhead) in each production department and assigns these costs to products using an averaging technique.

    a. A job order costing system accumulates costs by individual jobs.

        i. Chapter 8 presents and illustrates the two methods of assigning costs in a process costing system: weighted average and FIFO.

        ii. The only difference between the two methods is the treatment of beginning Work in Process inventory.

2. Both cost systems (job order and process) use materials requisition and employee time cards (Exhibit 8-2) as source documents.

    a. Costs are assigned to jobs in a job order costing system; however a per unit cost is not always determinable because of the potential variety of the units within a job.

    b. In a process costing system, a unit cost will follow since all products are similar in nature.

        i. The formula for the unit cost is by dividing a process' production costs by the quantity of units produced as measured by equivalent units of production(EUP).
    c. Process costing does not require that all units be fully complete in order for a unit cost to be found; the system uses EUP to compute unit costs.

        i. An EUP is an estimate of how many complete units could have been produced if all effort had been expended on producing only whole units.

Chapter 8: Process Costing: Weighted Average, Fifo and Standard

        ii. Equivalent units are computed by multiplying the number of complete or incomplete units produced times the percentage of completion. (Complete units would be multiplied by 100%, so they are automatically equal to the same number of "equivalent units".)

3. Weighted average and FIFO are two basic methods for calculating equivalent units. These methods use underlying assumptions about how costs are believed to flow through the production process. In all cases, units and costs are accumulated by production component (DM, DL, OH, or DM and conversion) and by department or process.

4. The weighted average method of accounting for cost flows computes unit cost by dividing the total (current and beginning work in process) production cost by the total number of equivalent units produced.

    a. The weighted average method includes the beginning work in process units as part of the number of production units for the period.

        i. The inclusion of these units is the difference in the weighted average and the FIFO computations.

    b. The weighted average method centers on the items completed in the current period and is not concerned

        i. with the amount of work performed last period on the beginning work in process.

        ii. Costs of the current period are combined with costs of the beginning work in process to determine total costs, which becomes the numerator in the per unit cost formula.

        iii. Total cost of the component is divided by its related weighted average equivalent units to find the average cost per cost component

        iv. The costs transferred to the next department is equal to the cost per unit multiplied by the number of units completed this period.

5. FIFO does not include beginning work in process units or costs in calculating cost per equivalent unit. This method directly on work performed during the current period and on costs of the current period.

    a. The FIFO method uses the reciprocal percentage when computing equivalent units of production for beginning work in process. Since FIFO deals with current period work and costs, the reciprocal percentage must be used to determine how much work must be performed on beginning work in process to complete production.

    b. To determine FIFO cost per unit, current period costs per process are divided by their related FIFO component EUP.

6. Computations for individual cost components should be done because material can be added at various stages of production and the points of addition must be known to determine what percentage of completion to use for EUP computation.

    a. For example, if material is added at a 20% completion point and the ending work in process is only 10% complete, the equivalency percentage for this material would be 0%. If the units are 45% complete, the materials equivalency percentage would be 100%.

    b. Direct labor and overhead may be added on a integrated basis, so one computation may be done for calculating conversion equivalent units.

Chapter 8: Process Costing: Weighted Average, Fifo and Standard

7. Regardless of which method (weighted average or FIFO) is used, there are six basic steps in process costing (see Exhibit 8-4).

    a. The first two of these steps (determining the units to account for and the units accounted for) require the use of whole physical units.
    b. The next step is that of computing EUP under one of the two methods.
    c. Step 4 determines the total costs to be accounted for and step 5 provides the cost per EUP per cost component.
    d. Concluding, the cost per unit is used to assign costs to units transferred out and ending inventory or to the completion of beginning work in process, units started and completed, and ending work in process as shown in Exhibits 8-6 and 8-7.

8. The bulk of the chapter addresses single production departments; however, most entities use multi-department production cycles.

    a. Computations in successor departments are the same as those in the first department except an additional cost component (transferred in) must be used.
    b. Costs are accumulated for all departments involved in production activities and, when the products are moved from one department to the next, the costs associated with those products must follow (see Exhibits 8-11 and 8-12).

9. Appendix 1 presents alternative calculations for computing EUP under the weighted average and FIFO methods. These alternatives can be used to check your answers or as shortcuts for dual computations.

10. Appendix 2 illustrates a standard process costing system (Exhibits 8-13 and 8-14). Standard process costing relies on a FIFO cost flow and allows variances to be determined during production. Standard cost variances are discussed thoroughly in Chapters 11 and 12.

SELF TEST

TRUE/FALSE

1. T **(F)**

    The two basic systems of accumulating costs are job order and FIFO costing.

2. **(T)** F

    In a process costing system, costs are accumulated in departments.

3. **(T)** F

    The source documents used in a process costing system include a materials requisition form.

4. T **(F)**

    The numerator in the formula for computing weighted average unit cost is total current period cost.

5. **(T)** F

    The numerator in the formula for computing unit cost when using FIFO process costing is total current period cost.

6. **(T)** F

    The numerator in the formula for computing unit cost when using weighted average process costing is total cost (beginning work in process cost and current period cost).

Chapter 8: Process Costing: Weighted Average, Fifo and Standard

7. **T** F

    The weighted average method of computing equivalent units of production adds the units in beginning work in process to the units worked on during the current period.

8. T **F**

    The FIFO method of computing equivalent units of production does not distinguish between units in beginning work in process and units worked on during the current period.

9. T **F**

    The sum of beginning inventory costs and current period production costs are assigned to units completed during the period.

10. T **F**

    The weighted average method of calculating EUP reflects the normal flow of units through a production process.

11. T **F**

    When using the FIFO method of calculating EUP, costing the completion of beginning work in process uses the percentage of work completed in the prior period.

12. T **F**

    A job order system collects costs by departments and a process system collects costs by jobs.

13. T **F**

    The FIFO cost-flow assumption merges any costs assigned to the beginning work in process with the costs of the current period to reach an average cost that is assigned to the output of the period.

14. T **F**

    To determine the number of units started into production in a period, subtract the ending inventory amount from the sum of the beginning inventory and the units transferred out.

15. **T** F

    A process cost accounting system accumulates costs by departments for a period of time.

16. T **F**

    Under the weighted average method, the cost of materials in the beginning work in process inventory is not used in the computation of the per unit cost for materials as shown on the production report.

17. T **F**

    Any difference in the equivalent units calculated under the weighted average and the FIFO methods is due to the units in the ending work in process inventory.

18. T **F**

    In process costing, the equivalent units computed for materials is generally the same as that computed for direct labor.

Chapter 8: Process Costing: Weighted Average, Fifo and Standard

MULTIPLE CHOICE

1. Process costing is used by companies that produce

    a. special order items.
    b. homogeneous items.
    c. items to customer specifications.
    d. heterogeneous items.

    B

2. Which of following is **not** a process costing method discussed in the text?

    a. FIFO
    b. Weighted average
    c. Strict FIFO
    d. LIFO

    D

3. When using the weighted average method in preparing a process cost report, which of the following would not be assigned costs?

    a. units completed during the period
    b. ending work in process units
    c. units sold
    d. transferred out units

    C

4. A difference between weighted average and FIFO process costing is that weighted average

    a. distinguishes between units in beginning work in process and units started this period and FIFO does not.
    b. uses only current period costs to compute cost per EUP.
    c. uses only transferred out costs to compute cost per EUP.
    d. combines current period costs with the costs of beginning work in process to compute cost per EUP.

    D

5. A difference between weighted average and FIFO process costing is that FIFO

    a. distinguishes between units in beginning work in process and units started this period while weighted average does not.
    b. uses only transferred out costs to compute cost per EUP.
    c. combines current period costs with the costs of beginning work in process to compute cost per EUP.
    d. always uses a conversion cost category in computing cost per EUP.

    A

6. Equivalent units are defined as the

    a. number of partial units completed during the period.
    b. number of whole units that could have been produced if all work had gone to produce whole units.
    c. total number of units produced last period.
    d. total number of units completed during the current period.

    B

7. Which of the following is used in computing equivalent units using the weighted average method?

	Beginning Work in Process	Ending Work in Process
a.	no	no
b.	no	yes
c.	yes	yes
d.	yes	no

    C

8. What ratio is used to determine the cost per unit under weighted average process costing?

    a. Total production costs divided by total EUP.
    b. Total units produced divided by total production cost.
    c. Current production costs divided by total units produced.
    d. Current production costs divided by units produced in the current period.

    A

80   Chapter 8:   Process Costing: Weighted Average, Fifo and Standard

9. What ratio is used to determine the cost per unit under FIFO process costing?

   a. Total production costs divided by total units produced.
   b. Total units produced divided by total production costs.
   c. Current production costs divided by total units produced.
   d. Current production costs divided by total units produced in the current period.

10. A production and cost report shows all of the following **except**

    a. all quantities and costs.
    b. computation of EUP.
    c. cost assignments.
    d. journal entries.

11. Process costing can be used for which of the following situations?

	Single Departments	Multi-Departments
a.	yes	no
b.	no	no
c.	yes	yes
d.	no	yes

Use the following information for questions 12 and 13.

The GSWS Co. has the following available for use in computing equivalent units of production:

    Beginning Work in Process   5,000 units
       (35 % complete)
    Started this period   11,500 units
    Transferred out   13,300 units
    Ending Work in Process   3,200 units
       (40% complete)

12. For how many units is GSWS accountable this period?

    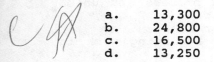

    a. 13,300
    b. 24,800
    c. 16,500
    d. 13,250

13. How many units were started and completed this period?

    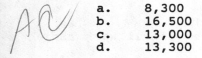

    a. 8,300
    b. 16,500
    c. 13,000
    d. 13,300

Use the information below for questions 14-23.

The following information is available for the Hammett Co. for the month of May:

    Beginning WIP (40%)   6,000 units
    Started   30,000 units
    Ending WIP(70%)   5,000 units

    Materials are added at the start of production.

    Costs:
    Beginning WIP
        Materials $ 12,500
        Conversion   20,400
    Current:
        Materials   30,000
        Conversion   110,000

Chapter 8: Process Costing: Weighted Average, Fifo and Standard

14. Using the weighted average method, compute equivalent units for materials.

    a. 33,500
    b. 32,100
    c. 36,000
    d. 30,000

15. Using the weighted average method, compute equivalent units for conversion costs.

    a. 35,000
    b. 30,000
    c. 32,100
    d. 34,500

16. Using the FIFO method, compute the equivalent units of production for materials.

    a. 32,100
    b. 30,000
    c. 36,000
    d. 34,500

17. Using the FIFO method, compute the equivalent units of production for conversion cost.

    a. 32,100
    b. 34,500
    c. 30,000
    d. 36,000

18. What is the total cost to be accounted for?

    a. $160,400
    b. $172,900
    c. $140,000
    d. $152,500

19. Using the weighted average method, what is the cost assigned to the units transferred out?

    a. $110,750
    b. $173,003
    c. $172,665
    d. $153,760

20. Using the weighted average method, compute the cost assigned to ending work in process.

    a. $17,360
    b. $17,005
    c. $19,130
    d. $24,800

21. How many units were started and completed during May?

    a. 36,000
    b. 25,000
    c. 31,000
    d. 30,000

22. Using the FIFO method, what is the cost assigned to the units started and completed?

    a. $110,750
    b. $153,000
    c. $173,003
    d. $172,665

Chapter 8: Process Costing: Weighted Average, Fifo and Standard

23. Using the FIFO method, what is the cost assigned to the units in ending work in process?

    a. $22,150
    b. $29,155
    c. $17,005
    d. $15,005

Use the following information for questions 24-28.

The Light Co. has the following available for the month of June.

Beginning Work in Process (45% complete)	7,500 units
Started	60,000 units
Ending Work in Process (65% complete)	5,000 units
Transferred out	?

Materials are added at the start of the process.

24. How many units were started and completed in June?

    a. 67,500
    b. 60,000
    c. 55,000
    d. 65,000

25. Using the weighted average method, compute total equivalent units for materials.

    a. 67,500
    b. 65,750
    c. 55,000
    d. 65,750

26. Using the weighted average method, compute total equivalent units for conversion costs.

    a. 67,500
    b. 65,700
    c. 65,750
    d. 55,000

27. Using the FIFO method, compute total equivalent units for materials.

    a. 67,500
    b. 62,375
    c. 65,500
    d. 60,000

28. Using the FIFO method, compute total equivalent units for conversion costs.

    a. 62,375
    b. 55,000
    c. 65,750
    d. 67,500

29. One fundamental reason for the evolution of a process cost system is that:

    a. Job order costing is too costly for some production methods
    b. Job order costing is more arduous to do
    c. Job cost sheets are less accurate than production reports
    d. Job order costing will not work in all situations

Chapter 8: Process Costing: Weighted Average, Fifo and Standard

30. When contrasting process costing to job order costing:

    a. Fewer material requisitions happen with process costing
    b. There are many work in process accounts with job order costing
    c. Equivalent unit computations are a major part of job order costing
    d. Material requisitions are not important with process costing

31. A non-manufacturing organization may utilize:

    a. Job order costing but not process costing
    b. Process costing but not job order costing
    c. Either job order costing or process costing
    d. Neither job order costing nor process costing

32. The beginning work in process inventory was 60 percent complete as to conversion costs, and the ending work in process inventory was 45 percent complete as to conversion costs.

    The dollar amount of the conversion cost included in the ending work in process inventory (using the average cost method) is determined by multiplying the average unit conversion costs by what percentage of the total units in the ending work in process inventory?

    a. 100 percent
    b. 60 percent
    c. 55 percent
    d. 45 percent

33. In the determination of manufacturing cost per equivalent unit, the average cost method of process costing considers:

    a. Current costs only
    b. Current costs plus cost of ending work in process inventory
    c. Current costs less cost of beginning work in process inventory
    d. Current costs plus cost of beginning work in process inventory

34. In process costing, costs are accumulated by:

    a. Job
    b. Batch
    c. Product
    d. Department

35. If a company uses two different unit cost figures to cost transfers from one department to another under a process costing system, then it is reasonable to assume that:

    a. there was no beginning work in process inventory.
    b. processing centers are arranged in a sequential pattern.
    c. the FIFO cost method is being used.
    d. the weighted average cost method is being used.

QUESTIONS AND PROBLEMS

1. Define and briefly discuss equivalent units of production.

2. Discuss the calculation of equivalent units and cost per EUP using the weighted average method of process costing.

Chapter 8: Process Costing: Weighted Average, Fifo and Standard

3. Discuss the calculation of equivalent units and cost per EUP using the FIFO method of process costing.

4. What are the six steps in process costing?

5. List the information found on a production and cost report.

Use the following information for questions 6-10.

The Sullivan Co. has the following information available for the month of December:

Beginning Work in Process (30% complete)	4,000 units
Started	22,500 units
Ending Work in Process (60% complete)	5,500 units
Transferred out	?
Costs:	
Beginning Work in Process	
Materials	$ 6,500
Conversion	17,300
Current Costs:	
Materials	45,500
Conversion	80,000

Materials are added at the start of production.

6. Using weighted average and FIFO respectively, compute the equivalent units for materials.

7. Using weighted average and FIFO respectively, compute the equivalent units for conversion costs.

8. Using weighted average and FIFO, compute the cost per EUP for materials and for conversion.

Chapter 8: Process Costing: Weighted Average, Fifo and Standard

9. Using the weighted average method, compute the cost assigned to the units completed and ending work in process.

10. Using the FIFO method, compute the cost assigned to the units transferred out and ending work in process.

11. Define the following: Transferred-in Cost

COMMUNICATION PROBLEM

With one person of your class work group, explain how the FIFO method for process costing differs from the weighted average method for process costing. Next, your partner is to restate what you told him. You are to state whether you agree with him or why you disagree. This exercise will help you to practice oral communication skills with a cohort.

SELF TEST SOLUTIONS

TRUE/FALSE

1. F	6. T	11. F	16. F
2. T	7. T	12. F	17. F
3. T	8. F	13. F	18. F
4. F	9. F	14. F	
5. T	10. F	15. T	

MULTIPLE CHOICE

1. B	6. B	11. C	16. B	21. B	26. C	31. C
2. D	7. C	12. C	17. A	22. A	27. D	32. D
3. C	8. A	13. A	18. B	23. C	28. A	33. D
4. D	9. D	14. C	19. D	24. C	29. A	34. D
5. A	10. D	15. D	20. C	25. A	30. A	35. C

QUESTIONS AND PROBLEMS

1. Equivalent units of production approximate the number of whole units that could have been produced if all work had been expended in producing complete units. Equivalent units must be calculated for both materials and conversion costs to assign costs to the completed and incomplete units at the end of a period. In performing the EUP calculations, the degree of completion must be taken into consideration.

2. The weighted average method of computing equivalent units multiplies the whole units transferred out and the units in ending inventory times the percent of completion for individual cost components. The EUP for transferred out and ending inventory are added together to get the total EUP for each cost component. Since no differentiation is made between units in beginning inventory and units worked on during the current period,

Chapter 8: Process Costing: Weighted Average, Fifo and Standard

weighted average totals costs associated with beginning work in process and current costs for each cost component and divides by the respective EUP to compute the average cost per EUP.

3. The FIFO method of computing equivalent units makes a distinction between work performed on units in beginning work in process and working on units only during the current period. Beginning work in process is multiplied by the reciprocal percent, units started and completed are always multiplied by 100%, because these units were started and totally completed during the current period. Ending work in process is multiplied by the percent of work completed on those units during the current period. Since FIFO separates out work performed last period, the method divides current period costs of each cost component by the respective EUP for that cost component when determining the cost per EUP.

4. The six steps that are used in process costing are as follows:

   (1) Calculate the number of units to account for.
   (2) Calculate the units accounted for.
   (3) Calculate equivalent units using one of the two methods.
   (4) Calculate total costs to account for.
   (5) Calculate the cost per equivalent unit.
   (6) Assign costs to inventories (transferred out and ending work in process).

5. A production and cost report will contain the following information:

   a. Total units to account for.
   b. Total units accounted for.
   c. Calculations for equivalent units.
   d. Total costs to account for.
   e. Calculations for cost per equivalent unit (broken down by cost component and by prior and current period).
   f. Assignment of costs to units transferred out and units in ending inventory.

6.
	Weighted Average		FIFO	
	Mat.	CC	Mat.	CC
Beg. WIP (4,000 30%)			0	2,800
Started and Com			17,000	17,000
Completed	21,000	21,000		
End. WIP (5,500 – 60%)	5,500	3,300	5,500	3,300
	26,500	24,300	22,500	23,100

   Answer: 26,500 and 22,500 respectively

7. 24,300 and 23,100 (for calculations see # 6 above).

8. Weighted Average
   Materials $52,000 / 26,500 = $1.96 (rounded)
   Conversion $97,300 / 24,300 = 4.00 (rounded)
   Total cost per EUP $5.96

   FIFO
   Materials $45,500 / 22,500 = $2.02 (rounded)
   Conversion $80,000 / 23,100 = 3.46 (rounded)
   Total cost per EUP $5.48

Chapter 8: Process Costing: Weighted Average, Fifo and Standard

9. Completed

    21,000 x $5.96 = $125,160

  Ending Work in Process
    5,500 x $1.96 = $ 10,780
    3,300 x $4.00 =   13,200
                      $ 23,980

10. Beginning WIP: $ 23,800
    Costs to Complete
     2,800 x $3.46   =   9,688
    Total cost of BI units   33,488

    Started and Completed
     17,000 x $5.48   =   93,160
    Total Transferred Out $126,648

  Ending Work in Process
    5,500 x $2.02 = $11,110
    3,300 x $3.46 =   11,418
                     $22,528

11. Transferred-in Cost: The dollar value assigned to units transferred into a department from a preceding department.

CHAPTER 9

SPECIAL PRODUCTION ISSUES: SPOILED/DEFECTIVE UNITS AND ACCRETION

CHAPTER OVERVIEW

Chapter 8 presented process costing in its basic form with only good units produced. Such exact production doesn't occur in reality. Chapter 9 presents the subjects of spoilage, defective units, and accretion which changes the number of acceptable good units at some point in the process.

Spoiled units are defined as those that are unsatisfactory and cannot be economically reworked. Defective units are unacceptable but can be economically reworked to a salable condition. Finally, accretion is defined as an increase in units or volume during the production process which usually results from adding more material in the production process.

Normal and abnormal spoilage affects the number of units completed and their cost. To determine and account for spoilage requires knowledge of when the spoilage occurs in the production process and what type of spoilage (continuous or discrete) is involved. The accounting treatment for accretion is illustrated in the chapter. Defective units are then covered. Reworking defective units creates additional costs that are either added to WIP costs for good units, included as estimated OH, or assigned to a loss account. Exhibit 9-9 illustrates journal entries for a variety of rework situations.

CHAPTER STUDY GUIDE

1. New terms discussed in Chapter 9 are important for understanding spoilage in process cost accounting. These include normal and abnormal spoilage, discrete and continuous spoilage.

    a. Normal spoilage is spoilage that is expected or planned on by management.

        i. When normal spoilage (either discrete or continuous) is discovered, its cost is considered a product cost and part of the total cost of the good units produced. See EXHIBIT 9-3

    b. Abnormal spoilage is spoilage that exceeds what is expected (normal).

        i. Abnormal spoilage, however, is considered a period cost and is recognized as a loss in the period of production.

    c. Discrete spoilage occurs at a specific point in the production process.

        i. Discrete spoilage is deemed to occur at either the inspection point (which can be at any stage of the process) or at the end of the production process.

        ii. **Units past the inspection point are considered good units.** See EXHIBIT 9-4 for an example.

    d. Continuous spoilage occurs evenly throughout the process.

Chapter 9: Special Production Issues: Spoiled/Defective Units in Accretion

- i. If the production process produces spoilage on a continual basis, an inspection point must be established at the end of production so that customers will not receive spoiled units.
- ii. See EXHIBIT 9-2 for a chart that shows how continuous and discrete costs are accounted for.

e. Determining when spoilage occurs in the production process is necessary in order to handle it appropriately in equivalent unit calculations. Assignment of spoilage cost is necessary to properly account for production costs.

f. Normal continuous spoilage is not included in equivalent unit calculations. It is handled by the "method of neglect," which simply ignores the units.

- i. Normal distinct [discrete] spoilage is included in equivalent unit calculations, so that the cost can be spread out over all units that have passed the inspection point.

g. Abnormal spoilage (whether discrete or continuous) is always computed on an equivalent unit basis. Exhibits 9-2 and 9-8 summarize these factors. See EXHIBITs 9-6 and 7 for this type of spoilage in FIFO and Weighted Average methods.

2. Accounting for spoilage in a job order cost system depends on two factors: (1) whether it is incurred for most jobs or relates to specific jobs, and (2) whether it is normal or abnormal.

   a. If spoilage relates to all jobs, then the predetermined overhead application rate should include an amount for the net cost of normal spoilage.

   - i. The net cost of normal spoilage is equal to the cost of spoiled work less the estimated disposal of that work.
   - ii. If spoilage is related to specific jobs, the estimated cost should not be included in setting the predetermined overhead rate.
   - iii. The disposal cost of spoiled goods should reduce the cost of the specific job.
   - iv. The cost of abnormal spoilage should be written off as a loss of the period.

3. Accretion is caused by either the addition of materials to the production process or by essential factors of the production process (such as baking bread where yeast causes the dough to double in volume).

   a. When accretion occurs in a successor department, the number of units transferred in and the related cost per unit must be adjusted to reflect this occurrence. See EXHIBIT 9-10 for an illustration.

4. Defective units are those that can be reworked and can be sold as either irregulars or as quality products.

   a. The cost of rework is either a product or period cost, depending on whether the rework is considered normal or abnormal.

   - i. Normal rework costs may be estimated and included as part of estimated overhead when predetermined overhead rates are used or the actual rework costs are included as part of WIP costs in an actual cost system.

5. Controlling Quality and Spoilage

   a. To control quality, the following questions need to be asked:

Chapter 9: Special Production Issues: Spoiled/Defective Units in Accretion

- i. What does the spoilage cost?
    - (1) By excluding these units from the EUP determination, spoiled unit costs are buried in the good units.
- ii. Why does it occur?
    - (1) By believing the cause creates minimal spoilage, it may be treated as an acceptable level of bad output and error tolerances are built into the cost system.
- iii. How can it be controlled?
    - (1) Some variance is uncontrollable.
    - (2) Most spoilage can be controlled by bulding quality in the process using statistical process control(SPC).
    - (3) Production personnel become the quality control people that assure quality with each item produced and reduce the need for quality control inspectors.
    - (4) Quality costs to prevent or detect spoilage or defective units are called prevention and appraisal costs. Prevention costs tend to be less costly than appraisal costs and include employee training, customer serveys, machinery designed to detect defects, and quality parts suppliers. Appraisal costs include receiving inspections and monitoring the production process. See EXHIBIT 3-6 for a larger list of quality costs.
- iv. See Chapter 3 for further discussion of quality control costs.

SELF TEST

TRUE/FALSE

1. T **F**

   Spoilage is defined as a decline in the number of units lost in excess of normal expectations.

2. T **F**

   A defective unit is one that cannot be reworked and sold.

3. **T** F

   Economically reworked means that the incremental income from the sale of reworked units is greater than the incremental cost of the rework.

4. **T** F

   A spoiled unit is rejected at a control point when it fails to meet quality control specifications.

5. T **F**

   The difference between scrap and waste is that waste has a minimal disposal value.

6. **T** F

   Normal spoilage is usually computed on the basis of good output, regular output, or actual output.

7. **T** F

   Abnormal spoilage are those units that exceed normal expectations.

Chapter 9: Special Production Issues: Spoiled/Defective Units in Accretion

8. T **F**

    Normal spoilage is viewed as avoidable in the future.

9. T **F**

    Spoilage that takes place on a continuous basis requires an inspection point that is approximately midway through the production process.

10. **T** F

    The method of neglect does not include spoiled units in the equivalent unit schedule.

11. T **F**

    The cost of abnormal spoilage is computed on an equivalent unit basis and assigned to work in process.

12. T **F**

    The net cost of normal spoilage is equal to the cost of spoiled work less accumulated disposal costs.

13. T **F**

    The cost of normal spoilage is recorded in a loss account for the period of occurrence.

14. **T** F

    Accretion is defined as an increase in volume or units due to an addition of materials.

15. T **F**

    Direct material that evaporates during production is known as either abnormal spoilage or normal spoilage.

16. **T** F

    Units of production that become defective in the usual course of production are known as normal spoilage.

MULTIPLE CHOICE

1. A normal loss is

    a. unexpected.
    b. expected.
    c. above average.
    d. avoidable.

    B

2. Spoilage causes units that are

    a. unacceptable.
    b. acceptable.
    c. usable.
    d. normal.

    A

3. A defective unit can be reworked and sold as

	An irregular	A quality product
a.	yes	no
b.	no	no
c.	yes	yes
d.	no	yes

    C

Chapter 9: Special Production Issues: Spoiled/Defective Units in Accretion 93

4. Economically reworked means that the incremental income from the sale of reworked units is

D

a. equal to the incremental cost of rework.
b. less than the incremental cost of rework.
c. not a factor in the decision to rework or not.
d. greater than the incremental cost of rework.

5. Which of the following is **not** a cause of shrinkage?

B

a. evaporation
b. accretion
c. oxidation
d. leakage

6. Abnormal spoilage has been

C

	Planned	Unplanned
a.	yes	no
b.	yes	yes
c.	no	yes
d.	no	no

7. Spoilage that occurs at a specific point is known as

D

	Discrete	Normal
a.	no	no
b.	no	yes
c.	yes	yes
d.	yes	no

8. Since normal continuous spoilage is handled by the method of neglect, it is considered a

B

	Period Cost	Product Cost
a.	no	no
b.	no	yes
c.	yes	yes
d.	yes	no

9. Abnormal discrete spoilage is considered a

D

	Period Cost	Product Cost
a.	no	no
b.	no	yes
c.	yes	yes
d.	yes	no

Use the following information to answer questions 10-15.

The information that follows is for the Wood Co. for the month of March:

Started	500 units
Beginning Work in Process (60% complete)	60 units
Transferred out	380 units
Ending Work in Process (40% complete)	50 units
Normal spoilage (continuous)	130 units

All materials are added at the start of production.

Beginning Work in Process Costs:
Materials	$ 34,000
Conversion	200,000

Current Costs:
Materials	$ 56,000
Conversion	175,000

94 Chapter 9: Special Production Issues: Spoiled/Defective Units in Accretion

10. What are equivalent units of production for materials using FIFO?

    a. 370
    b. 364
    c. 320
    d. 560

11. What are equivalent units of production for conversion costs using FIFO?

    a. 370
    b. 560
    c. 364
    d. 320

12. What is cost per unit for materials using FIFO?

    a. $ 480.77
    b. $ 151.35
    c. $ 243.24
    d. $1,030.22

13. What is cost per unit for conversion using FIFO?

    a. $1,030.22
    b. $ 243.24
    c. $ 151.35
    d. $ 480.77

14. What is the cost assigned to the units transferred out using FIFO (rounded)?

    a. $407,507
    b. $202,278
    c. $447,816
    d. $ 11,538

15. What is the cost assigned to the ending Work in Process using FIFO (rounded)?

    a. $ 7,568
    b. $ 9,615
    c. $ 17,183
    d. $ 31,607

Using the following information for questions 16-21.

   The following information is for the Jones Co. for the month of April:

            Started   100,000 units
            Beginning Work in Process
                (70% complete)   12,000 units
            Ending Work in Process
                (30% complete)   24,000 units
            Spoilage (normal discrete)   3,000 units
            Spoilage (abnormal)   1,000 units
            Transferred out   84,000 units

            Beginning Work in Process Costs:
                Materials $ 85,000
                Conversion   140,000

            Current Costs:
                Materials $110,000
                Conversion   180,000
            All materials are added at the start of production.
            The inspection point is at the end of the process.

Chapter 9: Special Production Issues: Spoiled/Defective Units in Accretion 95

16. What are equivalent units of production for materials using the weighted average method?

    B
    a. 108,000
    b. 112,000
    c. 92,200
    d. 91,200

17. What are equivalent units of production for conversion costs using the weighted average method?

    A
    a. 95,200
    b. 91,200
    c. 109,000
    d. 108,000

18. What is the cost per unit for materials using the weighted average method?

    D
    a. $5.26
    b. $3.47
    c. $1.81
    d. $1.74

19. What is the cost per unit for conversion costs using the weighted average method?

    C
    a. $1.79
    b. $5.26
    c. $3.36
    d. $1.81

20. What is the total cost assigned to the units transferred out using the weighted average method?

    A
    a. $443,700
    b. $448,800
    c. $433,500
    d. $428,400

21. What is the cost assigned to the ending Work in Process using the weighted average method?

    A
    a. $ 65,952
    b. $122,400
    c. $ 48,240
    d. $ 37,128

22. The net cost of normal spoilage is equal to the

    B
    a. cost of spoiled work plus the estimated disposal value of the work.
    b. cost of spoiled work less the estimated disposal value of the work.
    c. net realizable value of the work less the cost of the spoiled units.
    d. net realizable value of the work plus the cost of the spoiled units.

23. If spoilage is related to a particular job, the disposal value of the spoilage should

    C
    a. reduce the cost of all work in process.
    b. reduce the overhead applied during the period.
    c. reduce the cost of the particular job.
    d. recognized as other income during the period.

24. Normal spoilage is defined as

    A
    a. Spoilage that results from normal operations.
    b. Uncontrollable waste as a result of a special production run.
    c. Spoilage that arises under inefficient operations.
    d. Controllable spoilage.

Chapter 9: Special Production Issues: Spoiled/Defective Units in Accretion

25. Abnormal spoilage is defined as

    a. Spoilage that is not expected to arise under normal, efficient operating conditions.
    b. Planned spoilage.
    c. Spoilage that results from normal operations.
    d. An inherent part of the production process.

QUESTIONS AND PROBLEMS

1. Define the following terms: spoilage, abnormal loss, normal loss, discrete spoilage, and continuous spoilage.

2. Discuss the handling of discrete and continuous spoilage, for purposes of equivalent unit calculations.

3. Define and give an illustration of accretion.

4. Define and discuss defective units.

5. Discuss how spoilage is accounted for in a job order system.

Chapter 9: Special Production Issues: Spoiled/Defective Units in Accretion

Use the following information to answer questions 6-10.

The following information is available for the Short Co. for the month of December:

Beginning Work in Process (20% complete)	5,000 units
Started units	60,000 units
Normal Spoilage (discrete)	500 units
Abnormal Spoilage	800 units
Ending Work in Process (40% complete)	9,500 units
Transferred out	54,200 units
Work in Process Beginning Costs:	
Materials	$ 22,000
Conversion	90,000
Current Costs:	
Materials	$ 64,000
Conversion	210,000

All materials are added at the start of production.

6. What are equivalent units of production for materials and conversion costs using the weighted average method? (The inspection point is at the end of the process.)

7. Compute the cost per equivalent unit for materials and conversion costs using the weighted average method? (The inspection point is at the end of the process.)

8. Using your answers to questions 6 and 7, determine the assignment of costs for the period. What is the cost per unit of each good unit transferred during the period? How is the cost of abnormal spoilage treated?

9. Compute EUP and cost per unit using FIFO. Assume the inspection point is halfway through the process.

98 Chapter 9: Special Production Issues: Spoiled/Defective Units in Accretion

10. Compute the cost assigned to the units transferred out, ending WIP, and spoilage using the FIFO method. Assume the inspection point is halfway through the process.

COMMUNICATION PROBLEM

With one member of your in class group, write down in 100-150 words one topic or procedure from this chapter you least understand. Be sure to state this clearly so that the other person knows your difficulty. The other person is to respond by writing a summary of what the other person wrote and try to explain how to deal with the problem. These two written statements is to be turned in to the professor.

The purpose of this project to enhance your ability to write clearly what you don't understand and why. The other person learns reading skills of fellow students writing and improves their ability respond to a knowledge problem in writing. The professor learns from this assignment what areas are causing problems so that they may decide to spend more time on the subject.

SELF TEST SOLUTIONS

TRUE/FALSE

1. F	6. T	11. F	16. T
2. F	7. T	12. F	
3. T	8. F	13. F	
4. T	9. F	14. T	
5. F	10. T	15. F	

MULTIPLE CHOICE

1. B	6. C	11. C	16. B	21. A
2. A	7. D	12. B	17. A	22. B
3. C	8. B	13. D	18. D	23. C
4. D	9. D	14. C	19. C	24. A
5. B	10. A	15. C	20. A	25. A

QUESTIONS AND PROBLEMS

1. Spoilage is defined as anything in the production process that causes units or items to be unacceptable. Abnormal loss is defined as a decline in the number of units over and above what is considered normal. Normal loss is defined as the quantity or percentage of loss that is expected by management. Discrete spoilage occurs at a specific point in the production process. Continuous spoilage occurs evenly throughout the production process.

2. If discrete or continuous spoilage is abnormal, its cost is written off as a loss based on equivalent units of production. If discrete spoilage is normal, its cost is absorbed by all units past the inspection point on an EUP basis. If continuous spoilage is normal, its cost is absorbed by all units produced during the period.

3. Accretion is the increase in volume or units because of adding materials or because of some inherent part of the process itself. Adding water to soft drink syrup to produce soft drinks is an example of accretion.

4. Defective units are those that can be economically reworked and are salable. The rework cost is classified as either a product or period cost, depending on whether the rework is considered normal or abnormal. Normal rework costs may be estimated and included as part of estimated overhead when predetermined overhead rates are used or the actual rework costs are included as part of WIP costs in an actual cost system. An example of a defective item might be a vase that does not have uniform coloring.

5. The treatment of spoilage in a job order cost system depends on two factors: (1) whether the spoilage is related to a specific job, and (2) whether the spoilage is normal or abnormal. If spoilage is related to all jobs in general, the predetermined overhead application rate should include an estimate of the net cost of spoilage. The net cost of spoilage is equal to the cost of the spoiled work less the estimated disposal cost of spoilage. If spoilage is not related to all jobs, the cost should not be included in setting the predetermined overhead application rate and the disposal value of the spoiled goods should reduce the cost of the specific job that created them. If the spoilage is considered normal, it is treated as part of product cost. If the spoilage is considered abnormal, it is treated as part of period cost (a loss).

6.
```
BWIP            5,000          TO              54,200
Started        60,000          EWIP             9,500
To acct. for   65,000          NS                 500
                               AS                 800
                               Acct'd for      65,000
```

	Mat.	CC
TO	54,200	54,200
EWIP	9,500	3,800
N.S.	500	500
A.S.	800	800
EUP	65,000	59,300

7. Material = $22,000 + $64,000 / 65,000 = $1.32 (rounded)

   CC = $90,000 + $210,000 / 59,300 = $5.06 (rounded)

8. Transferred Out:
```
   54,200 x $6.38    = $345,796
      500 x $6.38    =    3,190
                              $348,986
```

   (Cost per good unit = $348,986 / 54,200 = $6.49)

   EWIP:
```
   9,500 x $1.32    =   $12,540
   3,800 x $5.06    =    19,228
                              $ 31,768
```

   Abnormal Spoilage:
```
     800 x $6.38    =               5,104
```

   Total Cost Accounted for   = $385,858
   (off due to rounding)

9.
```
BWIP           5,000          BWIP            5,000
Started       60,000          S & C          49,200
Acct. for     65,000          EWIP            9,500
                              N.S.              500
                              A.S.              800
                              Acctd. for     65,000
```

	Mat.	CC
BWIP	0	4,000
S & C	49,200	49,200
EWIP	9,500	3,800
N.S.	500	250
A.S.	800	400
EUP	60,000	57,650

Material = $64,000 / 60,000 = $1.07 (rounded)

CC = $210,000 / 57,650 = $3.64 (rounded)

10. Transferred Out:
```
    BWIP                              $112,000
      4,000 x $3.64      =              14,560      $126,560

    S & C
     49,200 x $4.71      =            $231,732
    NS    500 x $1.07    =                 535
          250 x $3.64    =                 910      $233,177
    EWIP
      9,500 x $1.07      =         $    10,165
      3,800 x $3.64      =              13,832      $ 23,997
    Abnormal Spoilage:
        800 x $1.07      =         $       856
        400 x $3.64      =               1,456      $  2,312
    Total Cost Accounted for =                      $386,046
        (off due to rounding)
```

CHAPTER 10

COST ALLOCATION FOR JOINT PRODUCTS AND BY-PRODUCTS

CHAPTER OVERVIEW

Chapter 10 covers the topics of related product output (joint products and by-products) and the treatment of joint costs. Related outputs are normally generated by companies that utilize a process costing system simply, by virtue of the production process. Before deciding to undertake a joint production process, management must make certain decisions regarding the commitment of resources.

A joint process provides multiple outputs that are classified (based on their abilities to generate revenue) as joint products, by-products and scrap. It is a management decision as to how these outputs are classified. Outputs can be reclassified over time due to changes in technology, economic factors, and environmental concerns.

Once the classifications of joint output are made, joint costs must be allocated in a rational and systematic manner. The basic methods of joint cost allocation use physical or monetary measures. Joint costs are allocated for inventory valuation purposes only. Such allocations do not affect decisions such as whether to undertake the joint process or to continue to process output after the split-off point.

The chapter also discusses how to account for by-products and scrap under both process and job order costing systems.

Joint costs may also be incurred in service companies and not-for-profit organizations. Service companies may choose to allocate joint costs or not. However, not-for-profits are required (under an AICPA SOP) to allocate the joint cost of providing a multipurpose communication into program and support categories.

CHAPTER STUDY GUIDE

1. As with other chapters, some basic terminology must first be mastered. A joint process is one in which a single product can't be produced without others being produced through the same process. Joint costs are those materials, labor, and overhead costs that are incurred during the joint production process.

    a. Each type of joint process output will be classified as either a joint product, by-product, or scrap depending on its relative market value.

    b. Joint products are the primary output of a joint process; the sales value of these products is the reason the joint process was undertaken.

    c. Since a joint process creates costs while producing several identifiable outputs, the joint cost must be allocated among the various outputs. The point at which one can identify separate products is known as the split-off point. Some products may be sold at this point, while others may need further processing to be salable. At split-off, all joint costs must be allocated only to the primary products.

102   Chapter 10: Cost Allocation for Joint Products and By-Products

- d. By-products and scrap receive no joint cost allocation. Costs that are incurred after the split-off point are assigned to those particular products that caused the incurring of these costs.

- e. A residual output that has no market value is called waste. By-products and scrap are secondary outputs of a joint process with the former having more sales value than the latter.

2. Allocation of joint costs is accomplished through the use of either a physical or monetary measure. When a physical measure for allocation is used, a common base is established for all products. This base could be number of tons, pounds, board feet, units, etc. While the physical base provides a non-changing measure of output, it does not necessarily provide fair and reasonable allocations.

3. There are three monetary measures that can be used for the joint cost allocation process: sales value at split-off, net realizable value at split-off, and approximated net realizable value at split-off.

- a. The sales value at split-off method allocates joint cost solely on the relative sales value of the products at the split-off point. To use this method, all primary products must be salable at split-off.

- b. The net realizable value at split-off method allocates joint cost based on a product's proportional net realizable value at split-off. (Remember from other accounting classes that net realizable value is equal to sales revenue minus any costs necessary to prepare and dispose of a product.) All primary products must be marketable at split-off to use this method as was true with the first method. This method considers costs incurred past split-off that are needed to ready the products for sale.

- c. The third method is approximated net realizable value at split-off. This method requires the calculation of a simulated net realizable value at split-off and, as such, is appropriate for allocations to primary products that are not salable at the split-off point. The simulated NRV calculation is equal to final sales price minus incremental separate costs. Incremental separate costs are all costs incurred between split-off and sales point. The physical and all monetary methods of joint cost allocation are illustrated in Exhibits 10-6 through 10-8 of the text.

4. The sale of by-products and/or scrap is usually recorded using one of two methods: net realizable value or realized value method.

- a. When using the net realizable value method, an inventory value that equals selling price less processing costs, storage costs, and disposal costs is recorded for the by-products/scrap.

   - i. If income remains after these deductions, the joint cost of producing the primary products is reduced by the remainder.

- b. If the realized value method is used, no inventory value is recorded for the by-products/scrap until such product is sold. The advantage of the NRV method is that of the timing of recognition of by-products/scrap sales value; the advantage of the realized value method is conservatism. If a loss is incurred, this is added to the cost of the primary products.

5. While it is not common for a job order system to have joint products, it is possible for this system to have by-products and scrap. In accounting for this occurrence, either net realizable value or realized value can be used.

- a. The treatment of by-product/scrap value basically depends on whether those products are typical or atypical of the production process. If such output is typical, the value should serve to reduce manufacturing overhead.

Chapter 10: Cost Allocation for Joint Products and By-Products

        i. Crediting overhead causes it to decrease which will be spread overhead all good units produced.

   b. If uncommon, the value should reduce the cost of the specific job generating the by-product/scrap.

6. The final section of this chapter discusses service and not-for-profit organizations and accounting for joint costs. These organizations may incur joint costs, such as advertising or printing costs for multipurpose communication documents.

   a. Not-for-profit organizations are required by the AICPA to allocate joint costs between program and support activities while service organizations can elect not to allocate these costs.

SELF TEST

TRUE/FALSE

1. T F

    It is necessary to allocate joint costs to determine financial statement values for internal decision making.

2. T F

    Joint products are also known as primary products, because they have significant revenue-generating ability.

3. T F

    By-products, scrap, and waste all have sales value.

4. T F

    A certain amount of waste is considered unavoidable.

5. T F

    The point at which outputs are first identified as separate products is known as the split-off point.

6. T F

    Joint costs are allocated to all products that emerge from the production process.

7. T F

    When using the physical measurement method of allocating joint costs, one must determine the net realizable value of the joint products.

8. T F

    The physical measurement method is very useful when products have stable selling prices.

9. T F

    The three monetary measures that are used to allocate joint costs are: net realizable value at split-off, approximated net realizable value at split-off, and cost at split-off.

10. T F

    A disadvantage of using a monetary measure to allocate joint costs is that the measurement unit is not constant.

Chapter 10: Cost Allocation for Joint Products and By-Products

11. T F

    Incremental costs refer to all costs that are inherent to the production process.

12. T F

    The most flexible monetary measurement basis is the approximated net realizable value at split-off method.

13. T F

    A not-for-profit organization is required to categorize expenses as either program or support costs by the AICPA.

14. T F

    By-products/scrap are primary outputs of a joint process.

15. T F

    The FASB requires all service organizations to allocate advertising costs among the various items advertised, either by-product lines or store locations

MULTIPLE CHOICE

1. Primary products are also known as

	Joint Products	Main Products
a.	no	no
b.	no	yes
c.	yes	yes
d.	yes	no

2. A single process that produces more than one product con-currently is called a/an

    a. allocation process.
    b. joint process.
    c. selection process.
    d. JIT (just-in-time) process.

3. Which of the following correctly finishes the statement: Scrap is

    a. a primary output of a production process.
    b. an incidental output of a production process.
    c. a residual output of a production process.
    d. also called a co-product.

4. Waste is

    a. a primary output of a production process.
    b. also called a co-product.
    c. a residual output of the production process.
    d. an incidental output of the production process.

5. In deciding on refreshments for a birthday party, you bake a cake instead of ordering it from the bakery. In preparing the batter for the cake, you double the recipe so that you can have a cake and cupcakes. The cupcakes would be considered

    a. primary.
    b. secondary.
    c. waste.
    d. scrap.

Chapter 10: Cost Allocation for Joint Products and By-Products

6. In a meat processing plant, which of the following items could be considered a by-product?

	Steaks	Bones
a.	yes	yes
b.	yes	no
c.	no	yes
d.	no	no

7. Joint costs are allocated to which of the following classifications of products?

	Secondary	Residual
a.	yes	yes
b.	yes	no
c.	no	yes
d.	no	no

8. Which of the following is a disadvantage of the physical measurement method?

   a. It treats all products equally and assigns the same cost per physical unit measurement.
   b. It considers the revenue generating ability of the joint products in making the joint cost allocation.
   c. The basis used to allocate joint cost is constant.
   d. It considers the incremental revenues and costs between split-off and point of sale.

Use the following information for questions 9-12.

Abco Corp. produces three grades of lumber: A, B, and C. Joint processing costs for the production cycle are $7,500. Disposal costs will be incurred whenever the units are sold.

	Feet	Sales Price per Foot at Split-off	Disposal Cost per Foot	Further Processing per Foot	Final Sales Price per Foot
A	5,000	$ 5.00	$1.00	$1.50	$ 7.00
B	10,000	10.00	4.50	6.00	12.00
C	15,000	15.00	7.00	9.50	20.00

9. What is the allocation of joint costs to A, using feet as the physical measurement?

   a. $3,750
   b. $2,500
   c. $7,500
   d. $1,250

10. What is the allocation of joint costs to product B, using the sales value at split-off approach (round to the nearest dollar)?

    a. $2,500
    b. $2,143
    c. $ 536
    d. $4,821

11. What is the allocation of joint costs to product A, using the net realizable value at split-off approach (round to the nearest dollar)?

    a. $4,615
    b. $2,115
    c. $ 769
    d. $2,500

Chapter 10: Cost Allocation for Joint Products and By-Products

12. What is the allocation of joint costs to product C, using approximated net realizable value at split-off (round to the nearest dollar)?

    a. $2,500
    b. $4,821
    c. $4,375
    d. $4,875

13. Which of the following is a method that can be used for recording byproducts and scrap?

    a. realized value approach
    b. approximated net realizable value at split-off
    c. sales value at split-off
    d. both b and c

14. When using the net realizable value method for by-products and scrap,

    a. by-product/scrap revenue is revealed on the income statement.
    b. by-product/scrap expenses are revealed on the income statement.
    c. by-product/scrap revenues, expenses, and profits are revealed on the income statement.
    d. no information about by-product/scrap is revealed on the income statement.

Use the following information for questions 15-18.

The We-Bit Co. produces a concentrated soup base from tomatoes and two types of soup result from processing: T and U. Joint costs are $3,300 for the production cycle. At split-off T can be sold for $8.00 per gallon, while U can be sold for $6.00 per gallon. Disposal costs at split-off are $1.00 per gallon for T and $2.00 per gallon for U. Further processing costs for T and U, respectively, are $.50 and $1.25. After further processing T can be sold for $10.00 per gallon and U for $12.00 per gallon. During the current production cycle, 1,000 gallons of T and 500 gallons of U were produced.

15. Using a physical measure, allocate joint product costs to T.

    a. $1,100
    b. $1,650
    c. $3,300
    d. $2,200

16. What amount of joint cost is allocated to T using the sales value at split-off approach?

    a. $1,650
    b. $ 900
    c. $2,400
    d. $1,100

17. What amount of joint cost is allocated to U using the sales value at split-off approach?

    a. $ 900
    b. $2,400
    c. $1,650
    d. $1,100

18. What amount of joint cost is allocated to U, using net realizable value at split-off?

    a. $2,063
    b. $2,567
    c. $1,238
    d. $ 733

Chapter 10: Cost Allocation for Joint Products and By-Products

19. When using the net realizable value at split-off method, what amount is subtracted from selling price at split-off to derive the allocation bases?

    a. Further processing costs
    b. Disposal costs at split-off
    c. Approximate cost at split-off
    d. Average cost at split-off

20. A joint process produces 2 joint products and 2 by-products. The approximated net realizable value at split-off method is used when

    a. all joint products are not salable at split-off.
    b. some joint products are not salable at split-off.
    c. the by-products are not salable at split-off.
    d. a and b are correct

21. A joint process produces three products: D, E, and F which are all salable at split-off. Which joint cost allocation method does not have to be used?

    a. Sales value at split-off
    b. Net realizable value at split-off
    c. Physical measures
    d. Approximated net realizable value at split-off

22. The sales value of by-products/scrap is

    a. required by GAAP to be shown as "Other Revenue" on the income statement.
    b. generally not recorded because the net realizable value method is used.
    c. shown as a reduction of cost of goods sold on the income statement.
    d. ignored because market values are not used in accounting records.

23. Which of the following has the lowest value?

    a. scrap
    b. primary products
    c. joint products
    d. by-products

24. A department store runs a newspaper ad each Sunday promoting specials carried at 5 store locations. Which of the following would be the least acceptable basis for allocation of this cost?

    a. Sales volume of the stores advertised.
    b. Floor space occupied by the stores.
    c. Equal allocation among stores advertised.
    d. Total number of products carried by each store.

25. Which of the following organizations require not-for-profit organizations to categorize their expenses as program or support costs?

    a. CASB
    b. GASB
    c. AICPA
    d. both a and c

QUESTIONS AND PROBLEMS

1. Define the following terms: joint process, joint products, by-products, scrap, and waste.

Chapter 10: Cost Allocation for Joint Products and By-Products

2. Why is the split-off point important?

3. Why must joint costs be allocated?

4. Discuss the physical measurement approach to joint cost allocation.

5. How are by-products and scrap accounted for?

Use the following information for questions 6-10.

	Tons	Sales Price per ton at Split-off	Disposal Sep. Cost per ton	Costs if Processed Further	Final Sales Price
R	30	$1,000	$ 500	$ 100	$1,700
S	25	800	350	500	1,250
T	8	1,500	700	400	2,000

Joint costs for the production cycle are $12,500. Disposal costs are incurred at whatever point the products are sold.

6. What amount of joint costs are allocated to each of the products, using a physical measure approach? (Round to the nearest dollar)

7. What amount of joint costs are allocated to the products, using sales value at split-off? (Round to the nearest dollar)

8. What amount of joint costs are allocated to the products, respectively, using net realizable value at split-off? (Round to the nearest dollar)

Chapter 10: Cost Allocation for Joint Products and By-Products

9. What is the approximated net realizable value per unit of each of the three products.? Which of the products should be processed further?

10. What amount of joint costs are allocated to the three products, respectively, using approximated net realizable value at split-off (Round to the nearest dollar) Remember that this method uses the <u>most appropriate</u> sales value at split-off.

COMMUNICATION PROJECT

Your class group should contact a local firm that operates with joint costs and products. Find out what they do to account for joint costs. Write a condensed report that describes how they handles these costs. The report should be turned into the instructor a person in the group should present your findings to the class. Another person in group should respond to any questions asked by fellow classmates. This project should enhance your skills communicating with the business profession. It should help improve your written and verbal communication skills.

SELF TEST SOLUTIONS

TRUE/FALSE

1. F
2. T
3. F
4. T
5. T
6. F
7. F
8. F
9. F
10. T
11. F
12. T
13. T
14. F
15. F

MULTIPLE CHOICE

1. C
2. B
3. B
4. C
5. A
6. C
7. D
8. A
9. D
10. B
11. C
12. C
13. A
14. D
15. D
16. C
17. A
18. D
19. B
20. D
21. D
22. B
23. A
24. D
25. C

QUESTIONS AND PROBLEMS

1. A joint process produces two or more products from the same production cycle. This process may result in primary and secondary products, scrap and waste. Joint products are produced by the same process and are also called primary products, co-products, or main products. These products have substantial sales value and are the reason that management undertakes the production process.

   By-products and scrap are incidental to the production process. Both are salable, but their sales values are small compared to primary products. Management would not undertake the production process for by-products or scrap.

   Waste is a residual of the production process. Waste has no sales value and a normal amount is considered an unavoidable production cost.

Chapter 10: Cost Allocation for Joint Products and By-Products

2. The split-off point is important because this is the first place at which joint products are identifiable and may first be salable. Split-off point is where the decision is made for or against further processing of products and the point at which joint cost is allocated to the primary products.

3. Joint costs must be allocated to the goods produced by the production process only for valuation purposes. The allocation of joint costs is not relevant to decision making, especially about further processing.

4. The physical measurement approach to joint cost allocation uses a common tangible physical characteristic of the products to allocate costs. This method treats all products the same and assigns the same cost per unit of measure. It also provides an unchanging measure for the product output.

5. By-products and scrap are usually accounted for by use of either the net realizable value method or the realized value method. The net realizable value method requires that the NRV of the by-products or scrap be inventoried and treated as a reduction in cost of the primary products. When the realizable value method is used, no value is recognized for by-products or scrap until the products are sold.

6. R 30/63 x $12,500 = $5,952
   S 25/63 x $12,500 = $4,960
   T   8/63 x $12,500 = $1,587
   (off due to rounding)

7. R 30 x $1,000 = $30,000/62,000 x $12,500 = $6,048
   S 25 x $ 800 = $20,000/62,000 x $12,500 = $4,032
   T   8 x $1,500 = $12,000/62,000 x $12,500 = $2,419
   (off due to rounding)

8. R 30 x $500 = $15,000/32,650 x $12,500 = $5,743
   S 25 x 450 = 11,250/32,650 x $12,500 = $4,307
   T   8 x 800 =   6,400/32,650 x $12,500 = $2,450
                  $32,650
   (off due to rounding)

9. R $1,700 - $100 - $500 = $1,100
   S   1,250 -   500 - 350 =   400
   T   2,000 -   400 - 700 =   900

   Products R and T should be processed further.

10. R 30 x $1,100 = $33,000/51,450 x $12,500 = $8,018
    S 25 x   450 = 11,250/51,450 x $12,500 = $2,733
    T   8 x   900 =   7,200/51,450 x $12,500 = $1,749
                    $51,450

    This method uses a combination of approximated and actual NRV at split-off because some products (S) will be at split-off, while others (R & T) will be processed further and sold.

CHAPTER 11

GENERAL CONCEPTS OF STANDARD COSTING: MATERIAL AND LABOR STANDARDS

CHAPTER OVERVIEW

Companies may use actual or standard costs to value inventory and create decisions. Standard costs provide a benchmark against which to surmise the efficiency and effectiveness of current operations. Standards are also utilized in forecasting future operating results. Standard costing was mentioned in the chapters on job order and process costing(7 and 8). This chapter and the following one give a complete overview on the use of standard cost systems.

Chapter 11 covers two specific types of standards: direct materials and direct labor, while Chapter 12 covers standards for overhead. Chapter 11 includes the development of a standard cost system, how materials and labor variances are computed, and the suitable use of variances for performance evaluation.

The first appendix to this chapter illustrates standard cost variances when multiple materials or grades of labor are used in the production process. Quantities and types of materials and/or
labor may be combined in different ways to produce equal or equivalent output. Variations from the standards are called mix and yield variances.

Appendix 2 addresses the effects of learning on production--an occurrence known as a learning curve.

CHAPTER STUDY GUIDE

1. Standards development should be done on a group basis within the business entity. Before standards can be initiated, the quality of output must be determined. Once this has been found, standards for materials and labor can be calculated.

2. The first step is to identify the direct materials that are needed to produce the product.

    a. An analysis of materials must be performed and the following questions must be answered.

        i. What inputs are required?
        ii. What quantity of each input is needed?
        iii. What quality of inputs should be used?
        iv. What price should be paid for the inputs?

    b. Once these questions are answered and the standards established, materials variances can be calculated as production occurs. There are three material variances: total, price, and usage.

        i. The total variance is the difference between actual production price (inputs) and standard price of actual production (outputs).

        ii. The materials price variance is the difference between the amount paid for materials and the standard price of materials.

Chapter 11: General Concepts of Standard Costing: Material and Labor Standards

        iii. The materials usage variance is the difference between actual quantity used and the standard quantity of materials allowed for the production achieved.

        iv. This is converted to a dollar amount by multiplying the differential quantity by the standard price.

3. Material variances should be recognized when the materials are purchased rather than when they are used in production. In the preferred method, price variances are calculated on the quantity purchased (rather than used). Price variances involve the purchasing rather than the production function.

4. The quantity variance is computed based on actual usage in production operations.

5. In the development of labor variances, each production operation must be identified and analyzed. All necessary movement to produce the product is taken into consideration.

    a. All needless movement is dismissed in determining standards.

6. Questions comparable to those requested regarding materials are asked when developing standards for direct labor: how many hours are needed to produce one item and what should workers be paid per hour to manufacture one item?

    a. There are three labor variances: total, rate, and efficiency.

        i. The total variance is the difference between the actual wages paid during the period and the standard wages allowed for the production achieved.

        ii. The labor rate variance is the difference between the actual and standard rates for the actual hours worked.

        iii. The labor efficiency variance is the difference between the actual hours worked and standard hours allowed for the level of production attained multiplied by the standard wage rate.

        iv. All variances must be identified as being either favorable (credit balances) or unfavorable (debit balances).

7. Once variances have been calculated, journal entries must be prepared and recorded. These entries are illustrated in Exhibit 11-7.

    a. If the variances are small, they are closed to Cost of Goods Sold.

    b. Large variances are closed to Raw Materials (materials price variance only), Work in Process, Finished Goods, and Cost of Goods Sold on a prorated basis (similar to the disposition of significant under or overapplied overhead). The proration is based on the amount of materials or labor in these accounts.

8. Six benefits realized in using a standard cost system are discussed in the chapter: clerical efficiency, motivation, planning, controlling, decision making, and performance evaluation.

    a. To properly realize the benefits of a standard cost system, responsibility must be established for the variances computed.

    b. It is important to note that some variances are interrelated and, therefore, responsibility may not be attached as would appear at first observation.

        i. For example, a favorable material usage variance may result from the purchase of a higher quality input than was specified in the standard. The purchasing agent is responsible for both variances rather than only for the purchase price variance.

Chapter 11: General Concepts of Standard Costing: Material and Labor Standards

9. Appendix 1 introduces the concept of mix and yield variances. When a company uses more than one material in the production process, it attempts to use those materials in the combination that will achieve the most benefit.

    a. In the use of labor, all companies employ both skilled and unskilled workers. Labor can also be used in different combinations.

    b. In many production processes, it may be possible to make substitutions of materials and workers. Each possible combination of materials and/or labor is considered a mix.

    c. Yield is the quantity of output that results from a specific amount of input. Use of non-standard mix combinations can result in non-standard output and mix and yield variances are computed.

    d. The mix variance compares the actual mix of the achieved quantity of input at the standard price with the standard mix of the actual quantity of input at the standard price. See EXHIBITs 11-10 and 11.

    e. The yield variance focuses on the variation in the actual versus standard quantity allowed for the output achieved at the standard mix and standard prices. See EXHIBIT 11-12.

10. Appendix 2 discusses learning curves. A learning curve is a model that facilitates how the amount of time needed to perform a task will decrease as employees become more proficient. The learning curve considers declines in production time per unit based on the doubling of total production quantities.

    a. The time it should take to produce one unit or batch in a multiple unit or batch process is called predicted (cumulative) average time per unit. This average time is found from the following formula:

    $$Y = aX^b$$

The variables in this learning curve formula are:
    Y is the cumulative average time for one unit or batch
    a is the time to do the first unit or batch
    X is the number of units or batches to be done
    b is the learning exponent

$$b = \frac{\ln \textit{learning curve rate}}{\ln 2}$$

ln learning curve rate is the natural log of the learning curve rate.
The 2 above assumes the learning curve occurs with a doubling of the output level (units or batches produced).

SELF TEST

TRUE/FALSE

1. T F

    In a standard cost system, only standard costs are recorded in the records.

2. T F

    The difference between actual costs and standard costs is called a variance.

Chapter 11: General Concepts of Standard Costing: Material and Labor Standards

3. **T** F

   If a variance is small, standard costs are approximately equal to actual costs.

4. **T** F

   If a variance is large, it is closed at year end to Cost of Goods Sold and inventories on a prorated basis.

5. T **F**

   Materials price variances are usually determined at the point of usage.

6. T **F**

   Rigorous standards positively affect motivation.

7. **T** F

   Practical standards can be reached or slightly exceeded with reasonable effort by workers.

8. **T** F

   Ideal standards provide for no inefficiency and do not allow for normal delays or human limitations.

9. **T** F

   A material yield variance computes the difference between the actual total quantity of input and the standard total quantity of input allowed based on output at a standard price.

10. **T** F

    Ideal standards are not usually used by companies because the standard is set too high to motivate employees and not low enough to allow for normal interruptions.

11. T **F**

    If a variance is favorable, its dollar amount or its percentage amount is not of concern to management.

12. T **F**

    Ideal standards can be used in forecasting and planning whereas practical standards cannot be used for such purposes.

MULTIPLE CHOICE

1. A standard is used for which of the following?

   a. Planning
   b. Evaluating
   c. Controlling
   d. All of the above

2. A standard cost system uses which of the following in its accounting records?

   a. Standard costs and actual costs
   b. Actual cost and market values
   c. Market values and standards costs
   d. Opportunity costs and standard costs

Chapter 11: General Concepts of Standard Costing: 115
Material and Labor Standards

3. It is necessary to know which of the following in regard to materials?

	Quality of inputs	Quantity of inputs
a.	no	yes
b.	yes	yes
c.	yes	no
d.	no	no

4. A document that lists all necessary operations to make a unit of product and time allowed for each operation is called a/an

 a. bill of materials.
 b. job cost record.
 c. operations flow document.
 d. production and cost report.

5. A/An _____ summarizes the direct materials and direct labor standard quantities and prices needed to make one unit of product.

 a. job cost record
 b. standard cost card
 c. production and cost report
 d. bill of lading

6. The difference between actual costs and standard costs is known as a/an

 a. purchasing error.
 b. overrun.
 c. variance.
 d. production error.

7. Which of the following is **not** a function of a standard cost system?

 a. Collecting the actual costs
 b. Determining the achievement of the manufacturing operation
 c. Evaluating performance through reporting variances
 d. Determining the rate of errors in the system

Use the following information for questions 8-12. (Round all answers to the nearest dollar.)

The following information is available for Lake Co. for the month of January.

 Standards:
  Material: 1.0 pounds per unit @ $12.00 per pound
  Labor: 1.5 hours per unit @ $8.00 per hour

 Actual:
  Material: Purchased 8,900 pounds during January @ $11.75 per pound
            Usage in January 7,500 pounds
  Labor: 2.00 hours per unit @ $8.25 per hour

  Production for January was 7,000 units.

8. What is the materials usage price variance?

 a. $1,875 F
 b. $1,875 U
 c. $1,750 F
 d. $1,750 U

9. What is the materials usage variance?

 a. $6,000 F
 b. $6,000 U
 c. $5,875 F
 d. $5,875 U

Chapter 11: General Concepts of Standard Costing:
Material and Labor Standards

10. What is the materials purchase price variance?

    a. $ 350 F
    b. $ 350 U
    c. $2,225 U
    d. $2,225 F

11. What is the labor rate variance?

    a. $3,500 U
    b. $1,750 U
    c. $3,500 F
    d. $1,750 F

12. What is the labor efficiency variance?

    a. $28,875 F
    b. $28,000 F
    c. $28,875 U
    d. $28,000 U

13. What variance compares (at the standard rate per hour) the number of hours actually worked with the hours allowed for the production attained?

    a. labor rate
    b. learning curve variance
    c. total labor variance
    d. labor efficiency

14. Which of the following applies to unfavorable insignificant variances?

	Debit Balance	Closed to
a.	yes	Cost of Goods Sold
b.	yes	WIP, FG, and CGS
c.	no	Cost of Goods Sold
d.	no	WIP, FG, and CGS

15. Which of the following applies to favorable variances?

	Type of Balance	Reduction in Production Costs
a.	debit	yes
b.	debit	no
c.	credit	no
d.	credit	yes

16. If standard costs are about the same as actual costs, then standard costs can be used for which of the following?

	Financial Statements	Internal Reports
a.	yes	yes
b.	yes	no
c.	no	no
d.	no	yes

17. Variance analysis is performed in which function of management?

    a. Decision making
    b. Controlling
    c. Motivating
    d. Planning

Chapter 11: General Concepts of Standard Costing: Material and Labor Standards

Use the following information for questions 18-23.
(Round all answers to the nearest dollar.)

The following information is available for the T-Shirt Co. for the month of November:

Standards:
1 yard per X-Large T-shirt @ $3.50 per yard
.5 hours per shirt @ $4.50 per hour

Actual:
Materials used 5,040 yards; purchased at $3.45 per yard
T-shirts produced 4,800
Direct labor hours used 2,750
Rate per hour $4.75

18. What is the material price variance?

    a. $ 252 F
    b. $5,292 F
    c. $ 252 U
    d. $5,292 U

19. What is the material usage variance?

    a. $1,080 U
    b. $1,080 F
    c. $ 840 U
    d. $ 840 F

20. What is the total material variance?

    a. $1,092 F
    b. $4,212 U
    c. $ 588 U
    d. $4,452 F

21. What is the labor rate variance?

    a. $1,575 U
    b. $ 688 U
    c. $ 688 F
    d. $1,575 F

22. What is the labor efficiency variance?

    a. $1,035 U
    b. $1,575 U
    c. $1,663 U
    d. $1,093 U

23. What is the total labor variance?

    a. $ 887 U
    b. $1,723 U
    c. $ 975 U
    d. $2,263 U

24. (Appendix 1) The difference between the actual total quantity of input and the standard total quantity allowed based on output at a standard price is the

    a. materials mix variance.
    b. materials yield variance.
    c. materials usage variance.
    d. materials price variance.

Chapter 11: General Concepts of Standard Costing: Material and Labor Standards

25. The learning curve model can be used for which of the following classifications of employees?

    a. assembly
    b. manufacturing
    c. office personnel
    d. all of the above

26. All of the following are uses of standard costs except:

    a. Inventory valuation
    b. Critical cost analysis when setting standards
    c. Product differentiation
    d. Simplification of record keeping

27. A detailed listing of the quantity and quality of direct material needed to manufacture one unit of product is a:

    a. Purchase order
    b. Bill of materials
    c. Materials requisition
    d. Product materials standards sheet

28. The person who is most likely to be responsible for a materials price variance is the:

    a. Line supervisor
    b. Plant manager
    c. Controller
    d. Purchasing agent

29. If materials are of standard quality, the person who is most likely to be responsible for a materials quantity variance is the:

    a. Line supervisor
    b. Plant manager
    c. Controller
    d. Purchasing agent

30. The difference between an actual cost and a total standard cost is a (an):

    a. Favorable variance
    b. Standard variance
    c. Total variance
    d. Unfavorable variance

31. An unfavorable material quantity variance indicates that:

    a. actual usage of material exceeds the standard material allowed for output.
    b. standard material allowed for output exceeds the actual usage of material.
    c. actual material price exceeds standard price.
    d. standard material price exceeds actual price.

32. Using more highly-skilled direct laborers might affect which of the following variances?

    a. direct materials usage variance
    b. direct labor efficiency variance
    c. variable manufacturing overhead efficiency variance
    d. b and c
    e. a, b, and c

Chapter 11: General Concepts of Standard Costing: Material and Labor Standards

33. A major drawback to setting standards based on historical results is that such standards

    a. can perpetuate inefficiencies.
    b. are harder to compute than are engineered standards.
    c. are usually too hard to meet.
    d. are usually not well received by workers.

34. An unfavorable labor efficiency variance

    a. means that workers were inefficient and their supervisor did a poor job.
    b. causes a favorable variable overhead efficiency variance.
    c. might result from an action taken by a manager other than supervisor of the workers.
    d. should always be investigated and corrected.

35. Which kinds of variances should be investigated?

    a. Those that are large and unfavorable.
    b. Those that are large and either favorable or unfavorable.
    c. All variances, despite their size.
    d. Only use variances.

36. A learning curve of 80% assumes that production unit costs are reduced by 20% for each doubling of output. What is the cost of the sixteenth unit produced as an approximate percent of the first unit produced?

    a. 30%
    b. 40%
    c. 50%
    d. 60%

QUESTIONS AND PROBLEMS

1. Discuss what must be taken into consideration when setting standards for materials.

2. List and briefly discuss the benefits of a standard cost system.

3. Define the following terms: operations flow document, variance, standard quantity allowed, and labor efficiency variance.

4. Briefly discuss material mix and yield variances.

Chapter 11: General Concepts of Standard Costing: Material and Labor Standards

5. Define and briefly discuss the use of a learning curve.

6. For each of the following items, match the definition with the appropriate term: bill of materials, standard cost card, materials price variance, variance analysis, exception report.

   a. A document/procedure that indicates when actual costs exceed or fall below the acceptable limits set for costs by management _____.

   b. A document/procedure that indicates the components of material and the quality and quantity of materials to be used in production _____.

   c. A document/procedure that indicates the direct labor and direct materials needed to complete one product _____.

   d. A document/procedure that indicates that standard cost and actual cost differ _____.

   e. An indication that the actual price paid for materials differed from the standard price for materials _____.

Use the following information for questions 7 and 8.

The following information is available for the month of March for J & J Co.

   Standards:
      Materials: 1.25 feet per unit @ $4.00 per foot
      Labor: 2.5 hours per unit @ $6.00 per hour

   Actual:
      Materials: 3,000 feet purchased @ $3.90 per foot
                 2,500 feet used for the month
      Labor: 6,100 hours @ $5.80

   1,750 units were produced

7. Compute the preferred material price and usage variances.

8. Compute the labor rate and efficiency variances.

Chapter 11: General Concepts of Standard Costing: Material and Labor Standards

9. (Appendix 1) The Fly Away Co. manufactures hot air balloons. Fly Away employs both skilled and unskilled workers. The skilled workers (Class X) earn $8 per hour while unskilled workers (Class Z) earn $5 per hour. Each balloon takes 41.25 hours of skilled labor and 13.75 hours of unskilled labor. During the month of August, Fly Away produced 25 balloons. Actual data for the month are as follows:

    Skilled labor 580 hours at $8.50 per hour.
    Unskilled labor 870 hours at $5.25 per hour.

    Determine the labor rate, mix, and yield variances for the month of August.

10. (Appendix 2) Mary Smith owns a ceramic shop that instructs customers in the art of making greenware. Mary discovers that it takes her new helper 4 hours to get her first piece of greenware ready to fire. Mary knows that there is a learning curve of 80% for new helpers. How long will it take the helper to get 16 pieces ready to fire?

COMMUNICATION PROBLEM

From the questions at the end of the chapter in the Study Guide, be prepared to answer the true-false and multiple choice questions when your instructor calls on you in class. Be sure you have covered up the answer. Also provide a reason why you think your answer is correct.
This testing procedure helps you develop communication skills among your classmates. Furthermore, you must think through why you choose that answer and explain the reason for this choice.

SELF TEST SOLUTIONS

TRUE/FALSE

1. F   6. F   11. T
2. T   7. F   12. F
3. T   8. T   13. F
4. T   9. T
5. F   10. T

MULTIPLE CHOICE

1. D   6. C   11. A   16. A   21. B   26. C   31. A   36. B
2. A   7. D   12. D   17. B   22. B   27. B   32. E
3. B   8. A   13. D   18. A   23. D   28. D   33. A
4. C   9. B   14. A   19. C   24. B   29. A   34. C
5. B   10. C   15. D   20. C   25. D   30. B   35. B

QUESTIONS AND PROBLEMS

1. To properly establish standards for materials, one must identify the **materials needed** to manufacture the product. It is also **necessary to** determine what inputs are going to be used, what quality of inputs are desired, and what quantity of inputs are required. After these decisions are made, a standard price per unit of input must be determined (usually with the help of the purchasing agent).

Chapter 11: General Concepts of Standard Costing: Material and Labor Standards

2. There are 6 benefits of a standard cost system: (1) clerical efficiency - less clerical time is needed in a standard cost system than in an actual cost system; (2) motivation - when attainable standards are set, these tend to motivate employees to strive to meet the standards; (3) planning - standards aid in budget preparation; (4) controlling - variance analysis enables management to control and measure costs of the system; (5) decision making - standard costs enable management to make timely and reasonable decisions; and (6) performance evaluation - the system provides feedback to employees and management as to how well the system is working and where improvements need to be made.

3. An <u>operations flow document</u> lists all operations necessary to make one unit, including the time allowed for each operation. A <u>variance</u> is the difference between the standard cost and an actual cost; a variance can be favorable or unfavorable. <u>Standard quantity allowed</u> reflects the standard quantity of input that should have been needed to achieve the actual output. A <u>labor efficiency variance</u> compares the number of hours actually worked with the standard hours allowed for the production level achieved and measures this difference at the standard rate per hour.

4. When a company uses more than one material in producing its products, those materials may be combined in a number of ways. Each possible combination of materials and/or labor is called a mix. The yield is the quantity of output that results from a specific input. The materials yield variance computes the difference between the actual total quantity of input and the standard total quantity allowed based on output. The materials mix variance computes the effect of substituting a non-standard mix of materials during the production process. The labor mix variance presents the financial effect associated with changing the proportionate amount of higher or lower paid workers in production. The labor yield variance shows the monetary impact of using more or fewer total hours than the standard allowed.

5. A learning curve is a model that enables management to predict how long it will take a person to perform a specific task after a period of learning has taken place. Learning helps to eliminate inefficiencies that result because employees are unfamiliar with the tasks they are to perform. A learning curve indicates the percentage decline in production time per unit that will occur as total production quantities are doubled.

6.
   a. exception report
   b. bill of materials
   c. standard cost card
   d. variance analysis
   e. materials price variance

7. 3,000 x $3.90   3,000 x $4
      $11,700 $12,000
              $300F
      materials price variance

    2,500 x $4   1,750 x $4
      $10,000 $7,000
              $3,000 U
      materials usage variance

8. 6,100 x $5.80   6,100 x $6   4,375 x $6
      $35,380 $36,600 $26,250
            $1,220 F $10,350 U
         labor rate variance   labor efficiency variance

9. 580/1,450 = 40%
    870/1,450 = 60%
    1,450
    TOTAL ACTUAL COST
        40% X 1,450 X $8.50   = $4,930.00
        60% X 1,450 X $5.25   =   4,567.50
                                  $9,497.50

Chapter 11: General Concepts of Standard Costing: Material and Labor Standards

```
ACTUAL MIX AND HOURS: STANDARD RATES
    40% X 1,450 X $8        =        $4,640.00
    60% X 1,450 X $5        =         4,350.00
                                     $8,990.00
Labor Rate Variance= $9,497.50 - $8,990 = $507.50 U
41.25/55 =  75%
13.75/55 =  25%
55.00
TOTAL ACTUAL HOURS; STANDARD MIX AND RATES
    75% X 1,450 X $8        =        $ 8,700.00
    25% X 1,450 X $5        =          1,812.50
                                     $10,512.50
Labor Mix Variance= $8,990 - $10,512.50 = $1,522.50 F

TOTAL STANDARD
    75% X 1,375 X $8        =        $8,250.00
    25% X 1,375 X $5        =         1,718.75
                                     $9,968.75
Labor Yield Variance = $10,512.50 - $9,968.75 = $543.75 F
```

10.

QUANTITY	PREDICTED HOURS PER UNIT	TOTAL PRODUCTION HOURS
1	4.0000	4.0000
2	3.2000	6.4000
4	2.5600	10.2400
8	2.048	16.384
16	1.6384	26.2144

CHAPTER 12

STANDARD COSTING FOR OVERHEAD

CHAPTER OVERVIEW

Chapter 12 discusses and illustrates flexible budgets for use in planning and control of overhead costs and standard overhead cost variances. Flexible budgets can be used to calculate variable and fixed overhead costs (as well as other types of costs) at different levels of activity. Exhibit 12-1 illustrates how the straight line cost formula can be used to compute costs at differing activity levels within the relevant range. Note that as machine hours increase, viable costs increase but fixed costs remain constant. Flexible budgests are usually prepared on an input basis. Outputs are measures of units produced and the ratio of outputs to inputs is called a
yield ratio.

Predetermined overhead rates are discussed noting that their use facilitates more accurate costing and price quotes. The alternative is to use actual overhead costing. In Chapter 5, an other approach to assigning overhead was discussed(ABC for overhead). Chapter 12 notes that combined overhead rates can be used or separate variable and fixed overhead rates may also be used. The use of separate rates provides for more detailed analysis of overhead variances as discussed below.

Four different methods of overhead variance analysis are examined. These approaches depend on the degree of cost detail available and method of overhead application (one or two rates) in use. The four-variance approach overhead provides the most detail of all the approaches. Managers must understand the breadth to which information is given under each method so that they can correctly exercise control, designate responsibility, and evaluate performance. Because of the nature of overhead costs, these managerial functions are not as easily undertaken as they were in relation to materials and labor. Acknowledgment of the variances in the accounting records at the end of the period are illustrated in Exhibit 12-6.

CHAPTER STUDY GUIDE

1. Flexible budgets are a series of budgets displaying costs at different activity levels. Utilizing flexible budgets require mixed costs to be separated into variable and fixed cost components.

    a. The activity levels in a flexible budget cover the relevant range of activity for the budget period. If all levels of activity are within the relevant range, then costs at each successive level should equal the amount of the previous level plus a uniform dollar increment for each variable cost factor (unless step costs are involved).
    b. Activities outside the relevant range may result in changes in costs for either or both variable and fixed costs. See Chapter 4 for more discussion of relevant range.

2. A predetermined overhead rate (or rates) can be determined when a flexible budget is prepared for variable and fixed overhead cost components.

    a. This rate can be determined by dividing budgeted overhead (either variable and fixed or total) at a specific level of activity within the relevant range by that activity level. The level that is chosen most often is the expected annual capacity. (Remember that variable costs remain constant on a per unit basis and vary in total with changes in activity. Fixed costs vary on a per unit basis in an inverse relationship to changes in activity although they remain constant in total.)

    b. Other activity levels could be used such as normal capacity, practical capacity, or theoretical capacity.

3. Flexible budgets can be prepared on either an input or an output basis. The input basis focuses on successive levels of input activity and the related standard output yield and costs.

    a. The output basis focuses on the number of units produced and the standard levels of input activity and costs required for that production.

    b. A yield ratio indicates the relationship between the input and output; for example if it takes 3 hours of machine time to make one unit, the yield ratio is 3:1.

4. Control over all production costs is essential for proper product costing. Control extends not only to direct materials, direct labor, but to overhead as well. The difference between actual overhead costs and the standard overhead that should have been incurred for actual production is known as a total overhead variance.

    a. Overhead variances can be determined using a variety of calculations that provide minimal or substantial detail about cost differentials from standard.

        i. Four approaches to calculating overhead variances can be utilized and provide between 1 and 6 variances.

        ii. The approach that is referred to as the 4 variance approach really provides six variances because a total variable overhead variance and a total fixed overhead variance can be computed in addition to the sub-element variances.

            (1) As the number of variances increases, so does the amount of information that is obtained for managerial use.

5. The four variance approach presents separate analyses for variable and fixed overhead and provides specific price and usage subvariances for each.

    a. The total variable overhead variance is the difference between actual variable overhead and standard variable overhead allowed for the production achieved.

        i. This total variance can be further divided into variable spending and efficiency variances. The variable overhead spending variance is the difference between actual variable overhead and budgeted variable overhead based on actual input.
            (1) This variance is often caused by paying either a higher or lower price than the standard allows.

        ii. The variable overhead efficiency variance is the difference between budgeted variable overhead at the actual input level and budgeted variable overhead at the output level (or standard input allowed for the activity achieved).

            (1) This variance focuses on the use of more or less input activity than allowed by the standard and quantifies that excess or reduced utilization by multiplying by the standard overhead rate.

6. The total fixed overhead variance is the difference between actual fixed overhead and standard fixed overhead applied to production. This total

Chapter 12: Standard Costing for Overhead

variance can be further broken down into a fixed overhead spending and volume variance.

   a. The fixed spending variance is the difference between actual fixed overhead and budgeted overhead. Budgeted fixed overhead is a constant amount throughout the relevant range.

   b. The fixed overhead volume variance is the difference between budgeted FOH and applied FOH. Applied fixed overhead is computed by multiplying the fixed overhead application rate times the standard input allowed for the level of production achieved (often called standard hours or inputs allowed).

   c. Management has little control over fixed overhead unlike materials use or labor efficiency variances.

   d. The volume variance is a measure of plant utilization.

7. Using the four-variance approach requires overhead costs being separated into their variable and fixed components. Separate rates are used for variable and fixed overhead. If this level of detail is not available and a single overhead application rate is used, either the 1-, 2-, or 3- variance approach must be used to compute overhead variances. See Exhibit 12-5 for a synopsis of these variance methods.

8. The next variance discussed is the one variance approach. This variance calculates only the difference between total actual overhead and total overhead applied to production.

   a. Applied overhead is computed by multiplying the combined overhead application rate times standard input activity allowed for the level of production reached.

   b. The total variance approach provides no detailed information for managers to find out the underlying reasons for the variance. Managers need to obtain additional information from various sources for overhead for control or evaluation purposes.

9. The two variance approach divides the total overhead variance into a budget variance and a volume variance.

   a. The budget (or controllable) variance is the difference between total actual overhead and the flexible budget for overhead based on standard hours allowed for the level of production achieved.

      i. The budget variance is equal to the sum of the variable and fixed overhead spending variances plus the variable overhead efficiency variance, all of the 4-variance approach.

      ii. The volume (or noncontrollable) variance is the difference between the flexible budget of total overhead based on standard hours allowed for the level of production achieved and total applied overhead.

         (1) This amount is the same amount as the volume variance computed under the 4-variance approach.

         (2) Fixed overhead remains constant at all levels of activity within the relevant range. The budget figure for fixed overhead does <u>not</u> use input activity times the predetermined rate in its calculation; it uses the budgeted amount of fixed overhead.

10. The three variance approach breaks down the overhead budget variance into a spending and an efficiency variance.

    a. The total overhead spending variance is the difference between total actual overhead and the flexible budget based on the actual input activity.

Chapter 12: Standard Costing for Overhead

b. The efficiency variance is the difference between the flexible budget at the input level of activity and the flexible budget at the standard input allowed for the output achieved.

c. The volume variance is computed as mentioned above. The relationships among the different approaches to variance computations are shown in Exhibit 12-5. Once variances have been computed, they are recorded in the accounting records as shown in Exhibit 12-6.

11. As manufacturing firms move towards more automated manufacturing, machinery costs and overhead increase at the expense of direct labor (note the increase in use of robots in the auto assembly plants). In many cases, direct labor no longer drives overhead. Firms are adopting a cost system with two product costs: direct materials and conversion costs (which is direct labor and overhead combined). Conversion costs may still be separated into its fixed and variable components.

a. The variable conversion cost variances are divided into spending and efficiency variances.

b. The fixed conversion costs provide two other variances, fixed spending and volume variances.

SELF TEST

TRUE/FALSE

1. T F

   A flexible budget is a budget that presents one level of activity and the costs that should be incurred at that particular level.

2. T F

   A step fixed cost fluctuates in total with small changes in activity levels.

3. T F

   A variable overhead application rate can be computed by dividing total budgeted variable overhead at any level of activity within the relevant range by the related measure of activity.

4. T F

   A yield ratio relates to the relationship between input and output.

5. T F

   The application rate for variable overhead can be determined using any level of activity within the relevant range.

6. T F

   The application rate for fixed overhead can be determined using any level of activity within the relevant range.

7. T F

   If the difference between applied overhead and actual overhead is immaterial, it is closed at year end to Cost of Goods Sold.

8. T F

   The difference between applied overhead and actual overhead is called under- or overapplied overhead.

Chapter 12: Standard Costing for Overhead

9. (T) F

    The control process is undertaken to assure that actual operations are going according to what was planned.

10. (T) F

    The total fixed overhead variance equals the fixed spending overhead variance only if the actual production equals the expected or normal capacity level.

11. T (F)

    Whenever the fixed spending overhead variance is favorable, the variable spending overhead variance is also favorable.

12. T (F)

    Whenever the volume variance is favorable, the variable efficiency is also favorable.

13. (T) F

    Waste or excessive usage of overhead materials will show up as part of the variable overhead efficiency variance.

14. T (F)

    In a standard cost system, overhead is applied to work in process on a basis of the actual hours of activity.

MULTIPLE CHOICE

1. A budget can be prepared using which of the following levels of activity?

	Single Level of Activity	Multiple Levels of Activity
a.	yes	yes
b.	no	yes
c.	no	no
d.	yes	no

2. Which of the following is essential in preparing a flexible overhead budget?

	Total Fixed Overhead	Per Unit Variable Overhead	Relevant Range
a.	yes	yes	yes
b.	yes	yes	no
c.	no	yes	no
d.	no	no	yes

3. Which of the following costs remain constant per unit over the relevant range?

	Variable	Fixed	Mixed
a.	yes	yes	yes
b.	yes	no	no
c.	no	yes	no
d.	no	yes	yes

4. Which of the following costs vary in total over the relevant range?

	Variable	Fixed	Mixed
a.	yes	yes	yes
b.	no	no	yes
c.	yes	no	no
d.	yes	no	yes

Chapter 12: Standard Costing for Overhead

5. Which of the following is a variable cost?

	Direct Materials	Direct Labor	Supervisor's Salary
a.	yes	yes	no
b.	yes	yes	yes
c.	no	no	yes
d.	no	yes	yes

6. Which of the following is most likely to be a step fixed cost?

    a. electricity
    b. water
    c. supervisors' salaries
    d. sales commissions

7. Control of fixed overhead costs is most important at which of the following times?

    a. Production
    b. End of period
    c. Commitment
    d. Materials acquisition

8. The total variable overhead variance is the difference between which of the following?

    a. actual and budgeted overhead
    b. actual and fixed overhead
    c. actual and applied overhead
    d. actual variable and actual fixed overhead

9. In the four variance approach to overhead analysis, the total variable overhead variance can be divided into which of the following components?

    a. spending and volume
    b. volume and efficiency
    c. spending and budget
    d. spending and efficiency

10. In the four variance approach to overhead analysis, the total fixed overhead variance can be divided into which of the following components?

    a. spending and volume
    b. volume and efficiency
    c. spending and efficiency
    d. spending and controllable

Use the following information for questions 11-21.

Ryan applies overhead to production based on direct labor hours. During October Ryan produced 9,500 units, each unit requires 5 DLH. The following information is available for the Ryan Co. for October 1995:

Standard:
    Variable overhead rate
    (per direct labor hour) $ 2.00
    Fixed overhead rate
    (per direct labor hour) $ 3.00
    Budgeted fixed overhead $120,000

Actual:
    Actual variable overhead $103,000
    Actual fixed overhead   112,000
    Actual direct labor hours   49,750

Chapter 12: Standard Costing for Overhead

11. Use the one variance approach to determine the total overhead variance for 1995.

    a. $0
    b. $30,000 U
    c. $22,500 U
    d. $22,500 F

12. Use the two variance approach to determine the overhead budget variance.

    a. $0
    b. $22,500 F
    c. $ 4,500 F
    d. $29,250 F

13. Use the two variance approach to determine the overhead volume variance.

    a. $ 7,250 F
    b. $ 7,250 U
    c. $22,500 F
    d. $22,500 U

14. Use the three variance approach to determine the overhead spending variance.

    a. $ 4,500 U
    b. $29,250 F
    c. $29,250 U
    d. $ 4,500 F

15. Use the three variance approach to determine the overhead efficiency variance.

    a. $ 4,500 F
    b. $ 4,500 U
    c. $29,250 F
    d. $29,250 U

16. Use the three variance approach to determine the overhead volume variance.

    a. $22,500 F
    b. $22,500 U
    c. $ 7,250 F
    d. $ 7,250 U

17. Use the four variance approach to determine the variable overhead spending variance.

    a. $ 3,500 F
    b. $ 3,500 U
    c. $22,000 U
    d. $22,000 F

18. Use the four variance approach to determine the variable overhead efficiency variance.

    a. $43,000 F
    b. $ 4,500 F
    c. $ 4,500 U
    d. $43,000 U

19. Use the four variance approach to determine the fixed overhead spending variance.

    a. $ 8,000 U
    b. $37,250 U
    c. $ 8,000 F
    d. $37,250 F

Chapter 12: Standard Costing for Overhead

20. Use the four variance approach to determine the overhead volume variance.

    a. $ 7,250 U
    b. $22,500 U
    c. $ 7,250 F
    d. $22,500 F

21. How many units did Ryan expect to produce during October?

    a. 40,000
    b. 8,000
    c. 9,500
    d. cannot be determined from the information given

22. Management can use flexible budgets for which of the following functions?

	Planning	Controlling	Evaluating
a.	yes	no	no
b.	yes	yes	no
c.	no	no	no
d.	yes	yes	yes

23. The White Company has $15,600 of actual overhead costs. The company applies overhead to production at 120% of direct labor cost. During July, White Co. had 1,375 direct labor hours and paid wages that totaled $12,375. What is the amount of under- or overapplied overhead?

    a. $3,225 underapplied
    b. $3,225 overapplied
    c. $ 750 underapplied
    d. $ 750 overapplied

24. TriCo. uses a standard cost system and applies overhead to production based on direct labor hours. TriCo. produces one product that requires 6 direct labor hours per unit. During the current month 5,500 units were produced that required 34,620 direct labor hours. TriCo. applies fixed overhead at the rate of $4.50 per direct labor hour. TriCo has actual fixed overhead of $158,000 and budgeted fixed overhead of $162,000. What is the amount of volume variance?

    a. $ 9,500 U
    b. $ 7,290 U
    c. $13,500 U
    d. $ 4,000 F

25. If the price a company paid for overhead items, such as utilities, increased during the year, the company would probably report a(n):

    a. favorable efficiency variance.
    b. favorable spending variance.
    c. unfavorable efficiency variance.
    d. unfavorable spending variance.

26. Tiger Company sells one product and uses a standard cost system. During 1996, the overhead volume variance was found to be zero. Given no volume variance, which of the following is correct?

    a. Actual variable overhead costs was equal to standard variable overhead costs.
    b. Total applied overhead was equal to total actual overhead.
    c. The denominator activity was equal to actual activity.
    d. The budgeted fixed costs were equal to the applied fixed costs.

Chapter 12: Standard Costing for Overhead

27. Which of the following variances would be useful in calling attention to a possible short-term problem in the control of overhead costs?

	Spending variance	Volume variance
a.	No	No
b.	No	Yes
c.	Yes	No
d.	Yes	Yes

28. When a flexible budget is used, a decrease in production levels within a relevant range would:

   a. increase total fixed costs.
   b. increase variable cost per unit.
   c. decrease variable cost per unit.
   d. decrease total costs.

29. An unfavorable volume variance

   a. signifies poor cost control.
   b. shows that sales were less than budgeted.
   c. shows that production was less than sales.
   d. shows that production was less than the level used to set the fixed overhead absorption rate.
   e. shows that production exceeded the level used to set the fixed overhead absorption rate.

30. In a factory operated largely by robots, the most appropriate basis for applying overhead is probably

   a. direct labor hours.
   b. direct labor cost.
   c. machine hours.
   d. raw material use.

31. When standard hours allowed for good production exceed the capacity measure used in computing a predetermined fixed overhead rate, the volume variance is

   a. unfavorable.
   b. favorable.
   c. not affected by the difference.
   d. not measurable

QUESTIONS AND PROBLEMS

1. Define the following terms: step fixed cost, flexible budget, mixed costs, and yield ratio.

2. What is the difference between the four and three variance approaches to overhead analysis?

Chapter 12: Standard Costing for Overhead

3. Discuss briefly flexible budgets and how they are used by management.

4. Discuss briefly how control over overhead can be obtained using variance analysis.

5. Discuss briefly the two variance approach to overhead analysis.

Use the following information for questions 6-8.

PolyPet produces pet products and has the following information available for the month of June 1996:

```
Standard:
    Variable overhead per DLH      $ 1.25
    Fixed overhead per DLH           2.25
    Direct labor hours per unit      2.50
    Budgeted fixed overhead                $ 78,750

Actual:
    Variable overhead                      $ 48,000
    Fixed overhead                           78,000
    Direct labor hours                       33,450
    Units produced                           13,900
```

Fixed overhead per unit was determined based on 14,000 units per month as capacity.

6. Use the following approaches to determine the appropriate variances:

   a. the one variance approach
   b. the two variance approach

7. Compute all the necessary variances using the three variance approach.

Chapter 12: Standard Costing for Overhead

8. Compute all the necessary variances using the four variance approach.

9. Supply the missing numbers for the flexible budget of the M & M Company. Sales price per unit remains constant at all levels of sale. Each units requires 2 machine hours.

Units	5,000	6,000	7,000
Sales	$100,000	_____	_____
Variable Costs (per machine hour):			
Electricity	9,000	_____	_____
Water	_____	$ 15,000	_____
Materials	_____	_____	$ 35,000
Labor	_____	$ 48,000	_____
Total Variable	_____	_____	_____
Fixed Costs:			
Depreciation	$ 1,200	_____	_____
Insurance	_____	_____	900
Prop. Taxes	2,100	_____	_____
Supervision	_____	5,000	_____
Total Fixed Costs	_____	_____	_____
Gross Profit	_____	_____	_____

10. If total actual overhead is $55,000 and total applied overhead is $61,250

    a. overhead is _____ applied.
    b. by $_____.

COMMUNICATION PROJECT

The class is broken down into larger groups of about six students each. Your group is to analyze the following case and come up with at least two alternative solutions. Within the group, each person's spontaneous comments are copied down verbatim. From subsequent study of the comments, those students offering more conflict resolving comments are identified.

Pickens Grinding Company needs to hire three people to work in the plant who can run robotic equipment and route products through processing. All factory space is on a single floor. Labor standards have been set for production.

At present, the firm has had 15 experienced people apply for the jobs. One person is John Gordin who is paralyzed and uses a wheel chair for movement. He has many years of experience using the robotic machinery but must have the control box lowered to chair level for his use. Tom Picker, the personnel supervisor, interviewed John and rejected him for the job because he feels John can not meet the labor standards that were set by the company.

What is the ethical implications of hiring the physically disable in perference to the nondisabled and vice versa? Remember the 1992 Americans with Disabilities Act and its implications.

The objectives of this assignment is to a) clearly identify the conflict; b) offer slolutions which resolve the conflict; c) sloutions which are realistic and practical and d) exhibit a personal disposition towards resolving conflict.

136   Chapter 12: Standard Costing for Overhead

SELF TEST SOLUTIONS

TRUE/FALSE
1. F   6. F   11. F
2. F   7. T   12. F
3. T   8. T   13. T
4. T   9. T   14. F
5. T   10. T

MULTIPLE CHOICE
1. A   6. C   11. D   16. A   21. B   26. D   31. B
2. A   7. C   12. A   17. B   22. D   27. C
3. B   8. C   13. C   18. C   23. C   28. D
4. D   9. D   14. D   19. C   24. C   29. D
5. A   10. A   15. B   20. D   25. D   30. C

QUESTIONS AND PROBLEMS

1. A step fixed cost fluctuates in total with large changes in activity levels. An example of a step fixed cost is maintenance and supervision costs.

   A flexible budget is a series of budgets that presents different levels of activity and their related costs.

   A mixed cost has both a fixed portion and a variable portion. An example of a mixed cost is water usage and its related expense.

   A yield ratio relates to the input/output flexible budgets. It indicates how much output should be produced from a given quantity of input.

2. The four variance approach breaks down total variable and total fixed overhead into their subvariances. The total variable overhead variance can be split into a spending and an efficiency variance. The total fixed overhead variance can be split into a spending and a volume variance.

   The three variance approach breaks the 2 variance approach budget variance into two components: a spending variance and an efficiency variance. The spending variance is equal to the total of the variable and fixed overhead spending variances under the 4-variance approach. The efficiency variance is equal to the VOH efficiency variance of the 4-variance approach. Both the four and three variance approaches contain a volume variance.

3. Flexible budgets present several different levels of activity within the relevant range. Flexible budgets help management control costs and production by providing information from sources within the entity.

4. Control over costs focuses on analyzing variances of all elements of product cost. This includes materials, labor, and overhead variances. A variance indicates a difference between actual costs and what was determined to be the standard for products. A deviation from standard can be favorable or unfavorable.

5. The two variance approach extends the one variance approach by inserting a middle column in the equation. This column represents information on the total overhead cost expected based on the standard input allowed for the output produced. The subvariances computed are the budget (or controllable) variance and the volume (or uncontrollable) variance.

6. a. Actual OH $126,000
        $3.50 x 13,900 x 2.5   -   121,625
                                                     $ 4,375 U

    b. Budget:
        Actual OH $126,000.00
        VOH
        (13,900 x 2.5 x $1.25) $43,437.50
        Bud. FOH   78,750.00   122,187.50
                                                     $ 3,812.50 U

Chapter 12: Standard Costing for Overhead

      Volume:
         VOH $ 43,437.50
         FOH (13,900 x 2.5 x $2.25)   78,187.50
                                                                                     $121,625.00

  $122,187.50 - $121,625 = $562.50 U

7. Spending:
    Actual: $126,000.00
        FOH $78,750
        33,450 x $1.25 =   41,812.50   120,562.50
                                                                                           $ 5,437.50 U

    Efficiency:
        (see above) $120,562.50
    (13,900 x 2.5 x. $1.25) = $43,437.50
    FOH   78,750.00   122,187.50
                                                                                                                      $ 1,625.00 F

    Volume:
        (see above) $122,187.50
        (see # 6 above)   121,625.00
                                                                                                   $ 562.50 U

8. VOH Spending:
    Actual: $ 48,000.00
    ($1.25 x 33,450)   41,812.50
                                                                                                           $ 6,187.50 U

    VOH
        (see above) $ 41,812.50
    ($1.25 x 13,900 x 2.5)   43,437.50
                                                                                                           $ 1,625.00 F

    FOH: Spending
        Actual $ 78,000.00
        Budgeted FOH   78,750.00
                                                                                                          $ 750.00 F

    FOH Volume
        Budgeted FOH (see above) $ 78,750.00
        ($2.25 x 13,900 x 2.5)   78,187.50
                                                                                                          $ 562.50 U

9.

Units	5,000	6,000	7,000
Sales	$100,000	$120,000	$140,000
Variable Costs:			
Electricity	$ 9,000	$ 10,800	$ 12,600
Water	12,500	15,000	17,500
Materials	25,000	30,000	35,000
Labor	40,000	48,000	56,000
Total Variable	$ 86,500	$103,000	$121,100
Fixed Costs:			
Depreciation	$1,200	$1,200	$1,200
Insurance	900	900	900
Property Taxes	2,100	2,100	2,100
Supervision	5,000	5,000	5,000
Total Fixed	$9,200	$9,200	$9,200
Gross Profit	$4,300	$7,800	$9,700

10.   a.   over
      b. $6,250

CHAPTER 13
ABSORPTION AND VARIABLE COSTING

CHAPTER OVERVIEW

This chapter contrasts two alternative product costing approaches: absorption and variable. Accounting regulators require absorption costing to be used in reporting to stockholders, lenders, and governmental units. Variable costing is often used for internal purposes because of the advantages discussed in this chapter. The difference between variable costing and absorption costing methods is the manner in which fixed factory overhead is treated. Absorption costing treats fixed factory overhead as a product cost, while variable costing considers fixed factory overhead as a period cost (see Exhibit 13-4).

The internal advantages of variable costing stem from the way it defines product cost: direct materials + direct labor + variable factory overhead. It is important to note that all three of these costs are variable. The advantages to management in using a definition of "product cost" that contains only variable costs will become more apparent in Chapters 14 and 15.

Organizations usually have one accounting system providing information to both internal and external users. This system is based solely on either absorption or variable costing concepts. Thus, the chapter provides you with the technical procedures to translate absorption costing information to variable costing information and vice versa (see Exhibits 13-12, 13-13, and 13-14).

CHAPTER STUDY GUIDE

1. The absorption and variable costing methods are contrasted in Exhibit 13-2 and Exhibit 13-3. Both methods compute the same amount of income before income taxes, **with two exceptions**. The difference in income before taxes between the two methods will be attributable to the way each method treats fixed factory overhead. Income is also affected by the amount produced versa the quantity sold.

2. Exhibit 13-3 shows that fixed factory overhead is a product cost and the amount of fixed factory overhead deducted from sales depends on how many units are produced and sold.

    a. The differences between these two methods is presented in Exhibit 13-4. Variable costing handles fixed factory overhead like other period costs, which deducts these costs for the period from sales.

    b. The two methods treat all other costs the same; therefore, the difference between the two methods is that the amount of fixed factory overhead deducted for a period is also the difference in income before income taxes for the period.

    c. The difference in income before income taxes between variable and absorption costing for a period is equal to the difference in the amount of fixed factory overhead the two methods charge against income for the period.

Chapter 13: Absorption and Variable Costing

3. Another important feature of Chapter 13 is featured in the comparison of Exhibit 13-3 and Exhibit 13-4. You will notice that the income statement format that is used for variable costing is different from the income statement format that is used for absorption costing.

   a. The variable costing income statement format classifies costs both by behavior (fixed or variable) and by function. All variable costs are charged against revenues in arriving at the line item "Total Contribution Margin."

      i. The Total Contribution Margin is the portion of the amount of income that remains after covering all of the variable costs; or the amount of income that is available to cover fixed costs and provide net income.

      ii. All fixed costs (including fixed factory overhead) are deducted from the Total Contribution Margin to arrive at the Income Before Income Taxes.

4. A major benefit of arranging the income statement in a format that permits variable and fixed costs to be identified is demonstrated in Chapter 13 in the discussion on cost-volume-profit analysis.

   a. Like the absorption costing income statement, the variable costing income statement also has costs grouped by function. Cost of Goods Sold, Selling, General and Administrative, etc. However, these costs are also presented by behavior which is useful for decision making.

5. Variable or absorption costing can be used in conjunction with either job order or process costing, and all three cost valuation methods: actual, normal, or standard.

   a. Standard costing could be used with both variable and absorption costing, and an example in Exhibits 13-7 and 13-8 demonstrates this costing approach.

6. Accounting information in a variable costing format will be more useful for some users (internal managers), while accounting information in an absorption costing format will be more useful for other users (primarily users outside of the firm).

   a. Organizations will only have one accounting system, which should be based on either variable or absorption costing. To satisfy the needs of all users, the accountant must be able to convert absorption based accounting information to variable based accounting information and vice versa. Both user groups will then receive the accounting information in the format that they prefer or require. An illustration of journal entries that converts variable to absorption costing is presented in Exhibits 13-13 and 13-14.

7. Exhibit 13-12 shows how to reconcile variable costing and absorption costing information. This exhibit builds on the standard costing example presented in the earlier exhibits.

   a. Only when the number of units produced is equal to the number of units sold will absorption costing and variable costing deduct the same amount of fixed factory overhead in a period. In this instance, net income would also be the same under both methods.

   b. If the number of units produced exceeds the number of units sold, an income statement compiled based on the absorption costing method would report a higher net income than an income statement prepared based on variable costing. The absorption method inventories the fixed factory overhead that is associated with the units produced, but not sold during the period.

   c. The variable costing approach expenses all fixed factory overhead cost for the period.

Chapter 13: Absorption and Variable Costing

   d. If the number of units sold in a period exceeds the number of units produced in that period (which could only happen if a beginning inventory is available), the use of absorption costing will result in a lower net income than variable costing.

      i. These relationships are summarized in Exhibit 13-10. The Demonstration Problem at the end of the chapter provides an example of the reconciliation of variable and absorption costing. Note that this example is based on actual costs.

SELF TEST

TRUE/FALSE

1. T F

   Another name for variable costing is full costing.

2. T F

   One accounting system can provide information which can be used to prepare income statements utilizing both the variable and absorption costing methods.

3. T F

   The major distinction between variable and absorption costing is in the treatment of variable factory overhead.

4. T F

   Both variable and absorption costing can be used with job order and process costing.

5. T F

   A major advantage of variable costing lies in the fact that it categorizes costs both by their behavior and their functional category.

6. T F

   In the variable costing income statement format, the total contribution margin is equal to the sum of total fixed costs plus income before income taxes.

7. T F

   Under variable costing, it is impossible to deduct more total factory overhead in a period than is incurred.

8. T F

   Using variable costing, all product costs are variable costs.

9. T F
   Absorption costing is as informative as variable costing to management when segment reporting is necessary.

10. T F

    Variable non-manufacturing costs are shown after the contribution margin on a variable-costing income statement.

11. T F

    Under direct costing, all variable costs are treated as product costs.

Chapter 13: Absorption and Variable Costing

12. T   F

Absorption costing views fixed overhead as having future service potential and adds this overhead to units of product.

MULTIPLE CHOICE

1. Under absorption costing, which of the following is not an inventoriable cost?

    a.   variable factory overhead
    b.   variable selling and administrative expenses
    c.   fixed factory overhead
    d.   direct labor

2. Which of the following explains the widespread use of absorption costing?

    a.   everyone recognizes that it is a conceptually superior method
    b.   it facilitates better internal decision making
    c.   it is prescribed by authoritative groups such as the IRS and FASB
    d.   it always permits firms to report higher levels of income

3. Which of the following accurately describes the relationship between the inventory valuation under variable costing as opposed to the inventory valuation under absorption costing?

    a.   The use of variable costing will always result in a higher inventory valuation.
    b.   The use of absorption costing can never result in a lower inventory valuation than variable costing.
    c.   The relationship depends on the number of units the firm produces relative to the number it sells in a period.
    d.   The relationship is indeterminate ex ante.

4. Variable costing facilitates cost classification by

    a.   functional group only.
    b.   behavior only.
    c.   functional group and behavior.
    d.   neither functional group nor behavior.

5. You would typically expect the use of variable costing to result in greater net income than absorption costing when

    a.   the number of units produced exceeds the number of units sold.
    b.   when process costing is employed.
    c.   when the number of units sold exceeds the number of units produced.
    d.   when this period's production exceeds last period's production.

6. Under absorption costing, when would you expect the amount of factory overhead charged against income to exceed the factory overhead incurred?

    a.   when production exceeds sales
    b.   when sales exceed production
    c.   when the current period's sales exceed the prior period's sales
    d.   when prior period production exceeds current period production

7. Using absorption costing, the fixed factory overhead that is incurred in a period may be found at the end of the period

    a.   only on the income statement.
    b.   only on the balance sheet as a liability.
    c.   only on the balance sheet as an asset.
    d.   on both the balance sheet and income statement.

Chapter 13: Absorption and Variable Costing

8. Using variable costing, the fixed factory overhead that is incurred in a period may be found at the end of the period

    a. only on the income statement.
    b. only on the balance sheet as a liability.
    c. only on the balance sheet as an asset.
    d. on both the balance sheet and income statement.

9. Which of the following best describes the relationship between the product contribution margin and the gross margin?

    a. The gross margin is always equal to or greater than the product contribution margin.
    b. The product contribution margin is always equal to or greater than the gross margin.
    c. The product contribution margin is always equal to the gross margin.
    d. It is impossible to make a general statement about the relationship.

10. In its first year of operation, firm X produces 2,000 more units than it sells. In year 2, it sells 2,000 more units than it produces. Which of the following statements is true?

    a. Variable costing must result in a greater net income in year 1 than absorption costing.
    b. Absorption costing must result in a greater net income in year 2 than variable costing.
    c. For the two years combined, absorption and variable costing will report the same income.
    d. For the two year combined, both methods will report a net loss.

11. Under absorption costing, which of the following would not include fixed manufacturing overhead costs?

    a. work-in-process
    b. finished goods inventory
    c. cost of goods sold
    d. period costs

12. When the number of units produced differs from the number of units sold in a period, which of the following would be equal under variable and absorption costing?

    a. total product costs deducted for the period
    b. total period costs deducted for the period
    c. total selling and administrative expenses deducted for the period
    d. the total contribution margin and the gross margin

13. To convert the absorption costing income to variable costing income in a period where unit sales exceeds unit production, you would

    a. need to do nothing.
    b. add back the difference between the amount of fixed factory overhead included in the cost of goods sold and the amount of fixed factory overhead incurred during the period.
    c. subtract the difference between the amount of fixed factory overhead included in the cost of goods sold and the amount of fixed factory overhead incurred during the period.
    d. add back the difference between the gross margin and the total contribution margin.

14. Which of the following costs would you expect to vary directly with the number of units produced?

    a. total production costs
    b. total period costs
    c. variable period costs
    d. variable production costs

Chapter 13: Absorption and Variable Costing

15. A firm's income under absorption costing would potentially be much different than its income under variable costing if

    a. most of the firm's production costs were variable.
    b. most of the firm's selling costs were fixed.
    c. most of the firm's selling costs were variable.
    d. most of the firm's production costs were fixed.

16. Two basic differences between absorption and variable costing are found in

    a. their definitions of product costs and selling costs.
    b. their definitions of period costs and selling costs.
    c. the style of the income statement and the definition of selling costs.
    d. the style of the income statement and the definition of product cost.

17. The style of presentation of the income statement for variable costing is sometimes called

    a. the traditional format.
    b. the contribution format.
    c. the variable and fixed format.
    d. the cost behavior format.

18. Under variable costing, variable factory overhead can be found in all of the following except

    a. work-in-process.
    b. cost of goods sold.
    c. cost of goods manufactured.
    d. selling, general and administrative expense.

19. All of the following are treated the same by variable and absorption costing except

    a. direct materials.
    b. direct labor.
    c. variable factory overhead.
    d. fixed factory overhead.

20. The costing method used for external reporting is:

    a. Variable costing
    b. Direct costing
    c. Marginal costing
    d. Absorption costing

21. When using variable costing, the term "inventoriable costs" refers to:

    a. Direct materials and direct labor only
    b. Direct materials, direct labor, and total overhead
    c. Direct materials, direct labor, and variable overhead
    d. Direct materials, direct labor, and fixed overhead

22. A method of assigning manufacturing costs to production so that both variable and fixed manufacturing costs are included in inventories and cost of goods sold is:

    a. Process costing
    b. Absorption costing
    c. Direct costing
    d. Variable costing

23. Where there is no beginning inventory, the difference between variable costing and absorption costing is equal to the amount of:

    a. Fixed marketing costs allocated to cost of goods sold
    b. Variable overhead allocated to ending inventory
    c. Fixed manufacturing costs in ending inventory
    d. There is no difference if no beginning inventory exists

Chapter 13: Absorption and Variable Costing 145

24. If an income statement is prepared as an internal report, under which of the following methods would the term gross margin most likely appear?

   a. Both absorption costing and direct costing.
   b. Absorption costing but not direct costing.
   c. Direct costing but not absorption costing.
   d. Neither direct costing nor absorption costing.

25. Under absorption costing, fixed manufacturing overhead is recognized as an expense when:

   a. the cost is incurred
   b. the product is sold
   c. the product is completed
   d. none of the above

26. The level of production affects income under which of the following methods?

   a. absorption costing
   b. variable costing
   c. both absorption and variable costing
   d. neither absorption nor variable costing

QUESTIONS AND PROBLEMS

1. What are two differences between variable and absorption costing?

2. Why does the accountant need to know how to convert variable costing information to absorption costing information?

3. Why do managers often prefer financial information to be presented in a variable costing format?

4. Generally, when the number of units produced is different from the number of units sold, what is the relationship between the income under absorption costing and the income under variable costing?

The following information was extracted from financial data on the first two years of operations of McDaniel Corp. Use this information to answer problems 5-10.

	YEAR 1	YEAR 2
Units produced...............................	20,000	20,000
Units sold....................................	18,000	22,000
Direct labor cost/unit........................	$4	$4
Direct Material cost/unit.....................	$5	$5
Variable factory overhead cost/unit...........	$1	$1
Total fixed factory overhead cost incurred...	$100,000	$100,000

146   Chapter 13: Absorption and Variable Costing

5. For year 1, what was the finished goods inventory valuation if McDaniel used absorption costing?

6. For year 1, what was the finished goods inventory valuation if McDaniel used variable costing?

7. How much greater was income before income taxes if McDaniel had used absorption costing rather than variable costing in year 1?

8. For year 2, how much fixed factory overhead was deducted if McDaniel used absorption costing?

9. For year 2, how much greater was income before income taxes if McDaniel used variable costing rather than variable costing?

10. For years 1 and 2 combined, which costing method would have resulted in the greatest income before income taxes?

COMMUNICATION PROJECT

Without looking at the solutions to true-false and multiple choice questions, each person in the class will be asked give an answer to each question along with an explanation as to why the answer is correct. This class methodology is designed develop speaking ability in a group of peers.

SELF TEST SOLUTIONS

TRUE/FALSE

1. F	3. F	5. F	7. F	9. F	11. F
2. T	4. T	6. T	8. T	10. F	12. T

MULTIPLE CHOICE

1. B	6. B	11. C	16. B	21. C	26. A
2. C	7. D	12. B	17. D	22. B	
3. B	8. A	13. D	18. D	23. C	
4. C	9. B	14. D	19. D	24. B	
5. C	10. C	15. D	20. D	25. B	

Chapter 13: Absorption and Variable Costing 147

QUESTIONS AND PROBLEMS

1. The first difference is in the definition of product cost. Variable costing includes only the variable portion of factory overhead as a product cost while absorption costing includes all factory overhead as a product cost. The second difference is in the income statement format. Absorption costing utilizes the "traditional" income statement format and variable costing utilizes the "contribution" income statement format. The contribution format permits costs to be categorized both by their behavior and their functional category.

2. Any organization will have an accounting system that produces accounting information in only one format: variable or absorption. Since some users require information in the variable costing format and others require information in the absorption costing format, the accountant must convert the accounting system's output so that both variable and absorption based accounting information is provided.

3. The variable costing format lends itself to many important internal decisions involving cost-volume-profit analysis and the identification of relevant costs.

4. Generally, when the number of units produced exceeds the number of units sold, absorption costing will result in the higher income and variable costing will result in the higher income when the number of units sold exceeds the number of units produced.

5. If absorption costing is used, the unit cost would be:
   Direct labor...................................$ 4
   Direct materials.............................. 5
   Variable factory overhead..................... 1
   Fixed factor overhead: ($100,000/20,000)...... 5
       Total $15

   The ending inventory valuation would consist of 2,000 units each carrying a value of $15 for a total valuation of $30,000.

6. Under variable costing, the product cost would contain only the Direct labor, Direct materials, and Variable factory overhead. Hence, the ending inventory valuation would be ($4 + $5 + $1) or $10/unit. With a total of 2,000 units in inventory, the total inventory valuation would be $20,000

7. This question often confuses students because no information is presented on the sales value of the units produced or the selling, general, and administrative costs. However, you must remember that all of the costs and revenues are treated the same under variable and absorption costing with the exception of fixed factory overhead. Once you determine how much fixed factory overhead each method charges against revenues you will be able to determine the difference in incomes. Under variable costing, all of the $100,000 in fixed factory overhead would be deducted in period 1. Under absorption costing, only $90,000 (18,000 * $5) would be deducted in period 1. Thus, absorption costing would put $10,000 of the fixed factory overhead into the ending inventory and would report income which is $10,000 higher than the income under variable costing.

8. In year 2, McDaniel sold everything they produced in year 2 plus the 2,000 units they carried over from year 1. They would then deduct all of the fixed factory overhead they incurred in year 2 plus the $10,000 they inventoried in the prior period for a total of $110,000.

9. The income would be $10,000 higher under variable costing. Again, the difference is strictly attributable to the $10,000 of fixed factory overhead that was pulled out of inventory in year 2.

10. They would report the same amount of income. In year 1, absorption costing would result in a greater income by $10,000, but in year 2 variable costing would result in a greater income by $10,000.

CHAPTER 14
COST-VOLUME-PROFIT ANALYSIS

CHAPTER OVERVIEW

You were introduced to variable costing in Chapter 13. Major managerial benefits of variable costing, relative to absorption costing, become evident in Chapter 14. Variable costing requires costs to be categorized based on their behavior: variable or fixed. Variable costs are those that vary directly with either the volume of sales or the volume of production. Total fixed costs do not change as volume changes within the relevant range. With all costs categorized by behavior, managers are able to predict the total cost amount at different levels of production and sales. Such knowledge is useful in Cost-Volume-Profit (CVP) analysis. Typically, in CVP analysis managers are interested in the impact of total costs and volume on profit.

CVP analysis is a very useful tool in the planning and budgeting activity of managers. Planning is by definition oriented to the future and requires managers to rely on predictions regarding such important factors as the sales price that will be realized for products, demand for products, and the costs of producing and selling the products. With CVP analysis, managers can analyze how sensitive their plans (or budgets) are to errors or uncertainty in the predictions regarding these factors. Managers can also use CVP analysis to evaluate alternative production and sales plans.

As you read Chapter 14, pay careful attention to the assumptions that CVP analysis relies on. The importance of understanding cost terms such as relevant range, fixed, mixed, and variable should be obvious as you learn the assumptions.

CHAPTER STUDY GUIDE

1. Predicting what an organization's profits will be at different volume levels requires an understanding of how revenues and costs change with volume. We can only gain that understanding if we can determine how costs behave when volume changes. Within the relevant range, we assume that the price received for each unit of output will be constant. Within the relevant range, we also assume that the variable costs/unit will remain constant and that total fixed costs will remain constant. The variable costing approach (from Chapter 12) is well suited for CVP analysis because it requires costs to be categorized by behavior. Using variable costing, the profit at any specific volume level is simply the difference between total revenues and the sum of total fixed costs plus total variable costs.

2. An important term in CVP analysis is "the breakeven point." The breakeven point can be identified in several different ways. It is the level of volume at which total sales equal total costs. It is also the point where net income is equal to zero, or the point where the total contribution margin equals total fixed costs. Above the breakeven point, the company enjoys a net profit, and below the breakeven point the company suffers a net loss.

3. To find the breakeven point, or any other volume level of interest, we need to manipulate the following formula: Total Revenue - Total variable costs - Total Fixed costs = Net income.

Chapter 14: Cost - Volume - Profit Analysis

a. To illustrate, assume that we are dealing with a firm producing a single product that sells for $10/unit, incurs total variable costs of $6/unit and incurs $25,000 of fixed costs each year.

   i. How many units must the firm sell each year to breakeven? First, consider what net income would be if the firm produced and sold nothing. The income statement would appear as follows:

   Sales.........................$ 0
   Variable costs...............   0
   Contribution margin..........   0
   Fixed costs.................. 25,000
   Net income...................(25,000)

   ii. Now, what would the income statement look like if the firm produced and sold 1 unit? It would appear as follows:

   Sales.........................$ 10
   Variable costs...............   6
   Contribution margin..........   4
   Fixed costs.................. 25,000
   Net income...................(24,996)

   iii. Note that the net income improved by $4, which is also the contribution margin that is generated on the sale of 1 unit which is called contribution margin per unit (or CM). If the firm were to produce and sell 2 units, the total contribution margin would be $8 and the net loss would be $24,992. For each additional unit sold, the contribution margin will increase by $4.

   iv. Determine how many units must be produced and sold to yield a total contribution margin of $25,000 and identify the breakeven point. The production and sale of 1 unit yields a contribution margin of $4. A contribution margin of $25,000 would be achieved with the production and sale of $25,000/$4 units, or 6,250 units. The following income statement shows the effects of producing and selling 6,250 units:

   Sales (6,250 * $10).................$62,500
   Variable costs (6,250 * $6) 37,500
   Contribution margin................ 25,000
   Fixed costs........................ 25,000
   Net income......................... 0

   (1) The breakeven point is 6,250 units with zero net income. This is a logical approach to finding the breakeven point in units and it underlies the unit breakeven formula below:

   X = (FC + P)/ CM
   where:
   X is the number of units at breakeven
   FC is total fixed costs
   CM is contribution margin per unit
   P is desired profit

4. To find the breakeven point in dollars, using the variable costing data above for the sale of 1 unit:

Sales....................$10
Variable costs..........   6
Contribution margin   4

   a. The sales price/unit and the variable costs/unit remain constant as volume changes. The contribution margin will be a constant percentage of total sales. In this illustration, the contribution margin is 40% of total sales: $4/$10.

      i. When the contribution margin is stated as a percentage of sales, it is cited as the contribution margin ratio or CM%.

Chapter 14: Cost - Volume - Profit Analysis

    ii.   This firm's contribution margin ratio is 40%.

    iii.   When using the contribution margin ratio to find the breakeven point, the breakeven point in dollars is where the total contribution margin is equal to the total fixed costs.

    iv.   In the illustration, breakeven will follow where the total contribution margin is $25,000. How many sales dollars are required to produce $25,000 of contribution margin? The answer is found by solving the following equation:

Total sales(.40) = $25,000.

    (1)   Solving for total sales dollars yields $62,500 and a contribution margin of $25,000.

    (2)   The formula for breakeven point in dollars is:

Sales = (FC + P)/ CM %
where:
Sales is the sales dollars that achieves the desired profit (and in this case the profit is zero)
FC is total fixed costs
P is desired profit
CM % is the contribution margin ratio

    (3)   Using these two formulas help to find other levels of volume as well. You may find the number of units to produce and sell to generate a desired net income.

If P, the desired profit, is $10,000, find the sales in units or dollars.

X = ($25,000 + $10,000) / $4/unit = 8,750 units
and

Sales = ($25,000 + $10,000) / .4 = $87,500

5.   Modifications to these general approaches will permit CVP analysis in terms of after-tax income (see Exhibits 14-4 and 14-5) and analysis where profit or net income is stated as a percentage of sales (see Exhibit 14-6). By imposing additional assumptions, CVP analysis may be used in a company that produces and sells two or more products.

6.   Two important terms are introduced in Chapter 14 that apply to CVP analysis. The first is "Margin of Safety." Margin of safety simply refers to the extent which present or projected sales exceed the breakeven point. In the preceding example, the firm has a breakeven point of $62,500. If the firm projects sales in the coming period of $90,000, its margin of safety would be $90,000 - $62,500 =$27,500.

    a.   The other important term is "operating leverage." The operating leverage of a company refers to the relative levels of its variable and fixed costs. The degree of operating leverage is a measure of operating leverage and is the ratio of a firm's contribution margin (income after variable costs) to its profit before taxes (income after fixed costs).

    b.   Operating leverage is important because it affects the rate of change in profit as volume changes. A high degree of operating leverage indicates that total profit is very sensitive to changes in volume. A low level of operating leverage indicates that profit is less sensitive to changes in volume.

7.   CVP analysis relies on some very critical assumptions that may not be realistic in some situations. These assumptions are listed at the end of Chapter 14. These assumptions should be perused to determine how the results of CVP analysis could be misleading if an assumption was violated.

Chapter 14: Cost – Volume – Profit Analysis

    a.   Note the linear assumptions regarding selling price, variable cost per unit, and fixed costs.

        i.   In fact, fixed costs are long-term variable costs.

    b.   Mixed costs can be separated and sales equal production volume.

    c.   In a multi-product firm, sales mix is constant.

8.   The emphasis on product quality may, the short term, affect variable or fixed costs; but, in the long run, sales and price should increase while appraisal and failure costs should decrease (see Chapter 3 for more discussion on Quality Costs).

    a.   While CVP analysis assumes functions for costs, these assumptions must be monitored frequently when a firm adopts TQM programs.

SELF TEST

TRUE/FALSE

1.   T F

CVP analysis relies on the assumption that all costs are linear.

2.   T F

CVP analysis cannot be conducted unless costs can be categorized by function.

3.   T F

In CVP analysis, the breakeven point may be defined as the point where the gross margin equals total fixed costs.

4.   T F

CVP analysis usually relies on the assumption that the volume of sales and production are equal.

5.   T F

For a given cost structure, profit is always maximized at the maximum level of volume within the relevant range.

6.   T F

CVP analysis indicates that a firm can never experience an operating loss that exceeds its fixed costs.

7.   T F

The margin of safety is always a positive number.

8.   T F

Computing the breakeven for a company with multiple products requires an assumption that the sales mix will remain constant when total volume changes.

9.   T F

In CVP analysis, dividing total fixed costs by the unit contribution margin yields the breakeven point in dollars.

10.   T F

Variable costs ratio equals variable cost divided by units of sales.

11. T F

A profit-volume graph is used to ascertain the volume at which revenue equals costs.

12. T F

The degree of operating leverage is the sales revenue divided by net income.

13. T F

Sales and variable costs are linear, is one assumption of breakeven analysis.

14. T F

A shift in sales mix toward more profitable products will raise the break-even point.

15. T F

The margin of safety can be defined as the amount by which sales can decrease before losses begin to be incurred by the company.

16. T F

Operating leverage is the least in companies that have low fixed costs and high per unit variable costs.

17. T F

If a company has high operating leverage, then profits will be very sensitive to changes in sales.

MULTIPLE CHOICE

1. The breakeven point may increase if

    a. total fixed costs increase.
    b. variable costs/unit increase.
    c. the sales price/unit decreases.
    d. all of the above.

2. The breakeven point may be defined as the point where

    a. the contribution margin equals total fixed costs.
    b. total costs equal total revenues.
    c. net income equals zero.
    d. all of the above.

3. Within the relevant range, it is always more profitable to produce at the maximum volume level, rather than zero volume, when

    a. the sales price is greater than zero.
    b. the sales price/unit is greater than the total fixed fixed costs/unit.
    c. the sales price/unit is greater than the total variable costs/unit.
    d. the firm has no fixed costs.

4. Which of the following formulas would correctly yield the level of sales that would generate a profit of $10,000?

    a. $10,000 + (FC/CM)
    b. ($10,000 + VC)/CM
    c. ($10,000 +FC)/(CM/Sales)
    d. ($10,000 +FC)/VC

Chapter 14: Cost – Volume – Profit Analysis

5. Total contribution margin can be computed by subtracting

    a. total variable costs from total sales dollars.
    b. total product costs from total sales dollars.
    c. total variable product costs from total sales dollars.
    d. unit product costs from unit selling price.

6. The lower the margin of safety,

    a. the higher the degree of operating leverage will be.
    b. the lower the degree of operating leverage will be.
    c. the higher the contribution margin will be.
    d. the lower the contribution margin will be.

7. The breakeven point appears on a CVP graph where

    a. the total expense line crosses the horizontal axis.
    b. the total revenue line crosses the horizontal axis.
    c. the total expense line crosses the total revenue line.
    d. the total revenue line crosses the contribution margin line.

8. The contribution margin ratio is

    a. the contribution margin divided by total costs.
    b. the contribution margin divided by sales.
    c. variable costs divided by sales.
    d. variable costs divided by total costs.

9. A company estimates its margin of safety is $10,000. From this information you know

    a. the company's net income is $10,000.
    b. the company is profitable.
    c. the company is in great financial condition.
    d. the company's degree of operating leverage is negative.

10. Two companies are hoping for an increase of 4% in sales volume. The company with the higher degree of operating leverage can expect

    a. a greater absolute dollar change in net income than the other company.
    b. a smaller absolute dollar change in net income than the other company.
    c. a greater percentage change in net income than the other company.
    d. a smaller percentage change in net income than the other company.

11. When volume changes by one unit, net income changes by

    a. the sales price/unit.
    b. the sales price/unit minus the fixed costs/unit.
    c. the contribution margin/unit.
    d. the contribution margin ratio.

12. The slope of the total cost line in a CVP graph is 5. This indicates

    a. total costs are $5/unit.
    b. variable costs are $5/unit.
    c. The contribution margin/unit is $5.
    d. none of the above.

13. CVP analysis relies primarily on concepts from

    a. variable costing.
    b. absorption costing.
    c. standard costing
    d. process costing.

Chapter 14: Cost - Volume - Profit Analysis

14. Total sales minus the total contribution margin equals

    a. total fixed costs.
    b. total variable costs.
    c. net income.
    d. none of the above.

15. All other things equal, if a downturn in sales is anticipated, management would prefer that their company

    a. have a high fixed cost ratio.
    b. have a low contribution margin ratio.
    c. have a high degree of operating leverage.
    d. have no variable costs in its cost structure.

16. If the ratio of total costs/sales declines as volume goes up, then we can conclude that

    a. the company has no variable costs in its cost structure.
    b. the company is profitable.
    c. the company has some fixed costs in its cost structure.
    d. all of the above.

17. Linear functions are always assumed for

    a. total revenue.
    b. total variable costs.
    c. total fixed costs.
    d. all of the above.

18. If a company has a contribution margin ratio of 9%, a profit equal to 10% of sales

    a. cannot be achieved.
    b. can be achieved if the fixed cost ratio is below 9%.
    c. can be achieved if its degree of operating leverage is above 5.
    d. can be achieved if there are no fixed costs.

19. In comparing the level of the pre-tax breakeven with the after-tax breakeven, we discover

    a. that the pre-tax breakeven is lower.
    b. that the after-tax breakeven is lower.
    c. that they are the same.
    d. that the comparison varies from one company to another.

20. The degree of operating leverage is calculated as

    a. net income divided by contribution margin.
    b. contribution margin divided by revenues.
    c. contribution margin divided by fixed costs.
    d. contribution margin divided by net income.

21. Breakeven sales is the level of sales:

    a. Where variable costs equal fixed costs
    b. Where total revenue exactly equals total costs
    c. Where sales revenue equals fixed costs
    d. Which falls within the relevant range

22. An assumption of graphical breakeven analysis is that:

    a. Costs and revenues are linear within the relevant range
    b. The total cost line is downward sloping
    c. Both the x and y axis are in the same unit of measure
    d. Zero fixed costs will necessitate zero variable cost

Chapter 14: Cost - Volume - Profit Analysis

23. Dividing fixed costs by the contribution margin ratio results in the:

    a. Variable cost per unit
    b. Breakeven point in dollars
    c. Breakeven point in units
    d. Variable cost ratio

24. Break-even analysis assumes that over the relevant range:

    a. total costs are unchanged.
    b. unit variable costs are unchanged.
    c. variable costs are nonlinear.
    d. unit fixed costs are unchanged.

25. For a profitable company, the amount by which sales can decline before losses occur is known as the:

    a. sales volume variance.
    b. hurdle rate.
    c. marginal income rate.
    d. variable sales ratio.
    e. margin of safety.

QUESTIONS AND PROBLEMS

1. Why is breakeven analysis an important managerial tool?

2. Define the breakeven point.

3. Why are managers interested in operating leverage?

4. What are the major assumptions that underlie CVP analysis?

5. Why does the breakeven point play such an important role in CVP analysis?

Chapter 14: Cost - Volume - Profit Analysis

Use the following information for problems 6 - 9.

Maxwell Corp. produces and sells computers. Below is a projected income statement for the approaching year.

```
Sales...(based on 10,000 units).............$100,000,000
Variable costs:
    Sales commissions.......$10,000,000
    Production costs........ 30,000,000
    Administrative..........  10,000,000   50,000,000
Contribution margin............................ 50,000,000
Fixed costs:
    S,G&A ...............  10,000,000
    Production...........  25,000,000     35,000,000
Net income.....................................  15,000,000
```

6. Compute Maxwell's projected breakeven point in units and dollars.

7. Suppose the projected net income (as indicated above) is unacceptable to Maxwell's President. In fact, the president wants a net income of at least 30% of sales. What is the minimum level of sales that will meet the President's objective?

8. The company president is considering eliminating the payment of sales commissions and replacing them with a straight salary of $10,000,000. If implemented, what will be the effect of the change on the breakeven point?

9. At the projected sales level of $100,000,000, what is Maxwell's degree of operating leverage and its margin of safety.

10. A company presently produces and sells a high quality metal picture frame. The frame sells for $10/unit. With its existing production technology, the firm incurs variable costs of $4/unit and total fixed costs of $10,000/year. An alternative production technology is now available which would reduce the company's total variable costs/unit to $3, but would raise total fixed costs to $20,000/year. At what level of sales, would the company be indifferent as to which production technology it used?

Chapter 14: Cost - Volume - Profit Analysis

COMMUNICATION PROJECT

A member of your class group is to explain the meaning and nature of operating leverage and degree of operating leverage. Another member of your group is to repeat the context of what was said. A third member of the group is to confirm or state how the second person reiterate what the first person said. The purpose of this exercise is to improve your listening and communication skills.

SELF TEST SOLUTIONS

TRUE/FALSE

1. T	4. F	7. F	10. F	13. T	16. T
2. F	5. T	8. T	11. F	14. F	17. T
3. F	6. F	9. F	12 F	15. T	

MULTIPLE CHOICE

1. D	6. A	11. C	16. C	21. B
2. D	7. C	12. B	17. D	22. A
3. C	8. B	13. A	18. A	23. B
4. C	9. B	14. B	19. C	24. B
5. A	10. C	15. B	20. D	25. E

QUESTIONS AND PROBLEMS

1. CVP analysis plays an important role in the planning and budgeting activities of a firm. Such analysis is useful in all profit-oriented firms. CVP is particularly useful in evaluating and comparing alternative production and sales strategies. It is also useful in sensitivity analysis as management seeks to understand the possible affect of prediction errors on the planned results.

2. The most common ways to define the breakeven point is simply the level of sales where net income equals zero. Alternatively, the breakeven point is found at the point where total revenues equal total costs or where the total contribution margin equals total fixed costs.

3. Operating leverage tells a manager how a change in volume will influence net income. All other things equal, high operating leverage is desirable when an increase in volume is expected. Low operating leverage is desirable when a decrease in volume is expected.

4. The major assumptions are: total revenues, total variable costs, and total fixed costs are linear within the relevant range; all costs can be classified as fixed or variable; and sales and production volume are equal. Other assumptions are listed at the end of Chapter 14.

5. The breakeven point is important because it serves as a frame of reference. Below this point, the firm is operating at a loss. Above this point, the firm is operating at a gain. Comparing projected or present levels of operation to the breakeven point produces the margin of safety.

6. Let's try to get the breakeven in dollars first. Remember, the breakeven point is the point where the total contribution margin is equal to the total fixed costs of $35,000,000. From the data given, Maxwell's contribution margin ratio is 50%. This means that 50 cents out of each sales dollar remains after the payment of variable costs. The breakeven would be: $35,000,000/.50 or $70,000,000. In units, this equates to $70,000,000/$10,000 = 7,000 computers.

7. The president wants a return on sales of 30%. So let's begin by putting the president's constraint into the following equation: Sales - VC - FC = Net income. The equation would look like this: Sales - .50*Sales - $35,000,000 = .30*Sales. Notice that both variable costs and net income have been restated in terms of Sales. Solving the above equation we find that sales in

Chapter 14: Cost - Volume - Profit Analysis

the amount of $175,000,000 would produce the desired income. Let's prove that we've found the correct solution:

```
Sales.....................................$175,000,000
Variable costs ($175,000,000 * .50)....   87,500,000
Contribution Margin....................   87,500,000
Fixed Costs............................   35,000,000
Net income                                52,500,000
```

and 175,000,000 * .30 = $52,500,000

8. If such a change were implemented, at the present level of operations Maxwell's income statement would change to:

```
Sales.....................................$100,000,000
Variable costs............................   40,000,000
Contribution margin.......................   60,000,000
Fixed costs...............................   45,000,000
Net income                                   15,000,000
```

Note that the contribution margin ratio has increased to 60%. The new breakeven point would equal $45,000,000/.60 or $75,000,000 as compared to only $70,000,000 with the sales commissions instead of the salary.

9. The margin of safety is the projected level of sales of $100,000,000 minus the breakeven level of sales, $70,000,000. So the margin of safety is $30,000,000. The degree of operating leverage is the contribution margin divided by the net income. In this case it would be $50,000,000/$15,000,000 = 3.3333.

10. In this problem, you can ignore the sales price because it will be the same under both alternatives. Therefore, we would be indifferent between the two production technologies at the volume level where the two production technologies produce the same total costs. To find this level, let's just set the total cost equations for each production technology equal to each other. Let X represent the volume of production and sales:

$4X + $10,000 = $3X + $20,000.

Solving for X, we find that at 10,000 units of output both production technologies result in total costs of $50,000. Below 10,000 units of output, management would prefer the production technology that it presently has. Above 10,000 units of volume, the new production technology would generate a greater net income through lower total costs.

CHAPTER 15
RELEVANT COSTING

CHAPTER OVERVIEW

A major input to any decision process is information. The quality and quantity of this input will affect the quality of the resulting decision. Both quantitative and qualitative information are concerns in the decision process. An efficient decision maker will focus only on information that bears on the decision, and discard other extraneous information. In the area of cost accounting, the information that bears on the decision are the "relevant" costs.

Managers must make many different decisions. Some of these decisions recur daily or even hourly, other decisions recur annually, and still other decisions are made once in a lifetime. The costs that are relevant for one decision may not be relevant for another type of decision. Further, it may be more difficult to identify relevant costs for the decisions that do not recur on a frequent basis.

In Chapter 15, general guidelines are presented for identifying relevant costs in any context. Also, these guidelines are applied to six types of decisions that are common to most profit-seeking organizations. These six types of decisions are identified in the CHAPTER SUMMARY. The objective is to identify which costs are relevant for each type of decision. In this chapter, the guidelines are applied to short-run decisions. The guidelines will be applied to long-run decisions in the later chapters dealing with capital budgeting (Chapters 19 &20).

Every organization has a limited set of resources to maximize the organizational goals and objectives. The resources must be used efficiently. Firms must dedicate attention to those resources that provide the most significant constraints to the achievement of organizational goals.

The major resource **constraints** include labor, capital, technology, or materials. If only one resource (or a specific category of resources) is the most significant organizational constraint, firms will maximize their financial goals by maximizing the contribution margin for each unit of the scarce resource (as illustrated in EXHIBIT 15-6).

With more than one constraint is limited, the solution to the efficient allocation of resources is less obvious. The APPENDIX presents some linear programming techniques that can be used to solve the multiple resource allocation problem. These techniques are useful because they can simultaneously account for multiple company constraints that limit a firm's ability to achieve its goals.

CHAPTER STUDY GUIDE

1. Three characteristics of relevant costs are presented on page 3 of your text. In general, relevant costs are 1) future costs as opposed to historical costs, and, 2) costs that vary between the alternatives under consideration (incremental costs), and, 3) opportunity costs.

2. **Opportunity costs** are difficult costs to identify. They are not "real" costs. They represent benefits that are sacrificed to pursue one alternative over another. For example, a student buys a ticket (8 weeks in advance) for $25 to attend a local rock concert. On the day of the concert, another

student offers her $100 for the concert ticket (ticket values have risen because of a recent chart-topping record release). In this situation, the ticket holder is faced with a decision that involves two alternatives: sell the ticket or attend the concert. Which costs are relevant to her decision? Eight weeks ago, before she purchased the ticket, the $25 ticket price was relevant in the decision to purchase the ticket. Once she paid the $25, however, it became a "sunk" cost and it is not relevant to the present decision. The only cost that is relevant is an opportunity cost. If she attends the concert, the student sacrifices an opportunity (incurring an opportunity cost) to collect $100 for the ticket. She cannot collect the $100 and attend the concert.

3. **Sunk cost** is a special cost since it is a historical cost that is never relevant to a decision. The previous example illustrates how the $25 original ticket purchase became a sunk cost. Whether a cost is sunk or not depends critically on whether the cost is a future cost or an historical cost. As the prior example illustrates, before the ticket was purchased, the $25 ticket price was a relevant cost. After the ticket was purchased (and the cost was sunk), the $25 ticket price was no longer relevant. No action available could recover the $25 purchase. Another illustration of a sunk cost is found in your text on page 6.

   a. Another term related to this chapter concerning relevant cost is an **avoidable cost**. It is a cost that can be deleted by picking one alternative over another.

4. The general instructions to identify relevant costs can be converted to specific rules for specific decisions. Six specific types of decisions are developed. From the general instructions, specific rules for making a decision in each of the six contexts are presented. These six varieties of decisions are short-run managerial determinations illustrating the application of general instructions to six conventional short-run decisions. Both qualitative and quantitative factors influence the managerial decision.

   a. Relevant costs are those associated with different courses of action. Incremental costs and revenues are derived from different paths. The action with the highest incremental benefit should be chosen.

      i. One alternative is to "change nothing" as expressed in the NEWS NOTE on p. 13.

5. One routine situation involves technological innovations rendering existing equipment obsolete. Machinery with new technology requires managers to decide whether they will keep existing machinery and equipment or replace it with new technology. Acquiring new machinery may reduce operating costs or increase revenues through increased efficiency. The outcome of this decision is usually made by comparing the incremental costs of the new technology (purchase price less the market value of the old equipment) to the lifetime reduction in operating costs or the increase in revenues that would be generated by the new technology. Because these cash flows occur at different points in time, managers may use discounted cash flow analysis in the decision. See EXHIBIT 15-2 as an illustration.

6. In the **make or buy decision**, managers determine whether a part, material, or service will be produced internally or obtained from an outside vendor. This decision context is first introduced in EXHIBIT 15-3 where qualitative and quantitative factors are listed.

   a. Long-run factors may have to be considered as well as the short run effects a decision may have on profitability.

   b. Make-or-buy decisions may be used in service operations such as doctors or **dentists offices**. See the NEWS NOTE on p. 20 for further applications.

   c. A specific example is shown in EXHIBIT 15-5.

7. The influence of constraints on production capacity will also require managerial decisions. Capacity can be constrained by the availability of:

Chapter 15: Relevant Costing

labor time, machine time, raw materials, energy, the capacity of distribution channels, or any other production input.

   a. The major managerial decision, with respect to capacity constraints, is how the scarce resource will be allocated.

   b. The **scarce resources** should be allocated to maximize organizational profits which means maximizing contribution margin per unit of the scarce resource. See EXHIBIT 15-6 for as an illustration.

8. Companies that produce multiple products must decide what organizational resources will be dedicated to the production and sale of each product (**sales mix**). Profit maximization may be the key goal it used as a measure to allocate organizational resources.

   a. Significant organizational resources that can be allocated among products include marketing efforts, advertising dollars, sales commission dollars, and research and development dollars.

   b. When looking at sales mix, be attentive to the association of price and volume <u>and</u> the managerial actions that can influence these two variables. See EXHIBIT 15-7.

9. Management should distinguish between **special order decisions** and recurring orders (normal sales). Special product orders may support unique pricing because of: the size of the order, or the customization of the order.

   a. The key to pricing special orders is to identify the costs that are associated with the order. The price needs to be sufficiently large to at least cover the incremental costs of the order. Incremental costs would include variable production and selling costs and any fixed costs that would not be incurred if the order was not accepted.

   b. Consideration also needs to be given to the impact of federal legislation (see the **Robinson-Patmen Act** on pricing special orders). If prices are too low, laws may be violated and subject the organization to significant fines and penalties.

10. Also with respect to products, the profitability of product lines is continually evaluated. While the direct revenues generated by a product may be easy to identify, the costs which should be associated with a specific product line are more difficult to identify.

    a. The difficulty arises from the fact that some costs are "allocated" to product lines, but would not be affected if the product line was discontinued. On the other hand, there are costs which can be traced to specific product lines but would also be unaffected if the product was discontinued. Neither of these categories of costs are relevant in evaluating whether a product line should be continued over the short-run.

    b. Any costs that would stop with the canceling of the product line is relevant in evaluating the viability of a product line. This includes all the variable costs and direct fixed costs associated with the product line. The **segment margin** is the direct revenues of the product line less the costs that could be avoided if the product line was discontinued. If the segment margin is positive, the product line should be retained for the time-being.

11. Linear programming is a mathematical technique used to limit the influence of multiple constraints on goal achievement.

    a. The linear programming steps include translating the goals of the firm into one **objective** function (such as maximize sales or maximize contribution margin) in mathematical terms. The objective function will be either maximized (as in this chapter) or minimized. Secondly the restricting resources are shown through **constraint functions**.

b. The following illustration assumes that a company produces two products: X & Y with contribution margins of $10 and $17 respectively. The objective function could be to maximize total contribution margin which could be expressed:

Max CM = $10X + $17Y

The variable X and Y are called decision variables which linear programming solves for.

The firm's limited resources restrict its ability to maximize the objective function. The goal of using linear programming is to identify the optimal resource allocation to maximize (or minimize) the objective function.

Alternative uses of the constraining resources are recognized in the constraint function equations. The company has available 300 pounds of a critical raw material which is a required input for both products X and Y. Three pounds of material are required for each unit of X and four pounds are required for each unit of Y. This constraint can be expressed in equation form as $3X + 4Y \leq 300$ pounds.

i. Similar equations can be formulated for all resources that may potentially be "binding" constraints on the achievement of the objective function. Constraints which are known to be non-binding are frequently called "redundant constraints" and can be ignored.

ii. Once equations have been developed for both the objective function and the set of all potentially binding constraints, an additional set of constraints, called the non-negativity constraints, are developed. The non-negativity constraints assure us that the linear programming solution will be feasible in the real life situation. In our example, we would add the following non-negativity constraints: $X \geq 0$, $Y \geq 0$.

Three types of equations are used: the objective function (in our example: Max CM = $10X + $17Y), the equations describing the resource constraints (our example: $3X + 4Y \leq 300$ pounds), and the equations which prohibit other infeasible solutions (in our example: $X \geq 0$, $Y \geq 0$). The linear programming solution is found by simultaneously considering (or solving) all equations.

c. The APPENDIX discusses two approaches to solving the system of equations. The first is a graphical approach. When all constraints can be stated in terms of two decision variables (such as products X and Y in our example) the graphical approach is viable. However, when the constraints are stated in terms of three or more variables (for example: products X, Y and Z), graphing is difficult because each variable requires its own axis (and you are probably already familiar with the problems of graphing in three or more dimensions).

i. All of the constraint equations are plotted on the same graph. The solution to the linear programming problem always occurs at a point on the graph where two constraint lines intersect (vertex) which is called a corner solution. The optimal solution is found by identifying the corner whose coordinates maximize the objective function. The constraint functions provide boundaries for the feasible solution.

ii. It is also important to note that the only feasible solutions to the set of constraints is in the upper right-hand quadrant of the graph (because of the non-negativity constraints). See EXHIBITs 15-16 and 17 for a graphical presentation.

iii. The solution to the problem lies on the boundary of feasible solution. Typically, the optimal solution lies at one of the corner points of the boundary. If the slope of the objective function is parallel to one of constraint functions, an indefinite number of optimal solutions exist. Otherwise, the

Chapter 15: Relevant Costing

optimal solution is found at one of the corner points. Coordinates inside the boundary are called interior points. They are not optimal solution points.

d. When three or more independent variables are involved in the linear programming problem, the graphing method becomes very complex. The second method discussed is the simplex method which used in linear programming with three or more independent variables. It is based on an algebraic perspective, but the simplex method can be very complex; conceptually, it is nothing more than an algorithm to compare the corner solutions and select the one solution that will optimize the objective function. It is normally solved using matrix algebra.

e. The third method of solving a linear programming problem is to utilize a computer program. Many software packages, including some of the more popular personal computer spreadsheets, offer a capability to solve linear programming problems. Many of these software programs are based on the simplex algorithm. Given the widespread availability of these software packages, it is unlikely that you will ever need to manually solve any linear programming problem that involves more than two variables.

SELF TEST

TRUE/FALSE

1. T F

    Costs that are relevant in any decision context are "sunk" costs.

2. T F

    Efficient decisions are made based on an analysis of "relevant" costs.

3. T F

    One specific type of sunk cost is "opportunity" cost.

4. T F
    In the analysis of a specific decision, a cost that can be avoided by taking one action rather than another is relevant.

5. T F

    Incremental costs are relevant costs.

6. T F

    The relevant costs in a special pricing situation may include some fixed costs.

7. T F

    In allocating scarce resources, the scarce resource is allocated to the products that product the highest contribution margin/product unit.

8. T F

    In equipment replacement decisions, the cost of the old equipment is relevant.

9. T F

    The segment margin measures income after the deduction of all variable and fixed costs that can be traced to a product line.

Chapter 15: Relevant Costing

10. T F

    In setting prices on special orders, managers need to be mindful of the effect of the special order on their regular business.

11. T F

    In linear programming, the objective function and the constraint equations are linear.

12. T F

    A corner solution is one that occurs at the intersection of two constraint equations.

13. T F

    A linear programming formulation is not necessary if there is only one constraining resource for the objective function.

14. T F

    The simplex method requires the manager to manually compute a solution to the linear programming problem.

15. T F

    The linear programming problem can have one or more objective functions.

16. T F

    The linear programming approach is only useful for objective functions that can be expressed mathematically (in an equation).

17. T F

    The solution to the linear programming problem must lie in the feasible region.

18. T F

    The solution to the linear programming problem is expressed in terms of the decision variables.

19. T F

    In allocating scarce resources among products, the contribution margin per unit cannot be used.

20. T F

    The purchase price of a new machine is a relevant cost.

21. T F

    Incremental costs can be either fixed or variable.

MULTIPLE CHOICE

1. Costs that bear on a decision are

    a. incremental costs.
    b. opportunity costs.
    c. relevant costs.
    d. all of the above.

Chapter 15: Relevant Costing

2. Relevant costs do not include

   a. future costs.
   b. opportunity costs.
   c. sunk costs.
   d. incremental costs.

3. Managers can make the best use of a scarce resource by

   a. producing products with a high contribution margin/unit.
   b. producing products with a high contribution margin ratio.
   c. producing products with low variable costs.
   d. producing products with a high contribution margin/unit of scarce resource.

4. If a cost has no influence on a decision,

   a. it is not a relevant cost.
   b. it cannot be a future cost.
   c. it is a sunk cost.
   d. all of the above could be true.

5. In evaluating the profitability of a product line, a cost is not relevant if

   a. it is fixed.
   b. it is allocated.
   c. it is an avoidable fixed cost.
   d. all of the above are true.

6. Sunk cost can include

   a. variable costs.
   b. fixed costs.
   c. product costs.
   d. all of the above.

7. In a special order pricing situation, a price should be sufficient to cover

   a. all variable production costs.
   b. all variable costs.
   c. all incremental costs.
   d. full absorption product cost.

8. Relevancy means that

   a. a cost is important.
   b. a cost has been precisely quantified.
   c. a cost is pertinent to a decision.
   d. all of the above are true.

9. When new technology becomes available, the potential cost savings from the new equipment represent

   a. irrelevant costs.
   b. an opportunity cost of keeping the old equipment.
   c. sunk costs.
   d. a cost of acquiring the new technology.

10. In deciding whether to make a part or purchase it, an opportunity cost that should be considered is

    a. the purchase price of the part.
    b. the variable costs to produce the part.
    c. the fixed costs to produce the part.
    d. the income that could be generated from idled production space.

Chapter 15: Relevant Costing

11. A change in sales mix could be achieved through

    a. reallocation of the advertising budget.
    b. a change in the sales commission structure.
    c. initiation of a sales discount program.
    d. all of the above.

12. An ad hoc sales discount is

    a. based on sales volume.
    b. a discount based on competitive pressure.
    c. an allowance for the inferior quality of goods that are marketed.
    d. a quantity discount.

13. An example of a fixed cost that would be relevant in deciding whether a product line is to maintained

    a. is the cost of raw materials.
    b. is the rental cost of production space acquired under a short-term lease.
    c. is an allocation of depreciation on corporate headquarters.
    d. is the depreciation on special-use equipment.

14. Normal sales price should be based on

    a. variable costs.
    b. incremental production costs.
    c. full absorption costs.
    d. all incremental costs - production and period.

15. The energy costs to operate an old machine run $50,000/year. A new machine which performs the same task only consumes $20,000 of energy/year. In an analysis of relevant costs, you would include energy costs of

    a. $20,000
    b. $50,000
    c. $30,000
    d. $70,000

16. In a make or buy decision affecting Part A, the salary of the production manager for Part A would be a relevant cost if

    a. he could be fired.
    b. he could be transferred to another division.
    c. he'll be eligible for retirement in the near future.
    d. any of the above conditions are met.

17. XY Company acquired an expensive machine three years ago for $1,000,000. Annual depreciation on the machine is $100,000. The machine has a market value of $250,000 and annual personal property taxes on the machine run $12,000. Which of these numbers are relevant in deciding whether the machine should be sold?

    a. the purchase cost and the property taxes
    b. the market value and the property taxes
    c. the market value and the annual depreciation
    d. none of the costs are relevant

18. On December 31, 1990, Z Company considers whether it should buy a particular machine. A short time later, the company purchases the machine. On January 28, 1991 they sell the machine. Of the two dates mentioned, the purchase cost of the machine is a relevant consideration on

    a. December 31, 1990 only.
    b. January 28, 1991 only.
    c. both dates.
    d. neither date.

Chapter 15: Relevant Costing

19. Refer to the information in question 18. On which dates would the resale value have been an important consideration in the decisions affecting the machine?

    a. December 31, 1990 only
    b. January 31, 1990 only
    c. both dates
    d. neither date

20. The objective of sales mix analysis is to

    a. maximize total organizational contribution margin.
    b. maximize total organizational gross margin.
    c. maximize segment margin.
    d. maximize total organizational profit.

21. The Robinson-Patman act may have an influence on

    a. the sales price on special orders.
    b. the make/buy decision.
    c. which resources are scarce in an organization.
    d. the asset replacement decision.

22. All other things equal, corporate profits will increase faster by selling those products that generate

    a. the most contribution margin per $1 of sales.
    b. the most contribution margin per unit.
    c. the most sales $ per unit.
    d. the most gross margin per unit.

23. Which of the following is not necessarily a characteristic of a relevant cost?

    a. it is associated with the decision.
    b. it is important to the decision.
    c. it is easily measured.
    d. it relates to the future.

24. A & B are two major ingredients used in the production of X & Y, two products manufactured by Hanley Co. In a profit-maximizing linear programming model, A & B will be represented as

    a. independent variables.
    b. constraints.
    c. surplus variables.
    d. dependent variables.

25. In a linear programming problem, the objective is to solve for the unknown quantities of

    a. slack.
    b. the dependent variables.
    c. the decision variables.
    d. the shadow prices.

26. Non-negativity constraints confine the feasible solution of the linear programming problem to

    a. the upper right hand quadrant.
    b. the lower right hand quadrant.
    c. the lower left hand quadrant.
    d. the upper left hand quadrant.

Chapter 15: Relevant Costing

27. Consider the following three equations:
    1. Max Sales = $100X + $35Y
       Subject to:
    2. 21X + 10Y ≤ 2,300
    3. 3X + Y ≤ 492

    In this set of equations, the objective function is represented by

    a. equation 1..
    b. equation 2..
    c. equation 3..
    d. equations 2. and 3..

28. Refer to the preceding problem. Assume X and Y are products. What is the maximum number of units of product X that can be produced?

    a. 492
    b. 2,300
    c. 109.5
    d. 164

29. In a profit maximization problem where all of the constraints are physical product inputs (materials), the optimal solution

    a. will be in the feasible region.
    b. will be a corner solution.
    c. will maximize the value of the objective function.
    d. will do all of the above.

30. Normally, inequalities would be used to mathematically represent

    a. the objective function.
    b. the non-negativity constraints.
    c. resource constraints.
    d. both b & c.

31. If the constraint line for a particular resource is not involved in the intersection (vertex) of the optimal solution to the linear programming problem, then

    a. the optimal solution will require consumption of less than 100% of the available resource.
    b. that resource is not part of any other corner solutions.
    c. the constraint line for the resource does not form part of the boundary of the feasible region.
    d. the constraint is represented by an isocost line.

32. Assume that an optimal solution to a linear programming problem lies at a point where the X axis intersects with exactly one constraint line. In this case,

    a. only two resource constraints are binding.
    b. only one resource constraint is binding.
    c. the solution to the linear programming problem is not a corner solution.
    d. none of the above statements would be true.

33. Linear programming is required to solve resource allocation problems when

    a. there are multiple products.
    b. there are multiple objective functions.
    c. there are multiple decision variables.
    d. there are multiple constraints.

Chapter 15: Relevant Costing   171

34. Finding the graphical solution to a linear programming problem becomes more difficult when

   a. there are more than 2 decision variables.
   b. there are more than 2 constraints.
   c. there are more than 2 dependent variables.
   d. all of the constraints but 1 are redundant.

35. When deciding whether to make a component part or to purchase it from an outside vendor, an irrelevant cost is:

   a. Variable costs of making the part
   b. Avoidable fixed costs
   c. Discretionary fixed costs
   d. Opportunity cost

36. A factor which limits production is a:

   a. Restraint
   b. Limit
   c. Restriction
   d. Constraint

37. A firm can continue to manufacture a component or buy the component from an outside supplier and rent the firm's unused manufacturing facilities to another company. If the firm continues to manufacture the component instead of buying it from an outside supplier, the rent the firm could receive for its manufacturing facilities is:

   a. a sunk cost
   b. an opportunity cost
   c. an avoidable cost
   d. none of the above

38. If the firm is at full capacity, the minimum special order price must cover:

   a. variable costs associated with the special order
   b. variable and fixed manufacturing costs associated with the special order
   c. variable and incremental fixed costs associated with the special order
   d. variable costs and incremental fixed costs associated with the special order plus foregone contribution margin on regular units not produced.

39. A segment should be kept if:

   a. segment revenues exceed segment variable costs
   b. segment revenues exceed segment variable costs and fixed costs
   c. the segment's revenues exceed avoidable costs associated with the segment
   d. segment operating profit is positive

QUESTIONS AND PROBLEMS

1. What is a relevant cost?

2. Why are sunk costs not relevant to decisions.

172   Chapter 15: Relevant Costing

3. Are all relevant factors quantifiable? Explain.

4. Why is the viability of a product line evaluated without regard to allocated fixed costs or certain direct fixed costs?

5. How is time an important determinant of whether a cost is relevant or not?

Use the following information for the next five questions:

The following cost information pertains to Harp Division of the Total Music Co:

	UNIT COSTS
Variable production costs:	
DM	$100
DL	125
V. overhead	50
Fixed production costs:	
(based on demand of 100 units/mo.)	
Factory depreciation	$ 20
Factory rent	40
Other	10
Total product cost	345
Variable Selling costs	20
Fixed SG&A costs	30
(based on monthly sales of 100 units)	

6. Assume for this question only, that the Harp Division does not exist, but is instead an aspect of Total Music Co.'s future plans. Total Music Co. will establish the Harp Division if the relevant information indicates the division will be profitable. For this decision, which of the costs listed above would be relevant?

7. For this question only, assume that the Harp Division is evaluating whether or not it will accept a special order for 10 harps at $325/unit. For this purpose, which of the costs would be relevant?

8. For this question only, assume that the original cost information pertains to 5 harps that have been produced this period. For purposes of setting a minimum sales price, which costs are relevant?

9. For this question only, assume that Total Music Co. is trying to decide if it should continue to produce the Harp in-house or contract with an outside manufacturer to build the Harp. One manufacturer has offered to produce any quantity of harps for Total Music Co. for $300/unit. Total Music Co. estimates that all of the factory rent paid by the Harp Division would be eliminated if the harps were purchased. The factory depreciation pertains to special equipment that has no alternative use and the "other" fixed factory costs pertain to the wages of the factory supervisor who has a union contract and cannot be fired. Assuming that Total Music Co. would experience no change in the sales (or selling costs) structure if they purchase the harps, based on forecasted monthly demand of 100 units/month, should the company make the harps or buy them? Show calculations.

10. Refer to question 9. Total Music Co. believes that there is a possibility for future demand to rise to 200 harps/month. Assuming that the Harp Division's relevant range extends beyond 200 harps, find the volume level where Total Music Co. would be indifferent (at least from a quantitative perspective) between making and purchasing the harps.

11. Why are linear programming techniques not required to optimally allocate a single scarce resource?

12. Why would an optimal solution never lie in the interior of the feasible region?

Chapter 15: Relevant Costing

13. How can you identify slack resources in a graphical presentation of the linear programming problem and solution?

14. Why is a graphical approach to the solution of a linear programming problem often infeasible?

15. Why are non-negativity constraints an important part of the formulation of the linear programming problem?

16. What are the major components of a linear programming problem?

Use the following information for the next 3 questions:

The Bell Manufacturing Co. is trying to determine which combination of products it should produce in the upcoming period. Two recent developments have created severe limitations on the availability of inputs that are crucial to the production of Bell's two main products: golf bags and vinyl seat covers. Both products are produced from a "plastic pellet" that is derived from a petroleum by-product. Because of recent events in the OPEC countries, petroleum-based products are in very limited supply. Bell's main supplier has stated that it would only guarantee Bell 10,000 lbs. of the plastic pellet in the coming period. Another problem that Bell is presently confronting has to do with its labor supply. Bell's main factory is currently plagued by a labor strike and is operating with managerial labor alone. Thus, in the coming period the company estimates that it will have no more than 8,000 available direct labor hours. Other information on the two products produced by the company follow:

	Golf bags	Seat covers
Expected unit sales price	$ 40	$ 30
Variable costs/unit (including materials and labor):	15	12
Estimated fixed costs for the coming period	10,000	15,000
Pounds of plastic pellets/unit	2	3
Direct labor hrs./unit	3	2
Estimated demand (in units) for the coming period	5,000	4,000

17. What is the objective function?

18. What is the solution to the linear programming problem that maximizes the objective function you described in 9. above? (Use any viable solution method).

COMMUNICATION PROJECT

Your instructor has access to video tapes associated with this text. From the Blue Chip group, Vol. 4, a segment on Culligan Water Conditioning is included and will be presented. You are to answer in writing the following questions:

1. Do you feel that Culligan focused more on their customers or their products?

2. Sometimes a company can turn a problem into an advantage. Can you suggest any examples of this with Culligan?

The goal of this exercise is to enhance your ability to accurately capture the information given.
You also learn to identify the intent behind the information being presented.

SELF TEST SOLUTIONS

TRUE/FALSE

1. F	4. T	7. F	10. T	13. Y	16. Y	19. T
2. T	5. T	8. F	11. Y	14. N	17. Y	20. T
3. F	6. T	9. F	12. Y	15. N	18. Y	21. T

MULTIPLE CHOICE

1. D	7. C	13. B	19. C	25. C	31. C	37. B
2. C	8. C	14. C	20. D	26. A	32. B	38. D
3. D	9. B	15. C	21. A	27. A	33. D	39. C
4. A	10. D	16. A	22. B	28. C	34. A	
5. B	11. D	17. B	23. C	29. D	35. C	
6. D	12. B	18. A	24. B	30. C	36. D	

QUESTIONS AND PROBLEMS

1. Relevant costs are simply those costs that are pertinent to a decision. These costs are future costs and vary across the possible decision alternatives. The set of relevant costs include opportunity costs.

2. Sunk costs are not relevant because no action that can be taken at the present time can influence them. They are not avoidable, and they do not differ between alternatives under consideration.

3. No. Some factors that are critically important are very difficult to quantify. These "qualitative" factors are important and relevant to decisions. For example, factors such as quality control, reliability of delivery schedules, and the type of production technology are important factors in the make/buy decision, but they are difficult to quantify. A firm would certainly not want to discontinue production of a crucial product component and purchase the part from a firm that rated low on these dimensions.

4. Allocated fixed costs are irrelevant because they do not differ between the alternatives under consideration: keep the product line/delete the product line. Some direct fixed costs are irrelevant for the same reason. For example, depreciation on production equipment can be a direct fixed cost of a product line, but irrelevant to the decision it has no alternative use. In other words, there is no opportunity cost associated with the use of the equipment.

Chapter 15: Relevant Costing

5. Whether a cost is relevant is critically dependent on whether the cost is to be incurred at some future time or whether it was incurred at some prior point in time. To be relevant, a cost needs to be a future cost. Not all future costs are relevant, but all prior costs (ignoring tax implications) are irrelevant.

6. All of the costs can be avoided.

7. The costs that are relevant are the ones that can be avoided by simply rejecting the special order offer. The avoidable costs would include the $275 of variable production costs and the $20 of variable selling costs. All of the other costs are irrelevant. Thus, the special order might be accepted if a sales price in excess of $295 could be obtained.

8. Once the harps have been produced, none of the production costs are avoidable. The only cost that can be avoided is the $20/unit in variable selling costs. All other costs are irrelevant.

9. The company should buy the harps. To identify relevant costs, we can first eliminate all period costs because they will remain the same whether the firm purchases or produces the harp. Of the production costs, all variable costs are avoidable if the harps are purchased and the $40/unit in factory rent is avoidable and therefore relevant. The other fixed production costs are irrelevant because they are unavoidable. Thus, by paying $300/unit to an external supplier, the firm could avoid $315 of internal costs.

10. This problem is easy to solve if you simply recast it as a CVP problem. What we are really comparing are two cost structures, one is a totally variable cost structure ($300/unit) and the other is a mixed cost structure ($275/unit + factory rent). To answer the question, we simply set the two cost structures equal to each other. We let the variable X represent the level of volume where the two cost structures would generate the same amount of total product costs:

    $300X = $275X + ($40 * 100)   [Note: $40 * 100 = total
    X = 160 units.   fixed costs at any level
                                        of activity.]

    If volume is projected to be above 160 units, the firm would be better off making the harps. If volume is projected at a lower level, the firm would be better off purchasing the harps.

11. If there is only one scarce resource, we learned in Chapter 19 that optimal allocation simply required using the scarce resource in the way that maximizes the contribution margin/unit of the scarce resource. In Chapter 22, we must consider tradeoffs that exist because there are _multiple_ scarce resource. Thus, we have the potential for substitution that did not exist in the Chapter 19 context. The linear programming is necessary to identify the optimal mix of scarce inputs.

12. The optimal solution would never lie in the interior of the feasible region because that would be tantamount to concluding that no resource is scarce (because the optimal solution required no resource to be 100% consumed). In other words, if several resources are scarce, the scarcest of those resources is going to be wholly consumed in an optimal allocation. Thus, if one resource is wholly consumed, the solution must be a corner solution rather than an interior solution.

13. Slack will be associated with all resources that are not part of the intersection at the optimal solution's vertex. The optimal solution vertex identifies those constraints that are wholly consumed in the optimal solution. All other constraints will have some slack.

14. There are two reasons that a graphical approach has limited applicability. The first reason stems from the obvious problems of graphing in four or more dimensions. Another practical reason is that computer programs are available to solve linear programming problems at a much quicker rate than a manual graphical approach.

15. The non-negativity constraints prevent an unreal solution from emerging in the LP analysis. For example, it is impossible to have negative labor hours, negative machine time, negative material inputs, or negative production. The non-negativity constraints preclude all corner solutions which contain such unreal numbers.

16. The major components of a linear programming problem are 1) an objective function that is to be maximized or minimized, 2) a set of equations that constrain the organization's ability to maximize the objective function, and 3) an additional set of constraints (such as non-negativity constraints) that confine the solution set to solutions that can actually be implemented.

17. Max CM = ($25 * Golf Bags) + ($18 * Seat Covers)

18. There are three corner solution to be evaluated:

	# of golf bags	# of seat covers
First corner solution	2,667	0
Second corner solution	0	3,333
Third corner solution	800	2,800

The first corner solution reflects the direct labor constraint, the second corner solution reflects the plastic pellet constraint, and the third corner solution is the intersection of the two constraints. The ultimate decision as to the combination of these products that should be produced will be based on the value of the objective function at each corner solution:

First corner solution: ($25 * 2,667) + ($18 * 0) = $66,675
Second corner solution: ($25 * 0) + ($18 * 3,333) = $59,994
Third corner solution: ($25 * 800) + ($18 * 2,800) = $70,400

The decision would be to produce 800 golf bags and 2,800 vinyl seat covers. This decision would maximize the objective function at an expected level of $70,400. At this level of production, all of the available direct labor hours and plastic pellets would be consumed.

CHAPTER 16
THE MASTER BUDGET

CHAPTER OVERVIEW

A major role of management is to initiate and control the process of change so that the organization continues to optimally serve those purposes for which it was created. This managerial activity is called "planning."

A formal system of organizational planning is often called a budgetary system. It gives managers a means by whcih to quantify the organizational plans and communicate the plans to employees of the firm. These plans may be classified as either operating plans (operating budgets) or plans to finance the operations (financial budgets).

This chapter provides an introduction to budgeting and organizational planning. You should be aware of what managers do to make a plan become reality. The managerial effort and activity directed at making the organizational plans become a reality is often referred to as "controlling." You should notice that managers can use the system of budgets for both planning and controlling purposes. The controlling aspect of budgets is evident in the chapters which deal with standard costing; Chapters 11 and 12, and Chapter 21 which deal with measuring organizational performance.

CHAPTER STUDY GUIDE

1. Formal planning or budgeting is found in nearly every type of organization: governmental, service, manufacturing, not-for-profit, etc. The number and type of budgets in use will vary from organization to organization. For example, firms which manufacture tangible products, such as automobiles, will have a different set of budgets from firms which prodive a service, such as insurance or banking.

    a. The important point to note is that each organization will have a set of budgets that captures the planned outputs (outputs are what the organization produces) and the planned inputs (inputs are what the organization consumes in its production).

    b. The budgeting process begins with a forecast of demand for a specific period of time for its output. This forecast is then developed into a sales plan or sales budget. The sales budget becomes the basis for preparing the budgets for the inputs such as capital, labor, and materials. The set of all budgets is referred to as the "master budget."

        i. An illustration of the general budgeting process is found in Exhibit 16-2. As this exhibit indicates, the planning or budgeting process serves the general purpose of achieving the goals and objectives of the organization. This exhibit depicts the budgetary process in two stages.

            (1) In the first stage, the planning stage, an organizational plan is adopted that is realistic given environmental and organizational (internal) constraints. Environmental

Chapter 16: The Master Budget

constraints include such things as availability of raw materials, anticipated actions by competitors, and governmental regulations. Organizational constraints include such items as available worker hours, plant capacity, and cash availability.

(2) In the second stage, the implementation stage, management strives to bring actual organizational performance in line with the adopted plan or budget. In this stage, any deviations from the plan are carefully evaluated. As a result of the evaluations, such deviations may influence individual employee performance evaluations as well as future budgets.

c. It is generally recognized that **participatory budgeting** is desirable because it involves managers in the process and they will be more committed to see to it that the budget is achieved. Yet at other times, **imposed budgets** may be the appropriate action. See Exhibits 16-22 and 16-23 in the Apendix for further discussion of these two types of budgets.

2. Exhibits 16-3 and 16-4 demonstrate how the budgeting process unfolds in a manufacturing organization. Notice that the budgeting process begins with a sales budget (budget for organizational output). Based on the sales budget, the budgets for all of the organizational inputs are determined. The required level of inputs is obviously dependent on the planned level of output. The required amount of each input for the budgeted output level may be partly determined by past experience, existing contracts or rate schedules, calculations by engineers, or perhaps through information supplied by vendors or other experts.

3. In Exhibit 16-4, the budgets in the manufacturing organization parallel the accounting cost categories. Look at the product cost budgets for factory overhead, materials, and direct labor. Other budgets will be compiled for various categories of period costs (selling, general, and administrative expenses). In addition to the budgetary categories for operating costs (operating budgets), Exhibit 16-4 indicates that there are interfaces with two important financial budgets: the capital budget and the cash budget.

a. A detailed discussion of capital budgeting is found in Chapters 19 and 20. Briefly, the capital budget is the organization's plan to acquire long-lived assets such as plant and equipment. The size of the capital budget for any particular period may be influenced by: planned changes in the level of production, availability of new production technology, restructuring of operations, planned replacement of existing facilities, etc..

4. A central feature in the system of budgets is the cash budget. To understand the importance of the cash budget is to understand that cash is the medium of exchange for inputs and outputs. Cash pays for the inputs consumed such as materials and labor, and cash is received for the output produced by the organization. Practically every budget affects the cash budget. See Exhibit 16-17 for an illustration of a cash budget.

a. A major purpose of the cash budget is to identify the timing of cash receipts and cash disbursements. By comparing the disbursements and the receipts, management can predict how the cash balance will change over some specific interval of time. This knowledge permits managers to plan for investing excess cash balances and to borrow, sell equity, or liquidate assets to meet cash deficiencies. When compiling a cash budget, be careful to exclude noncash expenses and accruals such as depreciation, amortization, and the expiration of prepaid insurance.

5. A detailed example of budgeting begins with the information contained in Exhibit 16-5. The example continues with Exhibit 16-7 which provides the sales budget for the first quarter of 1995 by month.

a. From the sales budget, the production budget is compiled. The production budget is merely management's planned level of production by period. See Exhibit 16-8 for a production budget. Initially, you might think that the number of units in the production budget would be the same as the number of units in the sales budget for each period. However, the level of production each period can differ from the level of sales if management wants to either liquidate or increase finished goods inventory.

    b. Having completed the production budget, a purchases or materials budget can be compiled for each component part or raw material that must be acquired outside of the organization (see Exhibit 16-9). These budgets also need to consider inventory levels and whether they will be increased or partially liquidated during the period.

    c. Also, based on the production budget, budgets for indirect and direct factory labor as well as other factory overhead are compiled (see Exhibits 16-10 and 16-11). Budgets for other operating costs (selling, general, and administrative expenses) are based on the sales budget and appear in Exhibit 16-12.

6. Following the completion of the operating budgets and the capital budget, the cash budget is assembled. The pattern of the cash budget is like the outline used to account for an inventory.

    a. The beginning cash balance for the period is like the beginning inventory. Cash deposits (cash collections) represent additions to the inventory(production or purchases). Adding the cash deposits to the beginning balance yields the total inventory of cash available for the period. Subtracting withdrawals (cash disbursements) from the cash available for the period yields the ending inventory of cash.

    b. Examine the cash budget in Exhibit 16-17 and notice how the format of that budget is similar to the way you would account for an inventory. The notable difference between cash and other types of inventory is that cash can be borrowed or invested. Consequently, the last section of the cash budget, the financing section, accounts for cash that is acquired through borrowing or asset liquidation and cash that is invested or used to repay debt.

7. After the operating and financial budgets are finalized, pro forma (projected) financial statements can be compiled for the period. Examples of these statements appear in Exhibits 16-18 through 16-20. The actual results of operations can be compared to these pro forma financial statements to evaluate organizational and segment performance. This comparison emphasizes the "control" dimension of budgeting. The specifics are detailed in the previously mentioned budgets such as the sales and production budgets. The pro forma statements may also indicate that plans need to be revised because projected profit levels are too low or specific costs appear to be unreasonable.

SELF TEST

TRUE/FALSE

1. T F

    One benefit of budgeting is that it coordinates that activities of the entire organization.

2. T F

    The financial and operating budgets of an organization are independent of each other.

3. T F

    The materials or purchases budget of a manufacturing firm is prepared based on the production budget.

Chapter 16: The Master Budget

4. T F

    The budgeting process is useful for both planning and performance evaluation.

5. T F

    An operating budget can be makde on a perpetual or continuous basis.

6. T F

    In creating the master budget, the first budget a company prepares is the materials purchases budget

7. T F

    The cash budget is one of the operating budgets.

8. T F

    The budgeting activity plays an important role in organizational communication.

9. T F

    The budgeting process is helpful in identifying organizational constraints.

10. T F

    The longer the time period covered by a budget, the more useful the budget will be for controlling operations.

MULTIPLE CHOICE

1. The set of all budgets in an organization is referred to as

    a. the operating budget.
    b. the financial budget.
    c. the master budget.
    d. the pro forma budget.

2. The sales budget is based on

    a. projected sales demand.
    b. the production budget.
    c. the selling and administrative expense budget.
    d. sales demand for the previous period.

3. The production budget is based on

    a. the sales forecast.
    b. the sales budget.
    c. the purchases budget.
    d. the cash budget.

4. The purchases budget is based on

    a. the sales budget.
    b. the cash budget.
    c. the selling and administrative expense budget.
    d. the production budget.

5. An imposed budget

    a. is a flexible budget.
    b. can lead to poor performance.
    c. is best for planning purposeds.
    d. is used to resolve conflicts.

Chapter 16: The Master Budget

6. If you were preparing a cash budget you should ignore

    a. the payment of cash dividends.
    b. the payment of stock dividends.
    c. cash expended for capital assets.
    d. cash collected from the sale of securities.

7. A budget is

    a. a quantitative expression of an organization's plans.
    b. a qualitative expression of an organization's plans.
    c. always prepared to cover a period of 1 year.
    d. useless in communicating managerial objectives.

8. An organization's pro forma financial statements represent

    a. budgeted results of operations.
    b. actual results of operations.
    c. results that can never be achieved.
    d. a qualitative performance standard.

9. The financial budgets of a firm include

    a. the sales budget.
    b. the production budget.
    c. the cash budget.
    d. the purchases budget.

10. The set of operating budgets include

    a. the cash budget.
    b. the purchases budget.
    c. pro forma financial statements.
    d. the capital budget.

11. Consider the following four budgets: cash budget, sales budget, purchases budget, and the production budget. Which of these budgets would logically be prepared last?

    a. cash budget
    b. sales budget
    c. purchases budget
    d. production budget

12. In a retailing organization, you would not expect to find which of the following budgets?

    a. sales budget
    b. production budget
    c. capital budget
    d. cash budget

13. A change in the sales budget would be least likely to affect which of the following budgets?

    a. selling, general, and administrative expense budget
    b. production budget
    c. cash budget
    d. capital budget

14. The production budget for a period will be influenced by

    a. management's policy regarding the level of raw material inventories.
    b. management's policy regarding the level of finished goods inventory.
    c. management's policy for accounts receivable collection.
    d. the sales budget only.

Chapter 16: The Master Budget

15. A very important role of the cash budget is

    a. to determine how to finance dividend payments.
    b. to help identify the timing of cash excesses and deficiencies.
    c. to determine the optimal source of financing for the organization's operations.
    d. none of the above.

16. Deviations of actual results from the budget may be a basis for

    a. revising future budgets.
    b. evaluating managerial and employee performance.
    c. changing budgetary assumptions.
    d. all of the above.

17. If you have access to monthly cash budgets for all 12 months of a year, an annual cash budget can be compiled. The ending cash balance in the annual budget would be equal to

    a. the sum of the ending cash balances for all 12 months.
    b. the ending cash balance for the 12th month.
    c. the beginning cash balance for the 12th month.
    d. the ending cash balance for the first month.

18. A pro forma income statement would require information from all of the following budgets except

    a. the factory overhead budget.
    b. the sales budget.
    c. the direct labor budget.
    d. the cash budget.

19. The budgets and pro forma financial statements must be prepared in a specific order. Which of the following would be prepared first?

    a. cash budget
    b. pro forma income statement
    c. pro forma balance sheet
    d. capital budget
    e. production budget

20. In the preceding problem, which of the five would be prepared last?

    a. cash budget
    b. pro forma income statement
    c. pro forma balance sheet
    d. capital budget

21. Slack in the operating budgets

    a. will cause an organization to operate more efficiently.
    b. is rarely found if the budgets are imposed.
    c. is lower in budgets developed with worker participation relative to budgets that are imposed.
    d. results from unintentional managerial computational errors.

22. When an organization maintains a constant 12 month budget horizon, the organization is utilizing

    a. continuous budgeting.
    b. perpetual budgeting.
    c. constant budgeting.
    d. periodic budgeting.

Chapter 16: The Master Budget

23. Managers may pay more attention to budgets when

    a. their compensation depends on the relationship of the actual results to the budgeted performance level.
    b. they don't have to participate in setting the budget.
    c. their superiors ignore variances or deviations from the budget.
    d. they are easily achieved.

24. Which of the following is not a good use of budgets

    a. as feedback devices.
    b. as investigating devices.
    c. as control devices.
    d. as planning devices.

25. In the cash budget, which of the following will not affect the "cash excess or inadequacy?"

    a. the beginning cash balance
    b. cash receipts
    c. cash disbursements
    d. financing

QUESTIONS AND PROBLEMS

1. Why is budgeting such an important organization activity?

2. What is the starting point in the budgeting process?

3. What is the purpose of the cash budget and why is it so important?

4. What are pro forma financial statements and what is their role in the budgeting process?

5. What are the components of the master budget?

Chapter 16: The Master Budget

6. Malachi Manufacturing produces a single product for which they have forecasted demand (in units) for the first four months of 1995 as follows:

JANUARY	FEBRUARY	MARCH	APRIL
12,000	11,000	10,000	12,000

   Malachi has a policy of maintaining an inventory of finished goods equal to 20% of the budgeted sales for the following month. On January 1, 1995 the company was in compliance with this inventory policy. Prepare a monthly production budget for Malachi for the first quarter of 1995.

7. Refer to problem 6 above. For each unit that Malachi manufactures, 3 pounds of raw material are consumed. Malachi maintains an inventory of raw material equal to 50% of the next month's production needs. Malachi was in compliance with the 50% inventory policy on January 1, 1995. Determine the quantity of raw material to be purchased by Malachi for the months of January and February.

8. The Johnson Co. has a sales budget for the first four months of 1995 as follows:

JANUARY	FEBRUARY	MARCH	APRIL
$100,000	$125,000	$90,000	$100,000

   All of the sales are made on account, and experience indicates that 30% of the receivables are collected in the month of sale, 40% in the following month, and 27% in the second month following the month of sale. The balance of 3% is never collected. How much cash should the Johnson Co. expect to collect in April?

9. Refer to the information in question 8 above. If the Johnson Company expects to collect $112,600 in February, determine the amount of total sales for the month of December 1995.

Chapter 16: The Master Budget

10. The following journal entries appeared in the Timberline Corporations's books for the month of July, 1995:

Accounts Payable	$100,000	
Cash		$100,000
Raw material inventory	30,000	
Accounts payable		30,000
Labor expense	20,000	
Wages payable		20,000

    Which of these entries would affect the cash budget for July? Explain.

SELF TEST SOLUTIONS

TRUE/FALSE

1. T 3. T 5. T 7. F 9. T
2. F 4. T 6. F 8. T 10. F

MULTIPLE CHOICE

1. C   6. B   11. A   16. D   21. B
2. A   7. A   12. B   17. B   22. A
3. B   8. A   13. D   18. D   23. A
4. A   9. C   14. B   19. E   24. B
5. B   10. B 15. B   20. C   25. D

QUESTIONS AND PROBLEMS

1. Budgeting is important for several reasons. The budget is a quantitative expression of the goals and objectives of the organization. Because budgets are quantitative, they provide a concrete standard of performance. As a performance standard, budgets are compared to actual results and become an important part of management control and performance evaluation. Also, because budgets are a concise expression of the organizational objectives, they are useful in communicating the objectives to organizational members and coordinating the efforts of organizational members.

2. The budgeting process always begins with an estimate of the demand for the organizational output. Such an estimate is translated into a budgeted level of output which is then used to compile budgets for the required inputs.

3. The cash budget identifies the timing of cash excesses and shortages. It is extremely important because cash is the medium of exchange for organizational inputs and outputs. If cash shortages exist, the organization cannot pay for its inputs and must make plans to obtain cash through borrowing, asset sales, etc.. If excess cash is available, the organization can plan to acquire investments.

4. The pro forma financial statements are financial statements which reflect budgeted operating and financial results. They are part of the master budget and are used as a performance standard, and as a basis for budget revision.

5. The master budget is simply the set of all budgets. It consists of the operating budgets, the financial budgets, and the pro forma financial statements.

Chapter 16: The Master Budget

6.

	JANUARY	FEBRUARY	MARCH
Budgeted sales	12,000	11,000	10,000
Desired ending inventory	2,200	2,000	2,400
Total needed	14,200	13,000	12,400
Less the Beginning inventory	2,400	2,200	2,000
Units to be produced	11,800	10,800	10,400

7. You must use the information from Problem 6. above to solve this problem. First, determine the total amount of raw material that will be required for each month's production:

	JANUARY	FEBRUARY	MARCH
Units to be produced	11,800	10,800	10,400
Multiply production by required quantity of raw material/unit	X 3	X 3	X 3
Material needed for production	35,400	32,400	31,200

Now, you are ready to actually compile the purchases budget:

	JANUARY	FEBRUARY	MARCH
Material needed for production	35,400	32,400	31,200
Budgeted ending inventory*	16,200	15,600	
Total material needed	51,600	48,000	
Less the Beginning inventory	17,700	16,200	
Materials to be purchased	33,900	31,800	

*Remember, the budgeted inventory levels are merely computed as 50% of the next month's production needs.

8.

	April cash collections
From February sales:	
$125,000 * .27	$33,750
From March sales:	
$90,000 * .40	36,000
From April sales:	
$100,000 * .30	30,000
Budgeted April collections	$99,750

9. In February, collections are made on sales which occurred in the months of February, January, and December. The collections would be 30% of February's sales, 40% of January's sales and 27% of December's sales. Use this knowledge to solve the problem:

Total February collections:	$112,600
Collected from February sales	
$125,000 * .30	(37,500)
Collected from January sales	
$100,000 * .40	(40,000)
Collected from December sales	35,100

Thus, $35,100 is 27% of December sales. Total December sales would have to be $35,100/.27 or $130,000.

10. Only cash inflows and outflows appear in the cash budget. Therefore, only the first entry would affect the cash budget. The second and third entries are merely accruals.

CHAPTER 17

COST CONTROL FOR DISCRETIONARY COSTS

CHAPTER OVERVIEW

Being familiar with the operations of several organizations, Focus on one of those organizations. What should this organization's total expenses be for its 1995 fiscal year? Without doubt, this is a difficult question to answer for any organization. Chapter 17 will provide you with some tools to answer this question.

For most organizations, we try to relate the cost of inputs (expenses) to the desired level of output (usually sales revenues). Chapter 17 banks on the Chapter 16 discussion of planning and budgeting. For many categories of expenses, using planning and budgeting concepts, standards can be developed (Chapters 11 & 12) that relate expenses to revenues. Thus, when asked what an organization's total expenses should be for 1995, an answer could be devised on the organization's planned output for 1995.

For one specific type of cost, discretionary cost, it is more difficult to draw a conclusion about the optimal level of the cost, given some desired level of output. They are fixed in nature making it difficult to develop standards for them as is done for direct labor or direct materials. Chapter 17 is primarily concerned with discretionary fixed costs. Several methods can be used to control and evaluate discretionary fixed costs.

CHAPTER STUDY GUIDE

1. In organizations that are profit-oriented, net income may be thought of as the difference between the organization's input (sales revenues) and the organization's outputs (expenses). Thinking of net income in this manner leads to interesting questions regarding the optimal level of net income. The level of net income depends on the level of revenues and expenses. For a given level of revenue, expenses must be contained below some threshold to achieve a desired level of net income. In other words, costs must be contained.

2. Chapter 16 shows budgets are useful for planning and control. When actual costs are compared to budgeted levels of costs, the budgeted level of costs represents a threshold for costs. If costs are contained below the threshold, the budgeted level of net income can be achieved. If costs exceed the threshold, the budgeted level of net income will probably not be achieved.

3. An organization can control costs by containing them below some level. The target level often is a standard or budgeted cost level. Stemming from this footing is the determination of the standards for various classes of costs. Standards can be developed from engineering estimates. For example, the direct material standard for the lumber required to build a certain birdhouse, can be determined based on: the size of the birdhouse; a reasonable allowance for waste, scrap, and spoilage; and the market price of each type of lumber.

Chapter 17: Cost Control for Discretionary Costs

    a.   Managers look at ways to reduce the waste, utilize less expensive alternative materials, and save labor time. Standards provide a benchmark for restraining costs, and a basis to compare alternative production materials and technologies for potential cost reductions.

4.   If a standard or budget cannot be easily developed for a particular cost, problems can occur regarding cost control. The costs may be discretionary fixed costs. Fixed costs are either discretionary or committed.

    a.   Committed fixed costs are related to the possession of basic plant assets or basic personnel. This category of costs includes such things as depreciation on plant equipment and the salary of the corporate president.

        i.   Recall from Chapter 11 the brief discussion of the capital budget (discussed in detail in Chapters 20 & 21). The capital budget of an organization accounts for much of its committed fixed costs. Changes in the capital budget will typically change the level of the committed fixed costs.

        ii.   Since committed fixed costs are related to the basic infrastructure of an organization, management cannot do much in the short run to control or change these costs.

    b.   Discretionary fixed cost can be controlled in the short run. The current chapter emphasizes concepts which can be used for discretionary cost control.

5.   Fixed costs are either exclusively discretionary or committed, but defining discretionary fixed costs may be difficult. If it is committed, the cost is not discretionary. Discretionary fixed costs are subject to management control in the short run and not directly related to the basic infrastructure of the organization.

    a.   These costs are frequently service-oriented. Examples include: repair and maintenance costs, personnel services, advertising, and research and development. For purposes of cost control, special attention should be spent on them because it is difficult to develop a standard for these costs that is based on a traditional ratio of inputs to outputs.

6.   Determining a standard for discretionary fixed costs on a ratio of inputs to outputs is difficult because the relationship between the cost and outputs if frequently not known or easily estimated.

    a.   For example, suppose a manufacturing company annually hosts a picnic for its employees and their families. The cost of the picnic is $10,000/year. This cost is discretionary because the company could easily eliminate it and the basic infrastructure of the organization would be unaffected. But should they discontinue the annual picnic? What are the benefits that the firm receives from this $10,000 cost? These questions may be impossible to answer fully.

7.   Managerial decisions affecting the incurrence and control of discretionary fixed costs must be made by relating the cost to the organization's goals. The contribution of a discretionary cost to the achievement of an organization's goals can be measured in terms of effectiveness and efficiency.

    a.   In regards to the company picnic, it's purpose is "to help maintain high employee morale." The company can find surrogates to measure employee morale: absenteeism, worker productivity, # of worker complaints, etc.. If these surrogate measures of employee morale indicate that morale has risen after the family picnic, we could conclude that the picnic was effective: it met the objective of maintaining high employee morale.

        i.   Whether the picnic was an **efficient** way to maintain high employee morale is another issue. The same level of morale could have

Chapter 17: Cost Control for Discretionary Costs

been attained by installing an employee recreation room at an annual cost of $100,000. In this case, the picnic was relatively efficient because it cost $90,000 less to achieve high morale. On the other hand, if the high employee morale could have been achieved by company sponsorship of an employee softball team at an annual cost of $3,000, the picnic would be regarded as inefficient because it cost the company $7,000 more than the softball team sponsorship.

8. Control of discretionary fixed costs in most organizations is achieved through: the use of budgets, consultation with experts, and efforts to relate the discretionary fixed costs to their contribution to organizational goals. As you read Chapter 17, pay particular attention to the roles of program budgeting and zero-base budgeting in controlling discretionary costs. Also, this chapter is filled with important terms. Refer to the glossary at the end of the chapter and make certain that you understand the definitions of the terms that appear there. Some discretionary costs occur in a particular pattern and repetitive. Standards may be developed and these costs are called **engineered costs**.

    a. Effective cost control systems have three control points: (1) before an event; (2) during the event; and (3) after the event (see EXHIBIT 17-1). Cost consciousness also affects control over discretionary costs as shown in EXHIBIT 17-2. An attitude and understanding of the cost can contain or reduce it.

    b. Other factors besides activity levels effect costs such as inflation, supplier cost adjustments.

    c. Cost containment should be used where possible. Seasonal cost increases should be avoided with advance purchasing.

    d. Service work such as repairs should be done on a preventive basis to avoid breakdowns. This practice is encouraged in JIT systems. Standardizing equipment can reduce training costs, maintenance and supply inventory size.

    e. Cost avoidance may be an alternative to cost containment.

    f. Cost reduction is the lowering of costs by finding others means to provide the service. The five steps of controlling discretionary costs are shown in EXHIBIT 17-3.

9. Benefits from discretionary costs may not be measurable in dollar terms. The benefits or outputs from these costs may be estimated in nonmonetary, surrogate measures. Examples of these measures are seen in EXHIBIT 17-4.

    a. Efficiency of discretionary activities is a comparison of actual output to actual inputs compared to planned output to planned input. A time lag may exist between outputs and inputs which makes efficiency comparisons questionable.

    b. Effectiveness is the comparison of actual output to planned output.

10. Committed fixed costs include fixed costs associated with plant assets or key plant or organizational personnel. They are associated with long-run management decisions. These costs are first controlled in the capital budgeting process; secondly, control is facilitated by comparing actual and expected results from plant asset investments.

SELF TEST

TRUE/FALSE

1. T F

    The term cost control is always synonymous with cost minimization.

Chapter 17: Cost Control for Discretionary Costs

2. T F

   Management may find discretionary fixed costs more difficult to control than committed fixed costs.

3. T F

   Cost control may result in increases in efficiency.

4. T F

   A starting point in cost control is preparation of a budget.

5. T F

   If costs decline from one period to the next, cost control in the organization must have been better in the second period than the first.

6. T F

   Cost containment programs work to minimize total costs.

7. T F

   All fixed costs can be categorized as committed or discretionary.

8. T F

   The level of discretionary fixed costs is more difficult to adjust in the short-run than committed fixed costs.

9. T F

   The benefits of discretionary fixed costs are easier to measure than the benefits of committed fixed costs.

10. T F

    Committed costs and discretionary costs are both semi-variable costs.

11. T F

    The philosophy of top management will determine to a large degree the classification of a fixed cost as discretionary or committed.

12. T F

    Contribution margin is defined as sales less discretionary fixed costs.

13. T F

    Committed fixed costs are those that relate to the investment in plant, equipment and the basic organizational structure of a company.

14. T F

    Discretionary costs usually exhibit step-variable behavior.

15. T F

    In zero-base budgeting, only changes from the prior budget must be justified.

Chapter 17: Cost Control for Discretionary Costs

MULTIPLE CHOICE

1. Managerial efforts to minimize period-by-period increases in per-unit variable and total fixed costs is called

    a. cost reduction.
    b. cost avoidance.
    c. cost containment.
    d. cost utilization.

2. Which of the following is cited as a reason for costs to change?

    a. technological change
    b. inflation/deflation
    c. supply and demand
    d. all of the above

3. The level of committed fixed costs will depend on

    a. the cash budget.
    b. the capital budget.
    c. the production budget.
    d. the sales budget.

4. Determining the optimal level of cost would be the most difficult for

    a. total discretionary fixed costs.
    b. total committed fixed costs.
    c. total variable period costs.
    d. total variable product costs.

5. Which of the following does not require a measurement of inputs?

    a. an efficiency measure
    b. an effectiveness measure
    c. cost standards
    d. cost control

6. Managerial control of discretionary costs is not likely to rely on

    a. zero-based budgeting.
    b. program budgeting.
    c. capital budgeting.
    d. expert judgment.

7. Program budgeting is often useful when

    a. an organization has mostly variable costs.
    b. an organization has no discretionary costs.
    c. an organization's output is difficult to measure.
    d. an organization has no stipulated goals.

8. If a discretionary cost is treated like an engineered cost, it may be controlled with the use of

    a. program budgeting.
    b. zero-base budgeting.
    c. budget appropriations.
    d. standards.

9. Most discretionary fixed costs are considered optional

    a. in the short run.
    b. in the long run.
    c. in the short and long run.
    d. under no circumstance.

Chapter 17: Cost Control for Discretionary Costs

10. Optimal control of a discretionary fixed cost is achieved when

    a. the cost is minimized.
    b. the cost is held at the same level as it was in the prior period.
    c. the cost is held below some threshold such as standard cost.
    d. the cost is optimal for the organization's goals and objectives.

11. Budgeting the cost of maintenance and repair at $3/machine hour is an example of a discretionary cost being treated as

    a. a fixed cost.
    b. an engineered cost.
    c. a period cost.
    d. a programmed cost.

12. An effective cost control system should function

    a. as a control before the event.
    b. as a control during the event.
    c. as a control after the event.
    d. as a control before, during, and after the event.

13. Cost containment is possible for changes resulting from

    a. inflation.
    b. technology.
    c. supply and demand adjustments.
    d. seasonality.

14. Discretionary fixed costs reflect

    a. the costs of the basic structure of an organization.
    b. an organization's frivolous expenses.
    c. expenses based on organizational policy or management preferences.
    d. expenses that benefit the current period only.

15. Which of the following can be reduced or eliminated in the short run without adversely affecting the long-term success of the organization?

    a. discretionary fixed costs
    b. variable selling costs
    c. variable production costs
    d. committed fixed costs

16. Which budgeting method starts with a minimal figure for funding?
    a. zero-base budgeting
    b. program budgeting
    c. traditional budgeting
    d. flexible budgeting

17. Which of the following is likely to be the most expensive budgeting method in terms of time and effort?

    a. zero-base budgeting
    b. program budgeting
    c. traditional budgeting
    d. flexible budgeting

18. Most discretionary costs are incurred

    a. to purchase and install equipment.
    b. to provide service activities.
    c. to provide management with perks.
    d. to create slack in the budget.

Chapter 17: Cost Control for Discretionary Costs

19. Opportunities to reduce costs in an organization will be increased if all employees are

    a. temporary.
    b. permanent.
    c. cost conscious.
    d. required to meet cost budgets.

20. For cost control purposes, it is important to examine differences between budgeted and actual costs

    a. to punish those responsible for the difference.
    b. to understand what caused the differences.
    c. so variances can be computed.
    d. to justify increases in budgeted costs for future periods.

21. Which of the following would reduce a company's committed fixed costs?

    a. slashing the firm's advertising costs
    b. closing the firm's legal department
    c. selling one of the firm's product warehouses
    d. reducing the size of the firm's research and development staff

22. An example of a committed fixed cost is:

    a. Advertising contracts
    b. Long-term computer leases
    c. Supervisory salaries
    d. Period to period warehouse rent

23. An example of a discretionary fixed cost is:

    a. Amortization of a purchased patent
    b. Long-term warehouse leases
    c. A janitorial services contract
    d. Ten-year computer services agreement

24. An example of a discretionary fixed cost would be:

    a. taxes on the factory.
    b. depreciation on manufacturing equipment.
    c. insurance.
    d. research and development.

QUESTIONS AND PROBLEMS

1. What is the difference between a committed and a discretionary fixed cost?

2. Why is the control of discretionary costs more difficult than other costs?

3. Why is cost control so important in an organization?

Chapter 17: Cost Control for Discretionary Costs

4. What is the role of the budgeting activity in cost control?

5. Why is the minimum level of cost not necessarily the optimum level of cost for discretionary costs?

6. Under what circumstances is program budgeting likely to make a valuable contribution to cost control.

7. What role does the capital budget play in controlling committed fixed costs?

8. Why can a cost be classified as discretionary in one organization and committed in another?

9. What do the terms effective and efficient mean in the context of cost control?

10. Classify each of the following fixed costs as discretionary or committed: advertising, salary of the corporate president, costs of a legal department, property taxes on a factory, depreciation on factory equipment, quality inspections, factory rent, costs of providing child care for employees, salary of the firm's market analyst, and the cost of a firm's advanced employee education program.

COMMUNICATION PROJECT

The instructor will call on you in class to answer a question in this chapter from the study guide. Cover the correct answers to the T-F and multiple choice questions.

The purpose of this exercise is enable you to be exposed to stress in meeting a deadline with no undue consequences. You will not be allowed to evade personal responsibility for preparing for the chapter.

Chapter 17: Cost Control for Discretionary Costs

SELF TEST SOLUTIONS

TRUE/FALSE

1. F	4. T	7. T	10. F	13. T
2. T	5. F	8. F	11. F	14. T
3. T	6. T	9. F	12. F	15. F

MULTIPLE CHOICE

1. C	6. C	11. B	16. A	21. C
2. D	7. C	12. D	17. A	22. B
3. B	8. D	13. D	18. B	23. C
4. A	9. A	14. C	19. C	24. C
5. B	10. D	15. A	20. B	

QUESTIONS AND PROBLEMS

1. A committed fixed cost is directly related to the fundamental purpose of the organization or the basic personnel in the organizational structure. Discretionary costs are frequently related to auxiliary activities of the organization and can be adjusted in the short run without affecting the long run viability of the organization.

2. Discretionary costs are more difficult to control because it is hard to specify the optimal level for the costs. Additionally, it is difficult to evaluate the control of discretionary costs with traditional input/output ratios.

3. In the long run, profit-seeking organizations must generate revenues that exceed their expenses. To be successful, the organizations must attempt to both increase revenues and control costs. Successful cost control strategies will not only control present costs, but will identify new technologies and methods to reduce future costs and keep the organization in a competitive position.

4. Budgets serve as a base line to which actual costs can be compared. Budgets give management an idea of what a cost should be for a specified output level and can be used to develop standards for costs. The differences between standard and actual costs can help identify organizational weaknesses and opportunities to achieve greater efficiency in the operations.

5. Many discretionary costs could be brought down to zero in the short run. In many cases, this would be unwise because it may substantially increase future costs. For example, discontinuing routine repair and maintenance service to machinery may result in immediate cost savings, but drive up future costs substantially due to breakdowns and premature machine obsolescence.

6. Program budgeting will probably be the most useful in organizations that have difficulty in defining or identifying their output. Frequently, this will include governmental and not-for-profit organizations.

7. Preparation of the capital budget gives an organization the opportunity to assess the impact of long-term investment on operations. The capital budget is a formal attempt to compare the costs and benefits of the investment opportunities presented to the firm. Once the investment is undertaken, many of the fixed costs associated with the investment are subject to very little management control. Therefore, management control for committed fixed costs is largely accomplished with the capital budget before the investment is undertaken.

8. The importance of a particular cost will vary from one organization to another. In one organization, a particular cost may be regarded as basic to the success of the organization, while it may be more of an auxiliary type of expense in another organization. For example, quality control costs would be very basic in a firm that collects and distributes human blood to hospitals, while quality control for a pencil manufacturer would be much less crucial.

9. An organization's activities will be regarded as effective if the organizational goals and objectives have been met. The operations of the same organization will be regarded as efficient if the goals and objectives have been achieved with actual inputs at or less than the level of budgeted inputs.

10. The following costs would be discretionary in most organizations: advertising, costs of a legal department, quality inspections, costs of providing child care for employees, salary of the firm's market analyst and the cost of a firm's advanced employee education program. All of the other costs would be committed.

CHAPTER 18

CONTROL OF INVENTORY AND PRODUCTION

CHAPTER OVERVIEW

This chapter introduces the related topics of controlling inventory and production levels, as well as their associated costs. Two major production control systems are discussed: push and pull. Traditionally, manufacturing firms have utilized "push" production control systems. In such a system, raw materials, work-in-process, and finished goods inventories are maintained at levels which balance the costs of an inventory shortage or outage with the costs of acquiring and carrying inventories. Inventories are used as buffers to protect the firm from unforseen events such as machine breakdowns, late deliveries by suppliers, unusually high product demand, or seasonal fluctuations in demand or raw material supplies. In line with the inventory buffer concept, the economic order size(EOQ) for raw materials(or merchandise inventory) is determined; otherwise, for manufacturing firms, the economic production run size(EPR) is demonstrated. A second facit for inventory pertains to when it should be reordered. The optimal point when to reorder inventory is called reorder point(ROP).

The second production and inventory control system discussed in the chapter is a "pull" system. One version was pioneered by Toyota in Japan. Called just-in-time, JIT, it considers inventory costly and strives to reduce inventory to the lowest possible levels. Reducing inventory levels identifies inefficiencies in the production process and deletes these wastes. Managers reduce lead times for raw material inputs by developing long-term relationships with suppliers. Every employee has a responsibility to maintain and improve the quality of the products. The firm adopts a total quality control(TQC) concept where work is done right the first time avoiding rework and defects along with corresponding costs associated with these activities. The firm and its emplyees must commit to continuous improvement in the efficiency of operations.

As you read this chapter, concentrate on the differences in the push and pull control systems. Also, note that there is a difference in the set of technical skills that is required to make each type of system successful. After reading the chapter, refer to the glossary of terms at the end of the chapter and see if you recall what each term means and to which system it relates.

CHAPTER STUDY GUIDE

1. Regarding the management of each inventory of raw materials, two issues must be addressed: **when to order, and what quantity to order**. Ideally, the quantity ordered should meet its daily needs, at a minimum cost for ordering(O) and carrying of the inventory(C). Examples of items included in O and C are shown in EXHIBIT 18-1 of your book.

    a. For example, consider a firm that estimates its usage of Material A for the coming year at 100,000 lbs.

        i. At one extreme, the firm could order all 100,000 lbs. at one time. If it did so, the ordering costs(O) of preparing and processing would be minimized. If all 100,000 lbs. were ordered at once, only one purchase order would need to be prepared for the entire year and only one order would be made annually. Thus, the ordering cost would be minimized. But the carrying costs would be augmented because of carrying this large inventory. The firm would need to provide storage, insurance, security, etc. for all 100,000 lbs..

    ii. At the other extreme: the firm could order just enough of Material A to produce one unit of product. If it did so, the costs of carrying inventory would be minimized due to reduced space needs, insurance needs, etc.. On the other hand, the costs associated with ordering inventory would be increased because the firm would need to process a purchase order for each unit it produced. Obviously, the least cost solution for the order quantity of Material A minimizes the total of the ordering and carrying costs and this quantity is called economic order quantity(EOQ). Mathematically this occurs when the total ordering cost equal the total carrying cost.

b. The EOQ model is designed to identify the order quantity that minimizes the total costs including both ordering costs and carrying costs. The EOQ model is presented below:

$$EOQ = \sqrt{(2QO)/C}$$

where
- EOQ = economic order quantity
- Q = estimated annual usage in units
- O = the cost of placing an order
- C = the annual cost of carrying one unit in inventory

EXHIBIT 18-4 illustrates a graph of the EOQ and EXHIBIT 18-5 illustrates the equation form of the EOQ.

2. The EOQ model is an aid to answer the question: How much do we order at one time? The other question about inventory concerns when the order should be placed. Typically, an order is placed for more material when the existing inventory reaches a level such that it will run out when the new order is received. It is called the "order point."

    a. The order point is determined by including the lead time, the average daily usage, and the required safety stock. Safety stock is carried to prevent stockouts or running out of inventory to meet customer's demand. To illustrate the order point calculation, let's continue with the example above using Material A.

    b. The term "lead time" refers to the time lag between the placement of an order for material and the receipt of the material. The lead time can vary from a few hours for some materials to weeks for other materials. With the adoption of JIT manufacturing, raw material suppliers are expected to be located a short distance away from the manufaturer so they can quickly deliver raw materials to the plant. For example, the new BMW plant in South Carolina, that will begin operations in 1995, has stated that local suppliers must be within 30 minutes of the plant.

    c. Assume that the lead time for Material A is 5 working days. If the firm has 200 working days in its factory each year, and consumes 100,000 lbs. of Material A each year, average "daily usage" would be: 100,000/200 = 500 lbs. If average daily use never exceeded 500 lbs./day and our supplier would deliver within 5 days of the order placement, reorder point would be equal to the 5-day consumption of Material A: 500 lbs. * 5 = 2,500 lbs. Reorder should be made when inventory reached 2,500 pounds. We would order an amount that was based on the EOQ model discussed earlier.

    d. If there was some probability that inventory use could exceed 500 lbs. in a day, or that the supplier would fail to deliver within the 5

Chapter 18: Control of Inventory and Production

working days, add an allowance for "safety stock" to the order point. Safety stock provides a buffer to prevent stockouts which create other costs to incur such as speedy delivery costs for materials and lost customer sales.

3. For companies that produce and sell multiple products, decisions must be made regarding the timing and quantity of production for each product type. Decisions regarding production run size are similar to EOQ decisions, except set up costs replace order costs in the EOQ model. The model and equation to use for this decision is called the economic production run model (EPR) and is useful for determining the quantity of each product to be produced in one production run.

   a. The equation is as follows:

   $$EPR = \sqrt{2QS/C}$$

   where
   - EPR = economic production run quantity
   - Q = estimated annual quantity produced in units
   - S = estimated cost of setting up a production run
   - C = estimated cost of carrying one unit in stock for one year

   For example, consider the case of a company that produces two products: X & Y. In its factory, the company can only produce one product at a time. Assume that the company estimates annual demand for product X at 10,000 units and demand for product Y at 10,000 units. At one extreme, the company could produce all 10,000 units of X and then all 10,000 units of Y. If demand is fairly constant throughout the year, this schedule is probably not realistic because the finished goods inventory of product Y would be fully depleted before production of product Y would begin, resulting in lost sales. At the other extreme, the firm could alternate, producing one unit of X and one unit of Y. Which costs are minimized and which costs are maximized in the first strategy? In the second strategy? The first strategy minimizes set up costs (the costs to switch from the production of one product to the other), and the second strategy minimizes the carrying costs of finished goods inventory. Likewise, scheduling the timing of each production run is based on the "order point" concepts discussed earlier.

   b. Pay careful attention in your text to the discussion of the additional tools (some of which are computer intensive techniques) that may be used in conjunction with the EOQ model to enhance the sophistication of inventory control: MRP, MRP II, Two-bin system, Red-line system and ABC listings.

4. The philosophy of the Just-In-Time, JIT, inventory control system is that inventory is undesirable. This includes finished goods, work in process, and raw material inventories. Proponents of the JIT system suggest that inventories hide organizational weaknesses and inefficiencies, and prevent organizations from recognizing such problems and solving them. In the JIT system, production is demand driven; it is a "pull" rather than "push" system. Production in each work center is paced by the next downstream work center. Raw material deliveries are reliably scheduled with suppliers to arrive just at the time they are needed for production. Effort is made to reduce the cost and time required for setups. Flexible manufacturing systems may be adopted to reduce setup time and allow for more variability in the products produced. Production schedules are driven by forecasts of product demand and are designed to keep materials flowing at an even pace. Decreasing setup time reduces the throughput time. This makes the producer more responsive to customer expectations.

   a. Production control in a JIT setting depends on related work centers having visual contact with each other. Manufacturing cells are established with machines grouped in families so they can perform a variety of operations in sequence. Products move from one machine to another from start to finish. The Kanban cards are a significant part of the visual communication between work centers. Major elements of the JIT philosophy are listed in EXHITIT 18-9. Study this exhibit carefully.

b. Accounting for the production activities in a JIT environment differs from the traditional system. Raw materials arrive and are put into production almost immediately; generally the distinction between materials in the work-in-process inventory and materials in a raw state are insignificant. One account, raw and in process materials, is used to account for both raw materials and materials in work-in-process.

c. Many JIT production systems are highly automated; direct labor may be insignificant relative to machine costs. Production expansion in the 1990's has not been followed by the traditional employment increase that follows an economic upturn.

d. One account, conversion costs, is frequently used to account for direct labor and factory overhead costs. In a JIT system, workers are expected to be multiskilled capable of performing many tasks. In fact, several functions traditionally done by service workers such as routine maintenance is done by the cell workers. Traditioally, service work is done by overhead workers whereas many of these tasks in a JIT system is done by the cell workers.

e. Another facet associated with JIT is the use of flexible manufacturing systems(FMS) consisting of groupings of several different types of machines together in a manufacturing cell so they can do a variety of operations in sequence. Products move from one machine to another until finished for that operation. The unit is then moved to another cell operation for additional work. Often the different cells are connected with an automated material-handling system(AMHS) which may be computer controlled (computer-integrated manufacturing system-CIM).

f. As a final point, if a company has a tremendous number of component materials and parts, it may be too costly to maintain a JIT control system for each part. In this case, the ABC inventory analysis can be used to prioritize parts based on unit and dollar volume. The higher priority parts become candidates for JIT control, and the other part inventories can be controlled with simple and inexpensive inventory techniques such as a red-line system.

SELF TEST

TRUE/FALSE

1. T F

    The EOQ model is designed to tell management when to place an order for materials.

2. T F

    The reorder point depends on the quantity of materials to be ordered.

3. T F

    JIT is a "pull" inventory control system.

4. T F

    Cost accounting in a traditional manufacturing environment will probably be different than in a JIT environment.

Chapter 18: Control of Inventory and Production

5. T F

    If a firm's lead time for ordering materials was increases, the order point decreases.

6. T F

    The JIT philosophy was imported to the United States from West Germany.

7. T F

    A stockout occurs when a company does not have inventory available for sale to its customers.

8. T F

    The basic EOQ model ignores relationships between various inventory items.

9. T F

    Just-in-Time is a philosophy about when to do something.

10. T F

    Two-bin and red-line systems are used to control the highest-cost production components.

11. T F

    Economic order quantity is the amount of materials needed to maximize the total of ordering and carrying costs.

12. T F

    EOQ can be used to compute an optimal production run which minimizes the total inventory carrying costs and production set-up costs.

13. T F

    Sources of supplies for a productin process are located near the firm is one requirement for just-in-time.

MULTIPLE CHOICE

1. Which of the following are costs associated with a stock outage?

    a. lost customer goodwill
    b. the contribution margin on lost sales
    c. shipping charges for special orders
    d. all of the above.

2. Which of the following would affect the EOQ?

    a. an increase in the required safety stock
    b. an increase in the lead time
    c. an increase in ordering costs
    d. all of the above

3. Which of the following are costs associated with inventory?

    a. ordering costs
    b. carrying costs
    c. stock outage costs
    d. all of the above

Chapter 18: Control of Inventory and Production

4. Which of the following is not a carrying cost of inventory?

    a. receiving costs
    b. handling costs
    c. insurance costs
    d. storage costs

5. Which of the following is not considered in the EOQ model?

    a. estimated annual quantity of material to be used
    b. cost of placing an order
    c. order lead time
    d. cost to carry one unit in stock for a year.

6. An increase in the lead time would directly affect

    a. the safety stock.
    b. the order point.
    c. the carrying cost.
    d. the EOQ.

7. If you were uncertain about the ability of a supplier to make a timely delivery of goods you would

    a. increase the lead time.
    b. increase the safety stock.
    c. increase the EOQ.
    d. decrease the EOQ.

8. The optimal level of safety stock is determined by comparing

    a. carrying costs to ordering costs.
    b. lead times to daily usage.
    c. the cost of a stock outage to the carrying costs of safety stock.
    d. the probability of a stock outage to the probability of having excess stock.

9. EOQ would not be used in conjunction with

    a. MRP
    b. MRP II
    c. CPM
    d. JIT

10. Which of the following is not a goal of most JIT production control systems?

    a. to increase production efficiency
    b. to eliminate activities that do not add value
    c. to maintain steady inventories
    d. to reduce the total production costs

11. If a company increases the frequency with which it purchase a particular part, this could indicate

    a. that the EOQ has went up.
    b. that the lead time has went up.
    c. that carrying costs have went up.
    d. that ordering costs have went up.

12. All other factors equal, an increase in set up costs would cause management to

    a. increase the order point.
    b. increase the length of production runs.
    c. increase the safety stock.
    d. increase the number of set ups.

Chapter 18: Control of Inventory and Production

13. Which of the following is not one of the expected benefits of MRP?

    a. reduced inventory levels
    b. improved labor and space utilization
    c. streamlined production scheduling and receiving
    d. less complexity in the planning process.

14. JIT works best when

    a. production inputs are consumed at a steady rate.
    b. product demand is difficult to forecast.
    c. last minute changes in production schedules need to be accommodated.
    d. a firm has poor relations with its suppliers.

15. To be efficient, a company switching to JIT may need to

    a. deal with fewer vendors.
    b. reduce set up times.
    c. change its product design.
    d. all of the above.

16. In a JIT production environment, a Kanban is

    a. a Japanese work station.
    b. a Japanese word for "quality control."
    c. a stock room.
    d. a card used for communication between work centers.

17. Inventory levels would naturally be higher in

    a. a pull system of production control.
    b. a push system of production control.
    c. a JIT system of production control.
    d. an efficient production control environment.

18. Fewer cost allocations are required in

    a. JIT systems of production control.
    b. traditional systems of production control.
    c. machine-intensive production environments.
    d. manufacturing environments where production is stable.

19. In the JIT production control system, monitoring the quality of the product is the responsibility of

    a. all laborers.
    b. vendors.
    c. managers.
    d. all of the above.

20. In an ABC inventory analysis, the items that would most likely be controlled with a JIT system are

    a. the A items.
    b. the B items.
    c. the C items.
    d. the items accounted for with a periodic inventory.

21. A JIT inventory control systems is easier to implement if the total number of vendors is small. To minimize the number of vendors, a company should

    a. select only vendors that provide a wide variety of parts.
    b. narrow its product line.
    c. standardize component parts of different products.
    d. store large inventories of high-volume components.

Chapter 18: Control of Inventory and Production

22. Effective implementation of JIT, requires employees to be

    a. skilled in more than one production task.
    b. quality conscious.
    c. alert for ways to improve operational efficiency.
    d. all of the above.

23. An increase in the purchase price of a major component part would directly affect all of the following except

    a. the costs of carrying stock.
    b. the costs of purchasing inventory.
    c. the EOQ.
    d. the ordering costs.

24. Which of the following does not affect the economic production run?

    a. ordering costs of raw material.
    b. production set up costs.
    c. costs of carrying finished goods inventory.
    d. total estimated annual production.

25. The probability of a stockout diminishes as

    a. the lead time increases.
    b. the safety stock increases.
    c. the lead time decreases.
    d. the safety stock decreases.

26. Just-in-time (JIT) inventory systems:

    a. result in a greater number of suppliers for each production process.
    b. focus on a "push" type of production system.
    c. can only be used with automated production processes.
    d. result in inventories being either greatly reduced or eliminated.

27. Japanese manufacturing has gained world attention as a result of the synergism created by the combination of automation and

    a. CIM systems.
    b. systems provided by CNC machinery.
    c. flexible manufacturing systems.
    d. the just-in-time philosophy.

28. Just-in-time is a(n)

    a. overall operating philosophy of management
    b. computerized program for maintaining raw materials inventories that is based on the optimization of order lead times.
    c. methodology that allows the implementation of CAM technology.
    d. totally automated production facility.

29. When a company moves toward a just-in-time management philosophy and environment,

    a. direct labor takes on a new meaning, "a person who manages a work cell."
    b. direct labor workers become responsible for many tasks that previously were indirect labor functions.
    c. the environment typically becomes more capital intensive.
    d. All of the above

Chapter 18: Control of Inventory and Production

30. A JIT environment has smaller inventories than the traditional manufacturing environment. As a result,

    a. larger production lot sizes are the rule, to realize the cost-effectiveness of long production runs.
    b. there are more work stoppages in the JIT environment because of more frequent machine setups.
    c. the JIT environment experiences a lower inventory turnover ratio than the traditional environment.
    d. the amount of working capital required increases.

31. An effective just-in-time work environment should

    a. set reasonable and attainable goals for direct labor employees.
    b. encourage continuous improvement of the work environment.
    c. generate more waste because of its high quality standards.
    d. ignore employees' suggestions.

32. The normal cost of finished goods sold should include actual cost of direct labor plus:

    a. actual cost of direct materials.
    b. applied costs of factory overhead.
    c. actual cost of factory overhead.
    d. both a and c above.
    e. both a and b above.

33. JIT manufacturing differs from traditional manufacturing in all of the following ways except:

    a. the treatment of direct materials and direct labor for product costing
    b. the level of inventories
    c. the approach to quality control
    d. the physical layout of the manufacturing process

34. Using the JIT philosophy, the entry to record the purchase of raw materials would be

    a. Purchases   XX
            Accounts Payable   XX
    b. Raw Materials Inventory   XX
            Accounts Payable   XX
    c. Raw-in-Process Inventory   XX
            Accounts Payable   XX
    d. Accounts Payable   XX
            Purchases   XX

QUESTIONS AND PROBLEMS

1. What costs affect the economic order quantity?

2. What are safety stocks?

Chapter 18: Control of Inventory and Production

3. What are the differences between push and pull inventory control systems?

4. Describe the differences between traditional inventory control systems and the JIT system.

5. How is the order point determined?

6. The Bowery company estimates that it will consume 300,000 bushels of rye in the coming year in the production of its new breakfast cereal. Each bushel of rye will cost the company $3.00. Insurance, storage costs, handling costs, and property taxes are expected to cost approximately $.50/bushel/year. The company purchases the grain from a local grain elevator. Each grain order (regardless of the quantity of grain ordered) will cost Bowery $500. If Bowery's cost of capital is 16%, compute the economic order quantity for the rye.

7. Refer to the information in the preceding question. What is the total sum that the Bowery company can expect to spend in the coming year for ordering and carrying costs?

8. Refer to the information in Problem 6 above. The Bowery company operates its production operations 300 days/year. The lead time between ordering the grain and receiving the grain is 10 working days. The company desires to maintain a safety stock inventory of 10,000 bushels. Compute the company's order point in bushels.

Chapter 18: Control of Inventory and Production

9. The McRyan Corp. produces a variety of components for electric motors. One component is a magnetic coil. The company estimates that it will require production of 20,000 magnetic coils in the coming year. Setup costs for producing the magnetic coils are estimated at $1,000. The costs of carrying one magnetic coil in inventory for a year are estimated at $2.00. What is the economic production quantity for the coil.

10. Refer to the information in the preceding problem. McRyan is concerned about a stock outage on the magnetic coil and has decided to examine the feasibility of carrying a safety stock inventory. The company is considering 3 alternative levels of the safety stock: 1,000 units, 2,000 units, and 3,000 units. The company estimates the cost of a stock outage at $2,000. It estimates the probability of a stockout occurring at 60% with no safety stock, 50% with a 1,000 unit safety stock, 40% with a 2,000 unit safety stock, and 20% with a 3,000 unit safety stock. Should the company carry a safety stock? If yes, at what level? [For this problem only, assume the company will have 5 setups during the year].

11. RedHot Company sells 20,000 units of a product annually. Incremental carrying costs are $2 per unit per year. Incremental ordering costs are $450 per order. There are 200 working days per year and the lead time is 12 days. Safety stock is 1,000 units.

    The cost of ordering five times per year is $_____ for carrying costs and $_____ for ordering costs.

    The EOQ is _____ units

    The reorder point is _____ units.

COMMUNICATION PROJECT

From the true-false and multiple choice questions at the end of Study Guide chapter, with the answers covered up with a sheet of paper, the instructor will go around the class and ask each student to stand up and answer a specific question along with an explanation of why that answer was chosen. This will be done until each question is answer by a student

210   Chapter 18: Control of Inventory and Production

SELF TEST SOLUTIONS

TRUE/FALSE

    1. T   3. T   5. F   7. F   9. T
    2. F   4. T   6. T   8. T   10. F

MULTIPLE CHOICE

    1. A   6. D   11. A   16. B   21. D   26. D   31. B
    2. D   7. A   12. B   17. D   22. C   27. D   32. E
    3. D   8. C   13. C   18. A   23. D   28. A   33. A
    4. C   9. A   14. B   19. D   24. A   29. D   34. C
    5. B   10. C   15. C   20. C   25. B   30. B

QUESTIONS AND PROBLEMS

1. The economic order quantity is determined by considering the carrying costs associated with inventory (such as insurance, property taxes, and storage costs), and the ordering costs.

2. Safety stocks are levels of raw, in process, or finished goods inventory that protect a firm from stock outages due to many potential factors: excess demand, errors in estimating lead times, actual production in excess of planned production during the lead time, excessive waste of materials, machinery breakdowns, etc..

3. In pull systems, the pace and level of production at each work center is controlled by the next down stream work center. The goal is to keep the production flowing through the work centers at a pace which is ultimately controlled by the last work center, which in turn is paced by market demand. The idea with a push system is to maintain production at a constant level and push the inventory down stream to the queue for the next work station. Higher levels of inventory would be expected in a push system at all stages of completion.

4. Traditional inventory and production control systems view inventory as a positive organization element. Inventory levels buffer the organization from judgmental errors, fluctuations in product demand, unexpected developments such as machine breakdowns or labor strikes, and provide assurances that shortages of key materials or components will not shut production down. JIT considers inventory to be an undesirable organizational element. The inventory prohibits managerial discovery of methods to improve quality and efficiency. Since the inventory hides problems that management should expose and solve, the more that inventory is reduced, the more potential there is for improving the quality and efficiency of the organization.

5. The order point is determined by comparing the lead time (the time that elapses between the placement of an order and the delivery of the material) to daily consumption of the material. If safety stock is desired, the equation to compute the order point is:

    Order point =(Lead time * Daily usage) + Safety stock.

6. Remember, the total carrying costs include the opportunity cost of capital. Therefore total carrying costs for one bushel of rye would be $.50 + .16*($3.00) = $.68

    The EOQ would be:
        EOQ = SQRT [(2*300,000*$500)/$.68] = approximately 21,000 bushels

7. The total costs would be the sum of the ordering and carrying costs. Since the EOQ is 21,000 bushels, we would need to order 300,000/21,000 times during the year = 15 times. Therefore, total ordering costs would be: 15 * $500 = $7,500 and the total carrying costs would be: (21,000/2)*.68 = <u>7,140</u> and total costs would be: $14,640

Chapter 18: Control of Inventory and Production

8. The order point is equal to the consumption of rye during the lead time plus the safety stock. If the company operates 300 days/year, daily consumption is: 300,000/300 = 1,000 bushels. The order point would be: (10 * 1,000) + 10,000 = 20,000 bushels.

9. To answer this problem, we adapt the EOQ model. The Economic Production Quantity is: EPQ = SQRT [(2 * 20,000 * $1,000)/$2] = 4,472 units (rounded)

10.

Costs of a stockout

Sfty stk	pr. stkout	# orders/yr.	wted pr.	stkout cost	total cost
0	.60	5	3	$2,000	$6,000
1,000	.50	5	2.5	2,000	5,000
2,000	.40	5	2.0	2,000	4,000
3,000	.20	5	1.0	2,000	2,000

Costs of carrying safety stock

Sfty stk	carrying cost	total cost
0	$2.00	$ 0
1,000	2.00	2,000
2,000	2.00	4,000
3,000	2.00	6,000

Costs of stockout and carrying costs combined

sfty stk	carrying costs	stkout costs	total costs
0	$ 0	6,000	$6,000
1,000	2,000	5,000	7,000
2,000	4,000	4,000	8,000
3,000	6,000	2,000	8,000

No, the firm should not carry any safety stock. The least cost alternative is to carry no safety stock.

11. [(20,000/5)/2] * $2 = $4,000 carrying costs
$450 * 5 = $2,250 ordering cost

EOQ = 3,000 units

$$EOQ = \sqrt{(2QO)/C}$$

EOQ = SQRT (2 * 20,000 * $450)/$2 = 3,000

ROP = [(20,000/200) * 12] + 1,000 = 2,200

CHAPTER 19
BASICS OF CAPITAL BUDGETING

CHAPTER OVERVIEW

Some of the most fundamentally important decisions made by managers are those which result in the selection of the organizational technology to design, produce, market, and distribute products and services. The capital budget is a very important tool to aid managers in this decision process.

The capital budget is management's plan to acquire long-lived assets. In Chapter 16, it was noted that the master budget could be subdivided into operating and financial budgets. The capital budget is one of the financial budgets. Several capital budgets may be compiled to cover various time horizons.

The concepts discussed in this chapter rely on the general discussion of budgets from Chapter 16 and the discussion of relevant costs in Chapter 15. The general idea is to determine which projects will be included in the capital budget and which projects will be rejected. This selection process relies on two types of decisions. The first decision requires selection of particular investments from a set of mutually exclusive alternatives. The second type of decision requires selection of investments by comparing investment returns to more general criteria. Chapters 19 and 20 present techniques and concepts that are useful in making the investment selection decisions.

CHAPTER STUDY GUIDE

1. The choices that an organization makes regarding its investment in fixed assets are crucial to the organization's success.

    a. These choices determine the technology that the organization will use to compete in its various product and service markets.

2. Most organizations rely on capital budgeting techniques that consider the time value of money. These techniques explicitly recognize that $1 received in the future is worth less than $1 received today, because $1 received today can be invested today and earn interest while $1 to be received in the future cannot be invested today.

    a. For example, if a dollar can be invested today to yield an annual return of 8%, in one year the investor will have $1.08; the investor is not indifferent between receiving $1 today or $1 in a year.

3. Capital budgeting techniques which recognize the time value of money use cash flow information rather than accrual accounting information about investments. No cash flow is connected with some accrual accounting expenses (such as depreciation) and revenues (credit sales). Only cash can be invested to yield a cash return. The timing of noncash expenses or revenues is irrelevant because no opportunity is sacrificed or obtained to generate cash returns.

4. Comparing cash flows occurring in different time periods must be restated so that each cash flow is measured in equivalent values at a specific point in time.

Chapter 19: Capital Asset Selection and Capital Budgeting

    a. For example, you are looking at a time line that runs from this moment to a point exactly 10 years in the future. Managers could restate each cash flow in terms of its future value in 10 years or 5 years or any other specific point in time. Normally managers prefer all cash flows to be restated in terms of what they are worth today (present value). Cash flows occurring at the initiation of an investment take place in time period 0; all other cash flows are referenced from that point in time. For example, if an investment is initiated on January 1, 1994, then January 1, 1994 is time period 0 and January 1, 1995 is time period 1, January 1, 1996 is time period 2, etc..

5. Restating future cash flows in terms of their present value is called discounting. To discount cash flows, managers first need to select a discount rate.

    a. A commonly used discount rate is a company's weighted average cost of capital. The cost of capital is the (weighted) average return required by all the investors who provide long-term capital to the organization. Discount factors to be used for various time periods and interest rates are found in Appendix B. Even cash flows occurring on an annual basis are called annuities. One set of tables in Appendix A are useful for discounting annuities and the other set of tables is useful for discounting single-sum cash flows.

6. Several techniques are used to a compare potential investments with each other or some preset criterion. Net present value (NPV) is a method that deducts the present value of all cash outflows from the present value of all cash inflows. The difference between the two is NPV. A positive NPV is means the project is acceptable. A negative NPV indicates the project is unacceptable. If NPV is used to compare two projects, the project with the larger NPV ranks highest.

7. Another popular discounted cash flow technique is the internal rate of return (IRR). IRR is the discount rate that equates the present value of cash inflows with the present value of cash outflows(oftentimes the initial investment). An investment is acceptable if the IRR is equal to or greater than some preset rate known as the hurdle rate (which is usually the cost of capital). The project is rejected if the IRR is lower than the hurdle rate. If IRR is used to compare two or more projects, the project with the highest IRR is selected.

8. The NPV method is often preferred to the IRR method because it relies on milder assumptions. Reinvestment of cash flows take place at the specified discount rate, not the IRR rate which may be higher than is currently obtainable.

9. The NPV method does not allow a very meaningful rank comparison of projects of unequal size. As a result, the profitability index (PI) was developed. The PI is a ratio of the net present value of all cash flows occurring in future periods to the time period 0's current net cash outflow net investment. A larger PI is an indication of a larger return for each $1 invested. The PI is used as a basis to compare two or more competing projects rather than as a general criterion to screen investments. Projects of unequal size can't be readily compared using only the NPV method.

10. Besides the three capital budgeting techniques which rely on discounted cash flow analysis, the text discusses two techniques which do not explicitly recognize the time value of money. These techniques are the "payback period" and the "accounting rate of return."

    a. The payback period is the amount of time that passes between the initial investment and the recovery of the net initial investment. By itself this method is ineffectual to select investments because it ignores the time value of money and all cash flows which occur after the payback. But it is useful as a companion to discounted cash flow techniques. It may measure an element of investment risk since managers have more information and more certainty about cash flows which occur in the near future than in the distant future. An increasing payback period increases the riskiness of the investment.

Chapter 19: Capital Asset Selection and Capital Budgeting

b. The accounting rate of return (ARR) is the last capital budgeting technique discussed in Chapter 19. The accounting rate of return is based on accounting data (which is readily available from accounting records) rather than cash flow data (which is not readily available from accounting records). If ARR is used as an investment criterion, the actual investment performance can easily be observed in the accounting records over the life of the investment, and the actual and estimated performance can be readily compared. Computationaly, many different versions of the ARR are used. The text identifies the relative advantages of computing ARR as the ratio of the average annual investment profits to the average annual investment.

11. Hi-Tech investments are automated equipment items which can be evaluated using discounted cash flow capital budgeting techniques but care must be used. The discount rate used may underestimate the desirability of the project. Interrelatedness of several hi-tech machines should be considered. Qualitative factors associated with these machine should also be considered. Finally the opportunity cost of not automating when compared to competitors should be considered.

12. To understand the contribution that each of these five capital budgeting techniques offer, it is important that one understand the assumptions that underlie each method and the limitations of each method. Exhibit 19-10 provides insight into these issues. Also, it is highly recommended that you become familiar with the terms in the Glossary, and carefully study the Solution Strategies and the Demonstration Problem at the end of Chapter 20.

SELF TEST

TRUE/FALSE

1. T F

    The payback method is based on accounting data rather than cash flow data.

2. T F

    An annuity is a cash flow that is repeated in two or more periods of an investment's life.

3. T F

    Discounted cash flow analysis normally relies on an assumption that all cash flows occur at the end of each period.

4. T F

    The profitability index ignores the time-value of money.

5. T F

    If the discount rate is zero, the future value and the present value of a cash flow are the same.

6. T F

    If a project's NPV = 0, the project's IRR = 0 also.

7. T F

    Discounted cash flow techniques (such as NPV and IRR) assume that cash inflows are not reinvested.

8. T F

    The accounting rate of return considers depreciation in measuring the average annual investment profits.

Chapter 19: Capital Asset Selection and Capital Budgeting

9. T F

    The profitability index is a ratio of the present value of all cash inflows to the present value of all cash outflows.

10. T F

    The payback method completely ignores all cash flows which occur after the payback period.

MULTIPLE CHOICE

Note: Please refer to Appendix A to obtain required discount factors.

1. A capital asset would include all of the following except

    a. inventory.
    b. a computer.
    c. a production machine.
    d. a long-term factory lease.

2. Most companies use _____ as the discount rate in evaluating capital projects.

    a. their bank's prime lending rate
    b. their cost of capital
    c. their return on stockholders equity
    d. the interest rate on U. S. treasury bonds

3. A certain project has a cash outflow at time 0 and cash inflows in time periods 1 to 5. All other factors equal, an increase in the discount rate that is used to evaluate the project will

    a. increase the project's NPV.
    b. decrease the project's profitability index.
    c. decrease the project's internal rate of return.
    d. all of the above.

4. If a project has a positive net present value, the project's internal rate of return

    a. will be less than the project's discount rate.
    b. will be the same as the project's discount rate.
    c. will be greater than the project's discount rate.
    d. will have a relationship to the project's discount rate that cannot be determined from this information.

5. If a project has major cash inflows in the early years of its life and major cash outflows in the latter part of its life

    a. it must have a negative net present value.
    b. it must have a negative internal rate of return.
    c. it must have a positive net present value.
    d. it may have multiple internal rates of return.

6. Which of the following capital budgeting techniques ignores the time value of money?

    a. internal rate of return
    b. net present value
    c. present value index
    d. payback

Chapter 19: Capital Asset Selection and Capital Budgeting

7. Which of the following capital budgeting techniques recognizes noncash revenues and expenses?

    a. payback
    b. accounting rate of return
    c. internal rate of return
    d. net present value

8. A comparison of competing investments can be made based on a comparison of

    a. net present values.
    b. internal rates of return.
    c. profitability indexes.
    d. all of the above.

9. In a comparison of two projects, one project would be considered less risky than the other if

    a. it has a lower payback.
    b. it has a lower NPV.
    c. it has a lower IRR.
    d. it has a lower PI.

10. When NPV is used as a criterion to evaluate investments, the method implicitly assumes that all cash inflows over the life of the project are reinvested

    a. at the internal rate of return.
    b. at the discount rate.
    c. in projects that yield no return.
    d. at the cost of capital.

11. If an analyst uses a discount rate of 12% compounded annually instead of a simple rate of 12%, future cash flows

    a. will have a lower present value.
    b. will have a larger present value.
    c. will have a lower present value if they are cash inflows and a larger present value if they are cash outflows.
    d. will have a larger present value if they are cash inflows and a lower present value if they are cash outflows.

12. Which of the following methods treat project cash flows as deterministic rather than probabilistic?

    a. IRR
    b. NPV
    c. Payback
    d. all of the above

13. Interpolation is a mathematical procedure that may be required to determine a project's

    a. NPV.
    b. PI.
    c. IRR.
    d. Payback period.

14. A $100,000 investment in working capital would appear in a discounted cash flow analysis as

    a. a cash outflow in time 0.
    b. a cash outflow in year 1.
    c. a cash outflow at time 0 and a cash inflow in the terminal year of the project.
    d. a cash inflow in the terminal year of the project.

Chapter 19: Capital Asset Selection and Capital Budgeting

15. A negative NPV indicates

    a. the total amount of cash outflows exceed the total amount of cash inflows.
    b. the PI is negative.
    c. the project's IRR is negative.
    d. the present value of all cash inflows is less than the present value of all cash outflows.

16. An NPV of 0 is an indication that

    a. there is no return of capital.
    b. there is no return on capital.
    c. the return on capital is equal to the discount rate.
    d. the PI = 0.

17. With respect to a specific project, which of the following changes would not result in an increase in both the project's IRR and NPV?

    a. a decrease in the discount rate.
    b. a decrease in the initial investment outlay.
    c. an increase in estimated future cash inflows.
    d. a decrease in estimated future cash outflows.

18. An analyst may need to resort to a trial and error process to determine a project's

    a. payback period.
    b. IRR.
    c. NPV.
    d. PI.

19. Differences between actual investment cash flows and estimated investment cash flows are disclosed in

    a. the firm's variance analysis.
    b. the post-investment audit.
    c. responsibility center evaluations.
    d. the firm's published financial statements.

20. A project consists of one cash outflow at the initiation of the investment followed by a sporadic series of cash inflows. An assumption that all future cash flows occur at the end of each period will result in

    a. a computed NPV that is less than the true NPV.
    b. a computed IRR that is greater than the true IRR.
    c. a computed accounting rate of return that is less than the true accounting rate of return.
    d. none of the above.

21. In a discounted cash flow analysis, to reflect uncertainty about the amount of a future cash outflow, an analyst could

    a. use a smaller estimate for the future cash flow.
    b. use a smaller discount rate.
    c. increase the discounting period.
    d. all of the above.

22. In an NPV analysis, if the IRR is used as the discount rate, the NPV will

    a. be negative.
    b. be positive.
    c. possibly be negative or positive.
    d. be equal to zero.

Chapter 19: Capital Asset Selection and Capital Budgeting

23. A change in depreciation method could affect a project's

    a. payback.
    b. NPV.
    c. accounting rate of return.
    d. payback and accounting rate of return.

24. A project's profitability is completely ignored by the

    a. IRR method.
    b. NPV method.
    c. payback method.
    d. accounting rate of return method.

25. A comparison of two competing capital projects should be based on

    a. all future cash flows.
    b. all future cash receipts.
    c. all relevant cash flows.
    d. all future cash disbursements and receipts.

QUESTIONS AND PROBLEMS

1. What is the relationship between a project's IRR and its NPV?

2. Why is NPV a poor basis to compare two projects which are not mutually exclusive?

3. Under what circumstances is the IRR more difficult to compute than other techniques discussed in Chapter 19?

4. Why is it important that the payback method be used in conjunction with other techniques to evaluate capital projects, rather than as a "stand alone" evaluation measure?

Use the following information for hte next three questions:

The Pupont Co. is considering an investment in the following project:

Required initial investment	$900,000
Net annual cash inflow	150,000
Annual depreciation	50,000
Estimated salvage value	150,000
Life of the project	15 years

Chapter 19: Capital Asset Selection and Capital Budgeting

5. Compute the payback period on the proposed investment.

6. Compute the accounting rate of return on the proposed project.

7. Compute the internal rate of return on the proposed project.

8. The Johnson Company recently completed the analysis of a project requiring an initial investment of $130,972, and determined that the project has an internal rate of return of 16%. The only cash inflow generated by this project is in the form of an annuity which lasts 5 years. If the Johnson Company uses their cost of capital of 12% as a hurdle rate, what is the NPV of the project?

Use the following information for the next two quesitons:

McDuck Enterprises is considering an investment in a new project. The investment is expected to generate annual savings in cash operating costs of $8,000 for the next seven years. The project would require an initial cash outlay of $34,048 and this cost would be depreciated fully over the project's life using the straight line method. The project is expected to have no salvage value at the end of 7 years. McDuck's cost of capital is 16%.

9. What is the NPV of the proposed project?

10. What is the IRR of the proposed project?

COMMUNICATION PROJECT

With one person of your class work group, explain how the NPV method differs from the IRR method of capital budgeting. Next ask your partner to restate what you just told him. If you disagree with him, explain how you disagree.

Chapter 19: Capital Asset Selection and Capital Budgeting

SELF TEST SOLUTIONS

TRUE/FALSE

1. F	3. T	5. T	7. F	9. F
2. T	4. F	6. F	8. T	10. T

MULTIPLE CHOICE

1. A	6. D	11. A	16. C	21. B
2. B	7. B	12. D	17. A	22. D
3. B	8. D	13. C	18. B	23. C
4. C	9. A	14. C	19. B	24. C
5. D	10. B	15. D	20. A	25. A

QUESTIONS AND PROBLEMS

1. A project's net present value is determined based on a specific discount rate. When that specific discount rate happens to be the IRR, the NPV on the project will be 0 (by definition of IRR). A lower discount rate will result in a positive NPV and a higher discount rate will result in a lower NPV.

2. NPV is an inferior basis to compare projects that are not mutually exclusive because NPV fails to capture the relative size of the projects and the lengths of the projects. For example, the project with the larger NPV may require a substantially larger investment than the project with the second highest NPV. NPV does not indicate relative profitability. The present value index is a much better basis to compare projects which are not directly competing with each other.

3. The IRR can only be computed on a trial and error basis unless all cash flows beyond time period 0 are in the form of an annuity. The cost of the trial and error process in time and effort can be minimized using computer-based technology.

4. The payback method ignores all cash flows beyond the payback period. If two projects have similar payback periods, the cash flows beyond the payback period will be very important in determining which project is selected, but the payback method does not consider these cash flows. If used in conjunction with discounted cash flow methods, the payback method can provide information about relative risk and the discounted cash flow methods can provide information about relative profitability.

5. The payback period is found by dividing the initial investment by the net annual cash inflow: $900,000/$150,000 = 6 years.

6. The accounting rate of return is found by dividing the average annual profit by the average annual investment. The average annual profit is the net annual cash inflow less depreciation: $150,000 - $50,000 = $100,000. The average annual investment is equal to the average book value of the investment: ($900,000 + $150,000)/2 = $525,000. The accounting rate of return = $100,000/$525,000 = 19.05%.

7. Since the cash inflows are irregular (because of the salvage value received in year 15), the IRR can only be found using trial and error or a preprogrammed calculator or computer. Through a trial and error process, you should determine that the IRR is just slightly below 15%.

8. First, determine the amount of the annual cash inflow. You must utilize the definition of IRR to make this computation. Given the initial outlay of $130,972 and the definition of IRR, we know that the present value of the cash inflows (using a discount rate of 16%) is also $130,972. We also know that the discount factor for an annuity discounted at 16% for 5 years is 3.2743 (from the tables in Appendix A). The annual cash inflow is found by dividing the present value of the net cash inflows, $130,972, by the discount factor 3.2743 = $40,000. Now, discount the $40,000 net annual cash inflow by the discount factor associated with a discount rate of 12% on an

annuity lasting 5 years. This yields a present value for the cash inflows of $144,192, and the NPV = $144,192 − $130,972 = $13,220.

9. The NPV is found by deducting the initial outlay from the present value of the cash inflows. The present value of the cash inflows is (4.0386 * $8,000) = $32,309. The NPV of the project is: $32,309 − $34,048 = ($1,739).

10. We know that the IRR for the project is the discount rate that will yield an NPV of 0. Since the company's hurdle rate is 16% and yields a negative NPV, the IRR must be somewhere below 16%. In this instance, we directly compute the IRR without resorting to a trial and error approach. If we divide the initial investment by the net annual cash inflow, the result is equal to the discount factor associated with the IRR for an annuity lasting 7 years. That discount factor is: $34,048/$8,000 = 4.256. Now, referring to the annuity tables, we discover that the discount factor of 4.256 lies between the discount factors associated with 14 and 14.5%. Using interpolation, we find that this project has an IRR of about 14.25%.

CHAPTER 20
ADVANCED CAPITAL BUDGETING TOPICS

CHAPTER OVERVIEW

One of the more difficult aspects of capital budgeting is setting the hurdle or discount rate. As mentioned in Chapter 20, the cost of capital is generally regarded as the minimum acceptable hurdle rate. Therefore, it is very important that the cost of capital be known to the analysts of potential capital projects. Unfortunately, the actual cost of capital is a visible number.

The best an analyst can do is to use a "good" estimate of the true cost of capital. One way to estimate the cost of capital is to use an average of the estimated cost of each capital component (capital components include debt, common equity, and preferred equity). Typically, this estimate of the cost of capital would use a "weighted" average of the estimated capital-component costs.

Chapter 20 provides a discussion of techniques that may be used to estimate the cost of each capital component and the weighted average cost of capital. The chapter also considers other factors that may be important in setting the capital budget. In particular, the chapter considers: the impact of uncertainty regarding cash flow estimates, the impact of income taxes on cash flows and accounting accruals, and issues to consider in attempting to rank alternative capital projects when insufficient capital is available to fund all available capital projects.

CHAPTER STUDY GUIDE

1. Before considering the issues that are involved in estimating the cost of capital, let's first consider the impact of income taxes on organizational cash flows. Income taxes are levied on some measure of "net income" (technically this is referred to as taxable income). Net income is an accounting concept, not a cash flow concept. This simply means that both cash flows and accounting accruals (such as depreciation, and book gains or losses on the disposal of an asset) can affect the magnitude of the tax payment.

    a. Depreciation is ignored in the "pre-tax" discounted cash flow analysis of Chapter 19. The tax effect of depreciation is considered in this chapter.

    b. To illustrate, assume that a company faces a marginal income tax rate of 40%. Also, assume that a potential project will generate a depreciation deduction of $100,000 in year 1.

        i. While the depreciation itself is ignored in a discounted cash flow analysis, the tax effect of the depreciation is not ignored. In this case, the depreciation deduction will reduce the firm's total tax liability (which is a real cash flow) by $40,000. The $40,000 is computed by multiplying the tax rate by the amount of depreciation: $100,0000 * .40.

        ii. In addition to accounting accruals such as depreciation, taxes also affect real cash flows. This is true whether the cash flows are inflows or outflows. For example, assume that a company is

Chapter 20: Advanced Capital Bugeting Techniques

considering a project that will decrease cash operating costs by $100,000/year. The after-tax benefit of the savings in operating costs is less than $100,000, because the tax liability of the firm rises as its income rises. If the firm faces a tax rate of 40%, the cost savings will generate additional taxes of $40,000 ($100.000 * .40). The cost savings are only $60,000 after-taxes.

iii. In general, the after-tax amount of a deductible cash outflow can be found by multiplying the pre-tax amount by the quantity: (1 - tax rate). The same formula applies to converting pre-tax revenue to after-tax revenue. Simply multiply the pre-tax revenue by the quantity: (1 - tax rate), and the result is the after-tax revenue. If a cash outflow is not deductible, or if a cash inflow is not taxable, the after-tax cash flow is the same as the pre-tax cash flow. [Note, also, tax laws often specify which depreciation methods are permissible and which cash flows are deductible.]

2. The most difficult aspect of estimating the cost of capital for any firm is estimating the cost of common equity. Estimating the cost of debt and preferred stock is relatively easy. The first thing to keep in mind in estimating the cost of capital is that it is a concept based on market values, and to estimate the cost of capital, market values of each capital component should be used rather than book values of each capital component.

a. For example, consider the book and market values of each capital component for the Frost Co.:

	Book Value	%	Market Value	%
Common stockholders equity	$1,000,000	33	$1,500,000	38
Preferred stockholders equity	500,000	17	250,000	6
Debt	1,500,000	50	2,250,000	56
Total	3,000,000	100	4,000,000	100

The relative weights of the capital components of Frost Co. are 56% debt, 6% preferred equity, and 38% common equity.

b. The cost of debt in the capital structure is found by dividing the total annual interest payment to the debtholders by the market value of the debt. For example, assume that the annual interest payment to debtholders of the Frost Co. totals $250,000. The interest payment is deductible for tax purposes. If the Frost Co. has a marginal tax rate of 30%, the after-tax payment to debtholders would be: $250,000 * (1 - .30) = $175,000. The cost of debt would be $175,000/$2,250,000 = approximately 7.8% (the after-tax interest cost is divided by the market value of the debt, not the book value).

c. Preferred equity is treated similarly to that of debt. The total annual dividend payment to preferred stockholders is divided by the market value of the preferred stock. Unlike debt, the dividend payment to stockholders (preferred or common) is not deductible for tax purposes. The pre-tax and after-tax payment to preferred stockholders is the same. For the Frost Co., the total annual dividend payment to preferred stockholders is $22,500. The cost of the preferred stock would be $22,500/$250,000 = 9%.

d. Estimating the cost of the common equity is more difficult because there is no contract that stipulates a specific periodic dividend that must be paid to common stockholders. Most companies have a dividend policy that is useful in estimating the cost of common equity.

i. Many methods can be used to estimate the cost of common equity, this text presents one of the most popular tools. The model assumes that the cost of equity is a function of the dividend yield (the annual dividend payment divided by the market value of the common equity) plus the expected growth rate in the dividend payment over time.

Chapter 20: Advanced Capital Bugeting Techniques

        ii.   For example, assume that the total dividend payment to common stockholders of the Frost Co. is expected to be $75,000 in the coming year. This payment is expected to grow at the rate of 9%/year in the future. The cost of the common equity would be: $75,000/$1,500,000 + .09 = 14%.

        iii.   The cost of the common equity is much greater than the cost of the other capital. This is reasonable because the common stockholders face considerably greater risk than preferred stockholders or debtholders.

    e.   The final step to find the weighted average cost of capital is to combine the costs of all three elements of capital. Market weights are used for finding the weighted average.

        i.   For the Frost Co. the weighted average cost of capital would be: (.38 * 7.8%) + (.06 * 9%) + (.56 * 14%) = 11.34%.

        ii.   This weighted average cost of capital is used in the capital budgeting models.

3.   When a company has a limited amount of capital for expansion, it must decide in which projects it will invest and which projects will be rejected. Initially, a company may simply "screen" all projects by comparing the expected return on each project to some preset criterion.

    a.   If the cost of capital is used as the criterion, the company would initially accept all projects that generate an IRR equal to or greater than the cost of capital. This is the equivalent of initially accepting all projects with an NPV that is greater than or equal to 0 (when using the cost of capital as the discount rate), or a present value index greater than or equal to 1.

    b.   From this initial set of projects, management will typically need to consider additional eliminations for two reasons. First, some projects may be mutually exclusive; second, the available supply of capital may be insufficient to fund all projects that passed the initial screening process.

    c.   By ranking the projects, management can determine which projects are "preferred" over others. While NPV, IRR, and PVI, can each be used to rank capital projects, it is very likely that no unique ranking of the projects will emerge if all three methods are employed (see the text's discussion on the different assumptions about reinvestment rates for each method).

        i.   Because NPV and PVI are based on milder assumptions about the rate at which cash inflows are reinvested and are more consistent with the goal of maximizing the value of the firm, they are generally the preferred methods to rank projects.

    d.   For projects that require a similar initial investment, NPV can be used as a basis of comparison.

    e.   PVI is preferred for a comparison of projects requiring different levels of initial investment.

    f.   Under capital rationing conditions, the IRR method in conjunction with NPV or PVI may improve the capital allocation process.

4.   The final topic in Chapter 20 deals with techniques that can be used to compare projects when the projects have cash flows that are unequal in terms of risk (uncertainty). Three specific techniques are identified to adjust project cash flows for risk; two of the methods involve formal approaches. All three methods involve subjective judgment on the part of the analyst.

    a.   One formal method to adjust for risk is to use a discount rate that is commensurate with the level of risk. In other words, a higher discount rate can be used for cash inflows that have higher levels of risk.

Chapter 20: Advanced Capital Budgeting Techniques

    b.   The other formal way to consider the impact of risk is to conduct sensitivity analysis. Sensitivity analysis systematically changes the estimates of the project life, cash flows, and discount rate to examine the "sensitivity" of the NPV or IRR to changes in these estimates.

5. There is a tremendous amount of information contained in Chapter 20. For a complete understanding of the important concepts, this chapter will require considerably more time than most of the other chapters. Make sure you commit the time to read the chapter several times and carefully study the examples.

SELF TEST

TRUE/FALSE

1. T F

    The Fisher rate is used to conduct sensitivity analysis on proposed capital projects.

2. T F

    From a mutually exclusive set of capital projects, only one project will be chosen.

3. T F

    The weighted average cost of capital is based on the "book" weights of the capital components.

4. T F

    The dividend growth method is a formal method of measuring the cost of preferred stock.

5. T F

    In a pre-tax analysis of cash flows, depreciation is ignored.

6. T F

    An after-tax cash flow can be found by multiplying the pre-tax cash flow by the quantity: (1 - the marginal tax rate).

7. T F

    In the screening decision, the three project evaluation methods (IRR, NPV, and PVI) are likely to provide conflicting indications of which projects are acceptable.

8. T F

    The IRR method of project evaluation assumes that all cash inflows can be immediately reinvested at the IRR.

9. T F

    For purposes of ranking projects, the NPV method is preferred to the IRR method, because it relies on milder assumptions about the rate that can be earned on the reinvestment of cash inflows.

10. T F

    All cash inflows and outflows are subject to income tax.

11. T F

    Payback Period is the reciprocal of Accounting Rate of Return.

12. T F

The primary difference between payback period and accounting rate of return is depreciation.

MULTIPLE CHOICE

1. In the following formula: X = Y(1-t), t is the firm's tax rate, and

    a. X is the pre-tax cash flow.
    b. Y is the after-tax cash flow.
    c. X is an accounting accrual only (X does not represent an actual cash flow).
    d. X is the tax on the cash flow.

2. In the formula k= (D/MP) + g, k is

    a. the weighted average cost of capital.
    b. the cost of preferred equity.
    c. the cost of common equity.
    d. the cost of debt.

3. A firm that anticipates a constant marginal tax rate of 40% for the foreseeable future, can increase the present value of a project by

    a. using an accelerated depreciation method.
    b. increasing the discount rate.
    c. using a lower rate of depreciation.
    d. pushing cash inflows to the latter years of a project's life and accelerating cash outflows to the early years of a project's life.

4. For a profitable firm, the after-tax payback period is likely to

    a. be shorter than the pre-tax payback period.
    b. be longer than the pre-tax payback period.
    c. be the same as the pre-tax payback period.
    d. go up as the tax rate goes down.

5. When managers are willing to consider all projects that have an IRR that exceeds the cost of capital, the IRR is being used as

    a. the Fisher rate.
    b. a judgmental method.
    c. a screening tool.
    d. a preference tool.

6. If only one project can be selected from a set of projects, the set is a

    a. mutually inclusive set.
    b. discrete set.
    c. indiscrete set.
    d. mutually exclusive set.

7. The interest rate that equates the present values of the cash flows from multiple projects under consideration is

    a. the discount rate.
    b. the cost of capital.
    c. the IRR.
    d. the Fisher rate.

8. If a project has a negative NPV, the rate at which cash inflows can be reinvested is assumed to be higher in which of the following?

    a. IRR
    b. NPV
    c. PVI
    d. NPV and PVI

Chapter 20: Advanced Capital Bugeting Techniques

9. On theoretical grounds, if one primary project evaluation measure is to be used, it should be

   a. the IRR.
   b. the payback method.
   c. the NPV.
   d. the accounting rate of return.

10. As the uncertainty about a future cash flow increases, so does the project's

    a. discount rate.
    b. risk.
    c. NPV.
    d. tax rate.

11. The minimal criterion for a project to be accepted is for

    a. the NPV to be positive.
    b. the PVI to be greater than 1.
    c. the IRR to be equal to or greater than the hurdle rate.
    d. the payback period to be less than 5.

12. In January, the Shield Co. issued bonds with a total face value of $100,000. The bonds bear a coupon rate of 9% per annum and investors paid a net amount of $95,000 for the bonds. If the Shield Co. faces a marginal tax rate of 30%, what is the after-tax cost of the bonds?

    a. 6.6%
    b. 6.3%
    c. 9.0%
    d. 6.0%

13. In the formula k = (D/MP) + g, g represents

    a. the growth rate in corporate sales.
    b. the growth rate in corporate net income.
    c. the growth rate in the corporate supply of capital.
    d. the growth rate in the market value of the common equity.

14. Once the portion of debt in the capital structure of a firm increases beyond the optimal level,

    a. the cost of debt will begin to rise.
    b. the cost of common equity will begin to rise.
    c. the cost of preferred equity will begin to rise.
    d. all of the above will occur.

15. Y company sells an asset with a book value of $30,000 for $50,000. If this company faces a tax rate of 50%, the after-tax cash flow from the sale of the asset will be

    a. between $30,000 and $50,000.
    b. greater than $50,000
    c. exactly $25,000.
    d. exactly $50,000.

16. If a company is unprofitable,

    a. at the margin, its pre-tax and after-tax cash flows will be the same.
    b. it should use a more accelerated depreciation method.
    c. it should lower its discount rate.
    d. its management should not consider undertaking any additional investments.

Chapter 20: Advanced Capital Bugeting Techniques

17. Sensitivity analysis can consider the affect of errors in the estimation of

    a. the discount rate.
    b. the life of the project.
    c. the amount of the annual cash flows.
    d. all of the above.

18. Which of the following measures are affected by depreciation (when considering after-tax cash flows)?

    a. the IRR
    b. the accounting rate of return
    c. the payback
    d. all of the above

19. In a pre-tax evaluation of a project, an NPV calculation would ignore all of the following except

    a. depreciation expense.
    b. the gain or loss on the sale of an asset.
    c. the sales price of an asset.
    d. an accounting accrual for salaries and wages.

20. If the selection of one project in a set requires the selection of all other members in the set, the projects are

    a. mutually inclusive.
    b. discrete.
    c. mutually exclusive.
    d. replacements.

21. The passage of pending legislation that increases the marginal tax rate would

    a. decrease the present value of future cash inflows.
    b. decrease the present value of future cash outflows.
    c. increase the present value of a project's depreciation tax shield.
    d. do all of the above.

22. The pre-tax and after-tax cash flows would be different for

    a. the initial cash outflow to purchase a machine.
    b. the initial cash investment in working capital.
    c. the annual rent payment on leased equipment.
    d. all of the above.

23. The affect of income taxes on the cost of capital is to reduce the **after-tax** cost of

    a. debt.
    b. common equity.
    c. preferred equity.
    d. all components of capital.

24. The after-tax cash flow from the depreciation deduction is found by multiplying the amount of depreciation by

    a. 1 minus the tax rate.
    b. the tax rate.
    c. 1 divided by the tax rate.
    d. the tax rate minus 1.

25. All other things equal, a decrease in the marginal income tax rate will

    a. decrease the tax benefit of the depreciation tax shield.
    b. increase the tax benefit of the depreciation tax shield.
    c. not affect the tax benefit of the depreciation tax shield.
    d. increase the pre-tax depreciation cash flow.

26. Capital budgeting risks include all of the following except:

   a. estimated asset life.
   b. timing of cash flows.
   c. expected salvage value.
   d. changes in the tax law.
   e. all of the above.

27. A probability distribution is a(n):

   a. average of future cash flows.
   b. expected value of future cash flows.
   c. range of possible future cash flows.
   d. a standard deviation of expected cash flows.

28. Standard deviations are:

   a. the expected value of future cash flows.
   b. another name for variance.
   c. a measure of variability about the mean value.
   d. the sum of the deviations about the mean.

29. The coefficient of variation is:

   a. another name for standard deviation.
   b. better, when comparing two projects, the higher its value.
   c. the ratio of expected cash flow divided by expected standard deviation.
   d. the ratio of expected standard deviation divided by expected future cash flow.

QUESTIONS AND PROBLEMS

1. Under what conditions would a firm prefer to use a slow rate of depreciation rather than an accelerated rate of depreciation?

2. What is the ultimate criterion in choosing one method over another to rank capital projects?

3. How can an analyst explicitly deal with the fact that she has much greater uncertainty about the amount of one specific future cash inflow than all other cash inflows associated with a project?

4. Why is the cost of capital based on market values of capital components rather than book values?

5. Since income taxes play an important role in capital budgeting, do you see a role for tax policy in influencing corporate investment? Explain.

6. If debt financing is so cheap relative to equity financing (because interest payments are deductible and dividend payments are not), why don't firms simply issue all debt and no equity?

7. Johnny invests $5,000 on January 1, 1991 in a stock that historically has paid no dividends. On December 31, 1992, Johnny decides to sell the stock and receives $6,400 (after-tax) for the investment. If Johnny's marginal tax rate is 40%, what was the gross price (pre-tax) Johnny received for the stock?

8. On November 13, 1990, Billy Joe purchased stock in the Markel Company for $15,000. He sold the stock on November 18, 1993 for $11,000. If Billy Joe can use the loss on the stock to offset other taxable income, what is his after-tax cash flow from the sale of the stock (assume Billy Joe faces a marginal tax rate of 30%)?

9. The ATC Co. is considering an investment in a labor-saving machine that will have an initial cost of $300,000. The machine is expected to reduce labor costs by $90,000 for the next 5 years. It will be fully depreciated according to the straight-line method and it is expected that the machine can

be sold at the end of 5 years for $40,000. Assuming that the ATC Co. has a marginal income tax rate of 35%, what is the after-tax payback period for the investment in the machine?

10. Refer to 9. above. Compute the NPV of the machine investment assuming the ATC Co. has a weighted average cost of capital of 15%.

11. How is coefficient of variation calculated and why might it be used.

COMMUNICATION PROJECT

Source: Blue Chip Vol. 3, Seg. 11

Farr Manufacturing builds custom industrial machinery. Farr is a start-up company that needed additional capital to finance the business. The owners sought difference sources of new capital. The company has been successful in raising money and new business. It's labor force has grown from 2 employees to seventy.

1. Why do you suppose the banks originally contacted refused to lend money on the basis of Farr's contract with DuPont?

2. What do you feel is Farr's most important resource?

3. What do you think has motivated Farr's owners to provide a generous employee benefits package and to share profits with employees?

From this problem, you will learn to observe presented material in a video format. You will learn to be observant to new material presented in a video form. Businesses are presenting more of this type of material to their employees so you should become accustomed to this form of gathering information.

SELF TEST SOLUTIONS

TRUE/FALSE

1. F 3. F 5. T 7. F 9. T 11.
2. T 4. F 6. T 8. T 10. F 12.

MULTIPLE CHOICE

1. D   6. D   11. C   16. A   21. D   26. E
2. C   7. D   12. A   17. D   22. C   27. C
3. B   8. D   13. D   18. A   23. A   28. C
4. B   9. D   14. D   19. A   24. B   29. D
5. C   10. B 15. A   20. D   25. A

Chapter 20: Advanced Capital Bugeting Techniques

QUESTIONS AND PROBLEMS

1. A firm would want to use a slow rate of depreciation when it desired to preserve depreciation deductions for future time periods. Motivation to preserve the deduction for future periods could come from an expectation of rising future tax rates or an expectation of increasing profitability in the future.

2. The ultimate criterion is to choose the method that will maximize the market value of the firm. The method that is most consistent with this criterion is the one that should be used.

3. There are several things she could do. In the interest of being conservative (and thereby not overestimating the present value of that risky future cash flow), she could use a larger discount (risk-adjusted) rate for that one cash flow. Alternatively, if she is uncertain about both the amount and the timing of the cash flow she could increase the discounting period (move the cash flow to time period 10 from time period 7). Lastly, she could experiment with a range of values for the cash flow (such as in a worst and best case scenario) and examine the impact of these changes on the NPV of the project.

4. The simplest answer to this question is that the cost of capital is a concept which requires the analyst to view the firm from the investor's perspective. Investors make decisions by comparing expected returns from many securities to the prices at which they can buy and sell those securities. To acquire new capital and maintain existing capital, the firm must attract outside investors. Obviously, outside investors transact at current market prices, not book values or historical prices. The cost of capital is therefore a measure that permits analysts to compare the potential return on new projects to the required return of investors.

5. It is probably obvious that national, state, and local governments use tax policy to a significant extent in influencing corporate and individual investment. Some of the more important tax provisions that have been used in the past include: changes in the rate of depreciation for specific kinds of assets, changes in the corporate and individual tax rate, changes in the tax rate on capital gains, tax credits for investments in certain kinds of assets, and tax holidays.

6. As a matter of fact, in recent years the ratio of debt in the capital structures of U.S. corporations has risen dramatically. However, as indicated in the text, the weighted average cost of capital is assumed to represent the least costly mix of debt and equity. Beyond some optimal level, additional increments of debt will actually increase the overall cost of capital. This is due to the fact that marginal investors will require larger and larger returns to offset the additional risk that they must bear. If a firm is financed with 100% debt, the risk characteristics of that debt are the same as if the firm were financed entirely with equity. In addition, the IRS would disallow a deduction for interest payments and treat the debt as if it were equity.

7. Only the profit on the sale is taxable. The after-tax profit is $1,400 ($6,400 - $5,000). The pre-tax profit can be found by dividing the after-tax profit by the quantity (1 - tax rate). In this case, the pre-tax profit would be: $1,400/(1 - .4) = $2,333.33. The total price received for the stock must have been: $2,333.33 + $5,000 = $7,333.33.

8. The after-tax cash flow will come from two sources: the cash from the sale of the stock and the tax savings generated from the $4,000 loss on the sale. The total after-tax cash flow will be $11,000 + (.30 * $4,000) = $12,200.

9. The after-tax cash flow from the annual savings in labor costs would be $58,500 ($90,000 * .65). The after-tax cash flow from the depreciation tax shield would be $21,000 [($300,000/5) * .35]. The total annual after-tax cash flow would be $79,500 ($58,500+$21,000). This would provide a payback of 3.77 years ($300,000/$79,500).

10. Use the after-tax cash flows from question 9 to compute the NPV:

cash flow	years	after-tax amount	discount factor	present value
Investment	0	($300,000)	1.00	($300,000)
Savings in costs	1 - 5	$ 79,500	3.3522	266,500
Salvage	5	$ 26,000	.4972	12,927
		Net Present Value		($ 20,573)

11. Coefficient of variation is calculated as follows:

    V = sigma/R
    Where V is the coefficient of variation sigma is the standard deviation R is the expected cash flow V is used to rank two or more projects have about the same standard deviation but expected cash flows that are substantially different. The project with the lower coefficient of variation is the better project since it has lower risk.

CHAPTER 21

RESPONSIBILITY ACCOUNTING AND TRANSFER PRICING IN DECENTRALIZED ORGANIZATIONS

CHAPTER OVERVIEW

A major focus of Chapter 21 is on responsibility accounting. In responsibility accounting, revenues and/or expenses are reported to managers who are responsible for these items. Performance measures are generated that companion the breadth of decision-making (type of responsibility center) of lower level managers. The four types of responsibility centers are: cost, revenue, profit, and investment. The name of the center implies the type of factors the manager has control over. Be aware that accounting information is a primary basis for evaluating responsibility center performance and for compensating or rewarding managers of responsibility centers.

The decentralized organizational structure creates a unique set of problems for management when one responsibility center in an organization conducts business with another responsibility center in the same organization. Two major problems that management must resolve are: 1) determine when organizational subunits should exchange goods and services, and 2) determine the price of the goods and services to be transferred that will maintain goal congruence.

One dogma of decentralization is that subunit managers should be evaluated only on factors that are under their control. A pivotal problem of top managers is to maintain the autonomy of the subunit managers and at the same time be assured that intra-company transfers of goods and services are consistent with general organizational goals.

A transfer pricing system is employed to maintain a harmony between subunit autonomy and the duty of all subunits to the realization of overall organizational goals (which may require top level managers to encourage, or discourage, intra-company transfers of goods and services). A variety of transfer pricing systems exist. This chapter provides an introduction to the various types of transfer pricing systems and descriptions of appropriate contexts where each system should be used.

CHAPTER STUDY GUIDE

1. Chapter 21 introduces the idea that decentralized organizations evaluate subunit managers on the basis of their subunit performance. To be evaluated on this basis, subunit managers must have a certain degree of autonomy in operating the subunit. The degree of decision making in these types of firms is discussed in Exhibit 21-1. The advantages and disadvantages of decentralization are found in Exhibit 21-2.

    a. Decentralization may have negative effects on the company goals. The goals of the subunit manager, the subunit and the company may not harmonize. This is called a lack of **goal congruence**.

2. The level of authority and the types of activities under the control of each subordinate manager will determine the type of accounting information that should be used to evaluate managerial performance. Four types of responsibility centers are discussed that may be used to control the activities in decentralized organizations.

Chapter 21: Transfer Pricing for Products

    a. In a **cost** center, managerial performance is evaluated (in part) by comparing actual costs to budgeted costs. The standard costing concepts discussed in earlier chapters are utilized.

    b. **Revenue** centers are evaluated by a comparison of actual results with planned or budgeted revenues.

    c. Managers of **profit** centers have control over both costs and **revenues**. The actual profit can be compared to a budgeted level of profit to evaluate the performance of the profit center and its manager.

        i. Normally, segment margin is the key figure measured (defined as revenue minus direct variable costs and avoidable fixed costs). Because segment margin can be manipulated (see the NEWS NOTE at the beginning of the chapter), care must be used when evaluating performance.

    d. An **investment** center manager has control over both costs and **revenues**, as well as the assets that are employed by the center.

3. Decentralization has the potential for subunits of an organization to provide goods and services to each other. Intra-company transfers create problems of goal congruence.

    a. Internal transfers may be in the best interests of both **subunits** involved in an exchange, but not in the best interests of the overall organization.

    b. A transfer can be in the best interests of the overall organization, but not in the best interests of one or more subunits.

    c. Preserving goal congruence is difficult when top management bases compensation or rewards on the relative achievement of its subunits. Upper management should encourage transfers that are in the best interests of the general organization and deter transfers that are not in the organizations best interests. Transfer pricing is used to encourage/discourage transfers within the company. The proper structure of the transfer pricing system maintains subunit autonomy <u>and</u> goal congruence.

4. Intra-company transfers are likely if one division produces a good or service that another division consumes. The general rule is that (from the perspective of the overall organization) a transfer should take place between the two divisions if the selling division can produce the product at a cost (including opportunity costs, which are discussed in Chapter 15) that is below the price of any outside supplier.

    a. The model in the chapter says that an internal transfer will be priced at a level that is between the sales price of the cheapest outside supplier (maximum or ceiling price) and the cost incurred by the selling division to produce the good or service (minimum or floor price).

    b. Whether the transfer takes place depends on the inducement facing the two division managers.

        i. An exchange will occur if both autonomous managers want to enter into the transaction. Otherwise it will not. The motivation of the managers will be decided by the influence the transfer will have on their performance evaluation.

5. Three potential bases may be used for a price on internal transfers: cost, market price, or negotiated price. Within each of these three categories, an infinite number of permutations exist.

    a. For example, cost can indicate: variable cost, absorption cost, cost + markup, product costs + period costs, etc..

Chapter 21: Transfer Pricing for Products 237

   i. The implementation of a cost-based transfer pricing system may involve more upper management arbitration than the other transfer pricing bases because of potential for pivotal conflict between divisions in defining "cost."

 b. A transfer based on market price may require only brief arbitration by upper management.

   i. A market-based price requires the existence of an easily parallel external market price for the internally transferred good or service.

   ii. If the good or service is unique, no outside market will exist. A negotiated price is tempting from the outlook of asserting subunit independence. A price that is negotiated between two divisions may be similar to market price but accounts for features of the internal transfer (such as savings on freight, selling costs, administration, etc..).

6. If a company can't arrive at a single transfer pricing base that will adequately provide encouragement for both the buying and selling division to enter into a transaction, management can use a dual pricing agreement.

 a. A dual pricing system will credit the transfer to the selling division at a different price than it charges the buying division.

   i. For example, the selling division may be credited for the transfer at market price, while the buying division is charged at full cost.

   ii. This creates artificial profits while it supports the incentives of the buying and selling division with overall organizational goals.

   iii. The biggest risk of such an arrangement is that it will encourage intra-organizational transfers that should not take place from an overall organizational perspective. The benefits of a dual pricing system are presented on page 45.

 b. In choosing between alternative transfer pricing arrangements, the four desirable characteristics listed on page 45 should be remembered. An apropos transfer pricing system maintains subunit autonomy and promotes goal congruence.

7. Transfer pricing for services is related to cost allocation schemes discussed in Chapter 6. Alternative transfer pricing systems will affect the type and quantity of services that are offered. Effective cost allocation schemes can provide the same results.

 a. Choosing between a cost allocation scheme and a transfer pricing system depends on the type of responsibility center established for the service-provider.

   i. If the service-provider is considered a profit or investment center, a transfer pricing system may be more suitable than cost allocations, definitely if the service center also provides services to external parties.

   ii. If the service-provider is a cost center, a cost allocation system can be just as effective as a transfer pricing system in accomplishing organizational objectives. Guidelines for setting a transfer price for services are presented in Exhibit 21-13.

 b. Advantages gained for transfer prices for services are discussed in Exhibit 21-14.

8. Multinational organizations have additional factors to consider in transfer pricing. The level of transfer prices can affect overall organizational profitability directly through taxes, tariffs, and exchange rates and

238   Chapter 21: Transfer Pricing for Products

indirectly by affecting the competitive position of foreign and domestic operations.

    a.   Multinational organizations need to consider both direct and indirect costs in setting transfer prices, as well as the motivational factors that bear on any intra-organizational transfer. These factors are all presented in Exhibit 21-15.

    b.   Details of transfer pricing systems are complex. The key objective is to achieve overall organizational goals and maintain subunit independence. The transfer price accomplishes this objective by providing a financial incentive to subunit managers to engage in intra-organizational transfers that are in their own best interests and the best interests of the organization.

SELF TEST

TRUE/FALSE

1.   T F

Three bases for transfer prices are market price, negotiated price, and cost.

2.   T F

Transfer pricing systems are also known as charge-back systems.

3.   T F

Promoting goal congruence is a primary objective of transfer pricing systems.

4.   T F

The maximum price of an intra-company transfer should never exceed the costs of the selling division.

5.   T F

A transfer pricing system can reduce subunit autonomy.

6.   T F

Transfer prices for services should always be based on cost.

7.   T F

Performance-based incentives can promote dysfunctional behavior in internal transfers of goods and services.

8.   T F

For external reporting, internal transfers should be valued at cost.

9.   T F

As the price of an internal transfer rises, so do total corporate profits.

10.   T F

A dual pricing system means that part of the goods are transferred at one price and part are transferred at another price.

11.   T F

Responsibility accounting directs the flow of information from the top level of the organization downward.

Chapter 21: Transfer Pricing for Products 239

12. T F

    If a firm is growing very rapidly, it should utilize a very centralized structure.

13. T F

    Responsibility centers are used to control decentralized organizations.

14. T F

    Decentrally-organized companies are likely to be large relative to centrally-organized companies.

MULTIPLE CHOICE

1. A transfer price that reflects an arms-length transaction is

    a. market price.
    b. full cost.
    c. negotiated price.
    d. a dual price.

2. A reporting system in which a cost is charged to the base level of management that can bear accountability for it is:

    a. Centralization
    b. Management by exception
    c. Variance analysis
    d. Responsibility accounting

3. A cost-based transfer could be at

    a. variable cost.
    b. standard full cost.
    c. full cost + a markup to cover period costs.
    d. any of the above.

4. Which of the following is not a problem in a market-based transfer price?

    a. There may be no external market for some goods transferred internally.
    b. Market price does not reflect possible cost savings on internal transfers.
    c. Market price is easily manipulated by division managers.
    d. Short-run and long-run market price can be substantially different.

5. Whether or not the selling division is operating at capacity will affect the level of

    a. opportunity costs in the buying division.
    b. opportunity costs in the selling division.
    c. fixed production costs.
    d. the maximum transfer price.

6. The minimum transfer price would not be affected by

    a. variable production costs.
    b. variable selling costs.
    c. any opportunity costs.
    d. fixed production costs.

Chapter 21: Transfer Pricing for Products

7. A buying division should acquire inputs from an internal selling division when

   a. the buying division has no idle capacity.
   b. the selling division is selling its output for a price that exceeds the price the buying division is paying for its input.
   c. the best price the buying division can obtain from an outside supplier exceeds the internal costs of production (including opportunity costs).
   d. the selling division has no idle capacity.

8. From the perspective of the buying and selling division, an internal transfer will take place when

   a. managers of both the buying and selling division are motivated to engage in the transaction.
   b. the manager of the buying division is motivated to engage in the transaction.
   c. the corporate president encourages the transaction.
   d. the transaction is in the best interest of the overall organization.

9. From the viewpoint of top management, an internal transaction should take place when

   a. managers of the buying and selling division are motivated to engage in the transaction.
   b. both the buying and selling division would be better off if there is an internal transaction.
   c. the transaction is in the best interest of the overall organization.
   d. corporate profits would not be lowered by the internal transaction.

10. Given that an internal transfer is going to take place, the transfer price level will not affect

    a. overall corporate profits.
    b. selling division profits.
    c. buying division profits.
    d. the performance evaluation of the buying and selling divisions.

11. In setting transfer prices, multinational corporations need to consider external factors such as the affect of the transfer price on

    a. goal congruence.
    b. corporate taxes.
    c. motivation level of managers.
    d. performance evaluation.

12. A transfer price between two cost centers is likely to be set at

    a. market price.
    b. a negotiated price.
    c. cost.
    d. arbitrated market price.

13. When top managers evaluate division managers on a comparative basis, division managers will evaluate the effect of alternative transfer prices on

    a. their division's performance measures.
    b. their division and the other transacting division's performance measures.
    c. overall corporate profits.
    d. overall corporate goals.

Chapter 21: Transfer Pricing for Products 241

14. If the relevant production costs in the selling division exceed the price at which the buying division can obtain the good from an outside supplier,

    a. the transfer price should be market price.
    b. corporate management would prefer that an internal transfer be priced at cost.
    c. corporate profits will decline if the two divisions transact.
    d. the profit of both divisions must fall if the two divisions transact.

15. Dual based transfer pricing

    a. encourages external transactions.
    b. reduces conflict between buying and selling divisions.
    c. increases competition between organizational subunits.
    d. all of the above.

16. Using a transfer price to allocate the costs of a service department may

    a. stimulate more interaction between providers and consumers of services.
    b. reduce excessive usage of service departments.
    c. forces users to perform cost/benefit analysis in contracting for services.
    d. all of the above.

17. The difference between the internal costs to produce a good and the external cost to purchase the good represents

    a. the potential increase in profit to the overall corporation from an internal transaction.
    b. the potential negotiating range for a buying and selling division.
    c. the motivation to engage in an internal transaction.
    d. all of the above.

18. Which of the following is an example of an opportunity cost that may be incurred by a selling division to engage in an internal transaction?

    a. variable production costs.
    b. fixed production costs.
    c. contribution margin on external sales that is sacrificed to accommodate the internal transaction.
    d. the gross margin that is lost on external sales to accommodate the internal transaction.

19. A transfer price should be set at a level that

    a. optimally allocates organizational resources.
    b. motivates divisional managers to be efficient.
    c. promotes goal congruence.
    d. all of the above.

20. When a buying division acquires goods in an internal transfer, it records the acquisition by

    a. debiting intracompany transfers.
    b. crediting intracompany sales.
    c. debiting inventory.
    d. debiting intracompany Cost of Goods Sold.

21. Division A offers to sell a certain product to Division B for $30/unit. Division B can acquire the same part from an outside vendor for $27. If Division B acquires the part from the outside supplier, what will be the effect on overall corporate profits?

    a. they will decline by $3/unit
    b. they will rise by $3/unit
    c. they will rise by $30/unit
    d. the effect cannot be determined from this information

Chapter 21: Transfer Pricing for Products

22. When the managers of two investment centers are negotiating transfer price, which of the following would probably have the least affect on the transfer price that is eventually set?

    a. the overall goals of the organization
    b. the presence of idle capacity in the selling division
    c. the performance evaluation measures
    d. the market price of the good

23. A reporting system in which a cost is charged to the base level of management that can bear accountability for it is:

    a. Centralization
    b. Management by exception
    c. Variance analysis
    d. Responsibility accounting

24. One essential difference between an investment center and a profit center is that:

    a. Profit centers control only revenues
    b. Investment centers control the purchase of assets
    c. Investment centers operate in centralized firms
    d. There is no dissimilarity

25. One detriment of decentralization is that:

    a. Top management is relieved of routine decision-making
    b. There may be duplication of efforts
    c. Employee morale is encouraged.
    d. Decision making is often more effective

26. A customary transfer price is:
    a. Negotiated price
    b. Full cost
    c. Cost plus markup
    d. All of the above

27. The goal of a transfer pricing system should be to:

    a. a. maximize the transfer price
    b. minimize the transfer price
    c. maintain goal congruence between the divisions and the entire firm
    d. none of the above

28. Which of the following types of transfer prices do not inspire the selling division to be proficient?

    a. transfer prices built upon market prices
    b. transfer prices built upon actual costs
    c. transfer prices built upon standard costs
    d. transfer prices built upon standard costs plus a markup for profit

29. Decentralization happens when:

    a. the firm's operations are situated over a large geographic area to reduce risk
    b. authority for important decisions is entrusted to lower segments of the organization
    c. important decisions are made at the upper levels and the lower levels of the organization are accountable for executing the decisions
    d. none of the above

Chapter 21: Transfer Pricing for Products   243

30. Goal congruence alludes to:

    a. the goals of the firm being compatible with the goals of its customers
    b. the goals of the suppliers being compatible with the goals of the firm
    c. the goals of the individual investment centers being compatible with the goals of the firm
    d. none of the above

31. One major difference between an investment center and a profit center is that

    a. investment centers control the purchase of assets.
    b. investment centers operate in centralized firms.
    c. profit centers operate in decentralized firms.
    d. profit centers control only revenues.

32. Which of the following is not a cost that is typically attributed to decentralization?

    a. the cost of poor decisions
    b. the cost of training lower level managers
    c. the cost of a sophisticated reporting system
    d. the cost of a slow response to a changing environment

33. The focus of responsibility accounting is on

    a. operating divisions.
    b. people.
    c. product costing.
    d. organizational departments.

34. Depreciation expense would not be found in a pure

    a. cost center.
    b. revenue center.
    c. profit center.
    d. investment center.

35. Which of the responsibility centers is responsible for the most monetary objects?

    a. investment center
    b. revenue center
    c. profit center
    d. cost center

QUESTIONS AND PROBLEMS

1. Describe the feasible region for a transfer price between two organizational units?

2. What are the possible bases that can be used to set a transfer price?

Chapter 21: Transfer Pricing for Products

3. What special problems do multinational companies have in setting transfer prices?

4. How do performance evaluation measures affect a division manager's incentives to engage in internal transactions?

Use the following information for questions 5 - 10:

S Division of Mega Corp. produces and sells an electronic motor. B Division of Mega Corp. consumes 10,000 electric motors/year of the type made by S Division in its production of electric razors. Currently, B division purchases the electric motor from an outside supplier for $7/unit. S Division has the capability to produce 30,000 motors/year. Presently, it is only producing and selling 15,000 units (that sell at an average price of $8/unit). The cost structure of S Division follows:
```
DM........................$1
DL........................ 2
Variable factory overhead  1
Fixed factory overhead.... 3 ( a total of $45,000/yr.)
Selling and Administrative 1 (all fixed - total $15,000/yr.)
```

5. What is the price range that will constrain the negotiations of the autonomous managers of A and B Division in a possible internal transfer of the motor?

6. How will Mega Corp.'s net income be affected if A and B division agree to an internal transfer of 10,000 electric motors whereby A and B will split the total company savings evenly? The transfer price will be how much?

7. If the transfer price is set at $6, how will the profits in each division be affected?

Chapter 21: Transfer Pricing for Products 245

8. Assuming that top management will not intervene, can we be 100% confident that the two divisions will mutually agree to a transfer price, and transfer 10,000 electric motors internally? Explain.

9. Now, assume that S Division is currently producing and selling 30,000 units to external buyers at $8/unit. What is the feasible range for a transfer price?

10. Continue with the assumption in 9. above: S Division is currently selling 30,000 units at $8 to external buyers. If these two divisions agree to an internal transfer, what will be the affect on Mega Corp.'s profits?

COMMUNICATION PROJECT

With members of your in class group, go to a local chain store such as a pizza restaurant. Ask the manager what price his store pays for supplies received from the main headquarters. These are transfer prices. Write up a brief report for your group summarizing your findings. In writing up your report, reach a consensus on what you found out and what you say in the report.

SELF TEST SOLUTIONS

TRUE/FALSE

1. T	3. T	5. T	7. T	9. F	11. T	13. T
2. T	4. F	6. F	8. T	10. F	12. F	14. T

MULTIPLE CHOICE

1. A	6. D	11. B	16. D	21. A	26. D	31. A
2. D	7. C	12. B	17. C	22. B	27. C	32. D
3. D	8. A	13. C	18. D	23. D	28. B	33. D
4. C	9. C	14. B	19. C	24. B	29. B	34. B
5. B	10. A	15. D	20. D	25. B	30. C	35. C

QUESTIONS AND PROBLEMS

1. The feasible region is bounded on the lower side by the incremental costs that the selling division would incur to accommodate an order from the buying division. Such incremental costs would include any opportunity costs. The feasible region is bounded on the top side by the lowest price that the buying division can obtain from an outside vendor.

2. The transfer price can be based on some definition of cost, market price, negotiated price, or on a combination of these bases. A combination of bases is referred to as a dual or hybrid transfer pricing system.

3. Transfers within multinational firms have all of the same problems of domestic transfers. The transfer price has to be consistent with overall organizational goals, motivate subunit managers, and to the extent possible, preserve their autonomy. In addition, multinational firms need to consider the impact of transfer prices on transaction costs such as taxes, tariffs, currency exchanges, and the influence of transfer prices on the competitive position of local units.

4. Performance evaluation measures play a major role in influencing the behavior of subunit managers in internal transfers. If an internal transfer will enhance a manager's performance evaluation, and increase his rewards he will be interested in an internal transfer. Otherwise, he will not. Individual subunit managers pay close attention to the affect of any action on their performance evaluation measures.

5. The top side of the negotiation range is determined by what the buying division is presently paying to an outside supplier. In this case, the top side of the range is $7/unit. The bottom side of the range is the sum of all incremental costs that the selling division would incur in accepting the business of the buying division. The incremental costs in this instance include the variable factory overhead, direct labor, and direct materials. The total of these costs is $4/unit. Therefore the price range would be $4 to $7.

6. Mega Corp.'s net income (before taxes) would rise by $30,000. This is simply the difference between the price that Mega Corp. would pay to an outside vendor, $7, versus the costs it would incur to produce the motor, $4, multiplied by the size of the order which is 10,000 units. The transfer price will be ($7-$4)/2 = $1.50 + 4 = $5.50 per unit.

7. If the negotiated price is $6, the selling division will experience a $20,000 increase in profits (10,000 * ($6-$4)), and the buying division will experience a $10,000 increase in profits (10,000 * ($7-$6)).

8. No, we can't be 100% confident that they will agree on a transfer price. Even though there is $30,000 of profits available to split between the two divisions, without understanding the performance evaluation measures, and the incentives of each manager, we can only speculate as to whether they will arrive at an agreement.

9. There is no feasible region. The selling division would be unwilling to accept any price below $8 (the $8 is composed of the variable costs, $4, and a $4 opportunity cost which represents the lost contribution margin on existing sales), and the buying division would be unwilling to pay any more than $7.

10. Total corporate profits would decline by $10,000.

CHAPTER 22
MEASURING ORGANIZATIONAL PERFORMANCE

CHAPTER OVERVIEW

A general theme throughout the text is that accounting information plays a major role in organizational planning and control. Two aspects of this role are to describe (in concrete terms such as dollars) what organizational performance should be and to measure actual performance. Another aspect of this role is to compare planned and actual performance. The discussion in Chapter 22 presents additional accounting and non-accounting techniques for measuring organizational and managerial performance and criteria for evaluating performance.

Managers recognize that solid links exist between individual performance measurement and evaluation, individual performance compensation, and organizational performance. Understanding these bonds is very important. In Chapter 22, techniques to measure the performance of organization segments are presented. These organizational performance measures are also used as measures of managerial performance and aid in determining managerial compensation. By associating managerial compensation with these measures, the personal financial goals of the managers and the organizational goals are closely affiliated.

While companies continue to use financial measures for performance evaluation, other nonfinancial measures are also being used. Preferably these measures are quantifiable. Financial measures focus on past events. Nonfinancial measures focus on a firm's performance activity which leads to increased stockholder wealth. Also they measure activity directly which leads to future cash flows. The list of nonfinancial performance measures (or NFPM) can be quite large so the ones used should be limited to the measures that are most useful to managers.

CHAPTER STUDY GUIDE

1. Location of decision makers within an organization leads to decision making being "centralized" or "decentralized."

    a. The authority to make decisions is centralized in an organization when most decisions are made by top management.

    b. When the authority to make decisions is passed down to lower level managers, the organization is described as decentralized.

        i. Organizations can fall anywhere on a continuum from excessively centralized to highly decentralized. Most of chapter 22 is dedicated to the discussion of accounting techniques that can be used to control decentrally-structured organizations.

        ii. When managers are given the authority to make decisions, they become accountable or responsible for making decisions that are consistent with the overall goals of the organization.

        iii. Their compensation will be dependent on how the consequences of their decisions match organizational goals.

Chapter 22: Transfer Pricing for Products

      iv. This dependence provides a strong incentive to make decisions that are in the best interest of the organization.

  c. With the recognition of world wide competition, firms that operate in a global economy realize they need to improve product quality. Thus, new measures of performance must be adopted (Appendix, Exhibit 22-17).

  d. A key factor in any performance evaluation system is that <u>timely</u> reporting be used. Managers must always be aware of how they are doing. They must know what measures are being used for evaluation purposes. If these measures are budgets, hopefully the managers participated in the budget setting process.

2. Two techniques have emerged to measure investment center performance: residual income (RI) measures and return on investment measures (ROI).

  a. ROI is a ratio of income to the assets that were employed to generate the income.

      i. In practice, different companies utilize different definitions of income and assets. The important considerations in selecting an income and asset measure are found in Exhibit 22-4.

      ii. The ROI measure suffers from the same problem as other accounting information -it is easily manipulated.

      iii. Another problem with the ROI measure is that it can induce subordinate managers to reject investment opportunities that top managers would prefer the organization accept. This situation is present in the example that begins on page 41 of your text.

  b. The RI measure is similar to the ROI measure but a major difference between the two measures is that ROI is a percentage number and RI is a dollar number.

      i. RI is equal to income minus a charge for the assets used to generate the income. RI can be a better measure compared with ROI because it overcomes the suboptimal investment problem. More specific limitations of RI and ROI are discussed in your text beginning on page 39.

3. The use of one performance measure for each type of responsibility center is desirable; however, the performance measures used are imperfect surrogates for the organization's goals.

  a. In actuality, the performance measures can influence managers to take actions that are contrary to organizational goals.

      i. The use of multiple performance evaluation measures (both quantitative and qualitative) help moderate the dysfunctional aspects of each single measure.

      ii. For example, a firm might use ROI and a qualitative measure such as percent of deliveries on time or throughput.

      iii. Global competition has made American firms more aware of product quality. Realizing the cost of quality requires recognition of these costs. See Exhibit 22-15 for a breakdown of these costs.

         (1) These quality costs include costs to prevent product failures: prevention and appraisal costs.

         (2) **Failure costs** including **internal** and **external failure** costs.

         (3) Failure costs are usually much higher than prevention costs.

      See Exhibit 22-12 and 22-17 for other measures.

Chapter 22: Transfer Pricing for Products

4. Measures to evaluate managerial performance should be selected based on the extent to which they "measure" a subordinate manager's contribution to the achievement of organizational goals.

    a. Having chosen specific measures, performance-based rewards are attached to various levels of performance (as measured), and because of the performance rewards, the performance measure becomes the important measure of goal attainment for the subordinate manager.

    b. Subordinate managers can receive the performance rewards by making and executing decisions that move the organization toward goal achievement, or by manipulating the performance measure. Either set of actions may be effective for the subordinate manager, but only the former actions are desired by upper level management.

5. Accounting performance measures based on accrual accounting concepts are more easily manipulated than cash flow information. For this reason (and because cash flow data provides better information on liquidity), cash-based performance measures are becoming more widely utilized. One such measure is the Statement of Cash Flows. This measure was first introduced in a prior chapter with the discussion of the cash budget and the capital budget.

6. Because cash flows can also be manipulated to some extent, some organizations are moving toward nonfinancial performance measures. One popular measure is throughput.

    a. **Throughput** is a measure of the number of units(of products or services) that are produced and sold during a period. Many organizations are also turning to qualitative measures of performance and are placing an emphasis on multiple measures of performance.

    b. Throughput time is the time required to turn materials into products. The use of a **flexible manufacturing system**(FMS) can reduce this time by grouping two or more automated machines in a **cell**. The machines are controlled by a computer. Setup changes for different orders can be easily be accomplished with computer-integrated manufacturing(CIM) systems.

    c. Consequently employees in firms using FMS must be better educated and able to read manuals and learn new techniques.

    d. Other nonfinancial performance measures (or NFPMs) are discussed in Chapter 22 and the APPENDIX. The NFPMs could be categorized into the follows factors:

        (1) product or service quality
        (2) customer satisfaction
        (3) manufacturing efficiency
        (4) technical excellence
        (5) rapid response to market changes

        i. Acceptable performance levels must be established to compare actual results against.

        ii. The number of performance measures should be limited to reduce evaluation and data collection time.
        iii. NFPMs will vary depending on the management level reported to.
        iv. See the APPENDIX and Exhibit 22-17 for further discussion activity cost drivers for NFPMs.

7. The technical aspects of this chapter are very simple. The conceptual aspects are more complex and deserve special consideration. In particular, you are encouraged to carefully consider the interactions of organizational goals, performance measures, performance-based compensation, and actual performance.

Chapter 22: Transfer Pricing for Products

SELF TEST

TRUE/FALSE

1. T F

    Centrally-structured organizations are likely to have more decision makers than decentrally-structured organizations.

2. T F

    Multiple performance measures can typically provide better control than single performance evaluation measures.

3. T F

    ROI is a performance measure that is used in profit centers.

4. T F

    An advantage of a throughput performance measure over financial performance measures is that it is more difficult to manipulate.

5. T F

    Variance analysis would be an appropriate tool to evaluate the performance of a cost center.

6. T F

    ROI can be influenced by sales price, sales volume, sales mix, expenses, and capital asset acquisitions and dispositions.

7. T F

    In ROI, the operating income includes the deductions for interest expense and income taxes.

8. T F

    ROI is improved by increasing sales revenue.

9. T F

    Residual income eliminates false signals generated by using a rate of return and failing to consider dollar amounts.

10. T F

    Distortions that may result when a manager's objectives conflict with organizational objectives are eliminated with the use of residual income.

11. T F

    Decision making takes place at all levels of management in a decentralized organization.

12. T F

    Responsibility accounting centers on the idea that an organization is a group of individuals working toward common goals.

13. T F

    The principle of controllability is less important to the internal reporting of a centralized firm than to a decentralized one.

Chapter 22: Transfer Pricing for Products

MULTIPLE CHOICE

1. If all other factors remain constant, which of the following will not increase ROI?

    a. Decreasing sales costs.
    b. Decreasing fixed costs.
    c. Decreasing operating assets.
    d. Decreasing variable costs.

2. The operating margin percentage is equal to:

    a. operating income divided by sales
    b. average operating assets divided by sales
    c. sales divided by operating income
    d. sales divided by average operating assets

3. A preferred definition of "income" in an ROI computation would be

    a. after-tax operating income.
    b. pre-tax operating income.
    c. after-tax segment income.
    d. pre-tax segment income.

4. The manager of a division who is evaluated solely on an ROI measure will accept a new project which

    a. has an ROI that exceeds the current corporate ROI.
    b. has an ROI that exceeds the current corporate cost of capital.
    c. has an ROI that exceeds the current divisional ROI.
    d. has an ROI that is positive.

5. Which of the following would cause a division's ROI to decline?

    a. expenses decline
    b. the asset base increases
    c. sales volume increases
    d. the sales price increases

6. Asset turnover is used to compute ROI. It is a ratio of

    a. assets/income.
    b. income/assets.
    c. sales/assets.
    d. sales/income.

7. The Statement of Cash Flows provides information about cash flows generated from

    a. investment activities.
    b. operations.
    c. financing activities.
    d. all of the above.

8. Which of the following is not a qualitative performance measure?

    a. acceptance of increased responsibility
    b. increased job skills
    c. new product features
    d. hours of professional education

9. Which of the following is not a desirable characteristic in performance evaluation measures?

    a. They should reflect organizational goals.
    b. They must be specific and understandable.
    c. They must be based on accounting information.
    d. They must promote harmony between organizational subunits.

Chapter 22: Transfer Pricing for Products

10. If management utilizes management-by-exception concepts,

    a. all variances will be investigated.
    b. all unfavorable variances will be investigated.
    c. all favorable and unfavorable variances will be investigated.
    d. all material variances will be investigated.

11. A manager of a subunit of an organization should be evaluated on

    a. all costs and revenues of the subunit.
    b. all direct costs and revenues of the subunit.
    c. all costs and revenues under the control of the manager.
    d. all costs and revenues that can be traced to the subunit.

12. The margin ratio used in the computation of ROI is a measure of

    a. income/sales.
    b. assets/sales.
    c. income/assets.
    d. sales/income.

13. All other factors equal, an increase in expenses would

    a. increase the margin ratio.
    b. decrease the turnover ratio.
    c. increase the turnover ratio.
    d. decrease the margin ratio.

14. A company uses a target rate of return of 14% to evaluate new investment opportunities. At the present time, C Division has a 17% ROI and the entire corporation has a 16% ROI. The corporate cost of capital is 13%. If the manager of C Division is evaluated on the basis of residual income, he would accept any project with an ROI in excess of

    a. 13%
    b. 14%
    c. 16%
    d. 17%.

15. Refer to the preceding problem. If the manager of C Division is evaluated on the basis of ROI, he will accept any project with an ROI in excess of

    a. 13%.
    b. 14%.
    c. 16%.
    d. 17%.

16. Comparisons between multinational units should be based on

    a. income.
    b. ROI.
    c. sales.
    d. nonfinancial measures of performance.

17. Throughput can be increased by

    a. increasing productive capacity.
    b. decreasing yield.
    c. decreasing productive processing time.
    d. all of the above.

18. The goal of synchronous management is to

    a. increase revenue.
    b. increase throughput and decrease inventory and expenses.
    c. provide job enrichment.
    d. promote goal congruence.

Chapter 22: Transfer Pricing for Products   253

19. Suboptimization is a problem created by

    a. incongruent goals.
    b. poor profitability.
    c. lack of cost containment.
    d. over investment.

20. If a manager is evaluated based on RI, she will invest in additional assets that

    a. increase her divisions's ROI.
    b. increase her division's residual income.
    c. increase her division's net income.
    d. increase the corporate ROI.

21. Company operates a factory that makes components for other ABC factories to assemble. The factory could be treated as

    a. cost center.
    b. an artificial profit center.
    c. either a or b.
    d. none of the above.

22. A responsibility center is

    a. any department.
    b. any manager.
    c. any area of activity for which a manager is responsible.
    d. only large departments.

23. A company that has very few profit or investment centers is probably

    a. centralized.
    b. decentralized.
    c. using only artificial profit centers.
    d. allocating indirect costs.

24. number of units that can be produced in a given period of time is called:

    a. throughput
    b. cycle time
    c. turnover
    d. efficiency
    e. manufacturing cycle efficiency

25. Types of responsibility centers include all of the following except:

    a. profit center
    b. contribution center
    c. investment center
    d. cost center

26. Cost centers can best be evaluated using:

    a. standard variable costing income statements
    b. budgets and standard costs
    c. return on investment
    d. residual income

27. The time it takes to produce one unit of product is called:

    a. throughput time
    b. delivery time
    c. manufacturing cycle time
    d. turnover
    e. manufacturing cycle efficiency

Chapter 22: Transfer Pricing for Products

QUESTIONS AND PROBLEMS

1. Why are decentrally-structured companies able to respond to changes in local conditions more rapidly than centrally-structured companies?

2. Why should managers be evaluated on the basis of multiple performance measures rather than a single performance measure?

3. Why is a throughput measurement potentially superior to many financial performance measures?

4. How are responsibility accounting and decentralization related?

5. How is the Statement of Cash Flows superior to many performance measures which rely on accounting accruals?

Use the following information for the next four questions:

XYZ Corp. is comprised of 5 autonomous operating divisions. Operations of Division A are summarized below:
```
        Assets available for use ..................$1,500,000
        Segment income............................    300,000
        Sales.....................................  4,000,000
        Corporate target rate of return............       16%
```

6. Compute the present ROI in Division A.

7. Compute the residual income in Division A.

Chapter 22: Transfer Pricing for Products

8. The manager of Division A is presently considering an investment in a new project. The new project promises to increase division sales by $1,000,000 and division net segment income by $100,000. If the manager of Division A is evaluated by ROI alone, what is the maximum amount he would spend to acquire the new project?

9. Refer to question 8. What is the maximum that the manager of Division A would spend for the new project if he is evaluated solely on the basis of RI?

10. Some information for the 1995 operations of Division T of Taga Corp. is listed below:

    ROI........................15%
    Profit margin..............10%
    Segment income............ $200,000

    If ROI is based on "assets available for use," what level of assets were available for 1995?

COMMUNICATION PROJECT

Break up into groups of two. You list the advantages of using ROI over RI in performance measurements of subunit managers of a company. Your counterpart of the group is to repeat what you said regarding the advantages of ROI vs. RI. The other person should tell you what RI overcomes as far as ROI is concerned. You are to state if you agree.

SELF TEST SOLUTIONS

TRUE/FALSE

1. F	3. F	5. T	7. F	9. T	11. T	13. F
2. T	4. T	6. T	8. F	10. T	12. T	

MULTIPLE CHOICE

1. A	6. D	11. C	16. D	21. B	26. B
2. A	7. D	12. A	17. A	22. C	
3. D	8. D	13. A	18. B	23. A	
4. C	9. C	14. D	19. A	24. A	
5. B	10. D	15. B	20. B	25. B	

QUESTIONS AND PROBLEMS

1. One of the major advantages of decentralization is that the authority to make decisions is pushed down to the lowest possible level in the organizations. This means that the people who are familiar with local conditions also make

local decisions. Response times are faster in decentrally-structured firms because the time required for information to be channeled up through the organizational hierarchy is saved.

2. Multiple performance measures are preferred because it reduces the possibility that managers will manipulate the performance measure. Also, it is difficult for all organizational goals and objectives to be captured in one performance measure.

3. Throughput measures are desirable because they can be excellent proxies for operational goals of organizations. Another advantage of throughput measures is that they are difficult to manipulate relative to accounting numbers.

4. Decentralization describes the authority structure in an organization. Top level managers in organizations that are decentralized need to devise ways to control operations. Responsibility accounting is a control mechanism which is frequently utilized in decentralized organizations.

5. The Statement of Cash Flows is potentially superior to many other financial performance measures because it is free of the accounting accruals which may be subject to managerial manipulation. An added advantage of the Statement of Cash Flows is that it not only measures profitability, but it measures liquidity as well.

6. The simplest way to compute the ROI is to divide income by assets: $300,000/$1,500,000 = 20\%$.

7. The RI is computed by subtracting a required target return from segment income: $300,000 - (.18 * \$1,500,000) = \$30,000$

8. The maximum amount that the manager would be willing to spend is the amount that would leave his existing ROI unchanged. He would be unwilling to spend an amount that would decrease his ROI. Therefore the maximum amount is found by solving the following equation (where X represents the maximum purchase price): $.20 = \$100,000/X$

   Solving for X, we find that the manager would spend no more than $500,000 to purchase the project.

9. If the manager is evaluated on the basis of RI, he would not want to have his current RI reduced. Therefore, the new project would need to generate at least an RI of 0. So we solve the following equation (where X is the maximum purchase price): $\$100,000 - (X * .18) = 0$

   Solving for X, we find that the manager would be willing to spend no more than $555,556 to purchase the new project.

10. Use the formula: ROI = Profit margin * Asset turnover
    $.15 = .10 *$ Asset turnover
    $1.5 =$ Asset turnover

    Next, use the profit margin formula to solve for sales:
    Profit margin = income/sales
    $.10 = 200,000/\text{sales}$
    $\$2,000,000 = \text{sales}$

    Now use the turnover ratio to solve for assets:
    Asset turnover = sales/assets
    $1.5 = \$2,000,000/\text{assets}$
    $\$1,333,333 =$ assets available for use

CHAPTER 23

REWARDING PERFORMANCE

CHAPTER OVERVIEW

Compensation plans should tie together organizational goals, performance measurements, and employee rewards. Organization goals are set by the board of directors and top management. They establish **compensation strategy** for the firm that shows how it fits into the company goals.

The strategy is differentiated into 3 categories: 1) top management; 2) middle managers; and 3) all other employees of the company. Top managers receive a salary plus a reward for achieving or exceeding target objectives. Middle managers receive a salary plus incentives for exceeding more narrow objectives. The other worker group receives a salary or hourly pay.

Historically, most compensation plans have been based on individual performance and short-run profits. Firms are moving toward group success. Non-financial performance measures are considered and long-run satisfaction methods are being used. The **periodic pay plan** is commonly used for hourly employees but provides little incentive for motivating employees to increase their performance. Another plan commonly used for non-management personnel is the **piece rate** pay plan which links work accomplished with employee rewards.

Compensation is also affected by the tax system. Pay is normally fully taxable to the employee. Fringe benefits may be tax-exempt to employees but fully deductible for the employer. Still other incentive compensation may be tax deferred.

Ethically, compensation must consider the change in the power structure of the corporate environment. Professional managers are replacing the traditionaly owner/management system. Stock ownership is dispersed among a larger segment of the population rather than ownership being concentrated among a limited number of people. Institutional investors (such as mutual funds and pension plans) are acquiring large blocks of stock but demonstrate little concern about management compensation policies in their investments. Excessive top management pay can result from a lack of interest by owners and can be counter-productive to the firm and the stockholders.

CHAPTER STUDY GUIDE

1. Compensation packages are based on strategic goals and critical factors that affect operational targets of a near term focus.

    a. Periodic compensation provides no incentive for employees to excel beyond the basic company expectations. These are typically salaried or hourly wage earners often supported by a union.

    b. Middle managers usually have a salary base plus incentive (such as a **bonus**) for segment performance above a specified targeted objective (often the objective is measured in financial terms).

Chapter 23: Rewarding Performance

      c.   Top management receives a salary plus incentives for company performance that exceeds specific financial accounting-related measures.

2. Pay for performance plans encourage employees to work better and lower overall costs of operation. The company's operational targets and compensation plans must be correlated.

    a. The long-run perception that will maximize stockholder wealth should be affected by compensation plans. Employee stock option plans that are a part of compensation should encourage long-run wealth maximization for the stockholders.

    b. Group and Individual Benefits

        i. Automation of operations reduces hands-on production. Production quality and performance is enhanced with **TQM** and quality circles. Small group incentives encourage cooperation. Results-based evaluations provide performance evaluations.

    c. Management ownership is reduced as professional managers evolve. Their interests may differ from the owners' interests regarding the use of a firms's resources.

3. Performance measures should be used that link with the operational plan. Performance measures should be based on output that is controllable by the manager.

    a. For basic level workers, performance measures should be **specific** and have a short-run focus.

    b. For higher level employees, the measures should be controllable by the person over a longer time frame.

    c. Performance compensation should be in accordance with the individual's hierarchial level.

    d. **Contingent pay** provides the employee with a base salary plus additional pay (or other benefits) if the base is exceeded.

    e. Overall long-term company performance should be encouraged. **Profit sharing** promotes this occurrence. **Stock options** and **stock appreciation rights** encourage long-term performance improvement in the company.

4. Managerial performance plans often proved compensation dependent on their results (for middle management) and the company's financial performance (for top-level management).

    a. Rewards to management should be based on monetary and nonmonetary measures for short-term and long-term factors.

5. Tax treatment of fringe benefits are often not taxed until later (which is called **tax deferred**) and some benefits are **tax exempt**. A summary of the different types of pay plans is shown in EXHIBIT 23-6.

    a. **Cafeteria plans** allow the employee to choose the benefits desired with no taxes charged on these benefits.

    b. Deferred compensation received by the employee is non-taxable when earned and the earnings in the plan are tax deferred until the employee receives payments from the plan.

Chapter 23: Rewarding Performance

SELF TEST

TRUE/FALSE

1. T F

   Compensation practices should be the same for top executives and middle managers.

2. T F

   Compensation plans are comparable among companies in the same industry.

3. T F

   Performanc reward systems are the first step in setting up a business.

4. T F

   Performance rewards for first line workers are never based on performance.

5. T F

   Financial incentives are rewarded for performance that at least equals targeted objectives.

6. T F

   Defined performance measures need not be correlated with an organization's goals.

7. T F

   Firms operating in the global environment are seeking perfromance rewards to get workers to work together in the firm.

8. T F

   Managers in the U.S. have the highest average salary in the world.

9. T F

   The relationship between CEO pay and manufacturing employees pay has created no problem in employee loyalty to their employer.

MULTIPLE CHOICE

1. Performance incentives work best for which of the following groups:

   a. top level executives
   b. middle level managers
   c. production line or hourly employees
   d. a and b

2. Employee stock ownership is commonly encouraged for which employee groups:

   a. top-level management
   b. middle level management
   c. line workers
   d. salaried employees
   e. all of the above

Chapter 23: Rewarding Performance

3. Stock ownership in a corporation are encouraged with

    a. golden parachutes
    b. periodic compensation
    c. piece rate pay
    d. perks
    e. stock appreciation rights

4. Pay which is guarenteed every month is

    a. contingent pay
    b. employee stock ownership plan
    c. merit pay
    d. stock appreciation rights
    e. periodic compensation

5. All of the following are incentive pay options except

    a. merit pay
    b. piece rate
    c. profit sharing
    d. periodic compensation

6. The country that places the most emphasis on quality as a primary factor effecting executive compensation is

    a. Japan
    b. Canada
    c. Germany
    d. United States

7. Global competition has placed a significant emphasis on

    a. productivity
    b. ownership interest
    c. quantity of output
    d. quality of the product or service

8. The following pay plans focus on the long-term:

    a. monthly salary
    b. contingent pay
    c. health insurance
    d. ESOPS

9. Pay plans that create a low level of motivation are:

    a. hourly wages
    b. merit pay
    c. cafeterial plan
    d. piece rate

10. The pay plan that is highly linked to performance is:

    a. merit pay
    b. pensions
    c. contingent pay
    d. pensions

11. The pay plan that is clearly tied to company objectives is:

    a. profit sharing
    b. stock options
    c. ESOPS
    d. all of the above

12. Cafeterial plans are:

    a. employee tax deductible income.
    b. the best food in the company town.
    c. allow for a selection tax exempt fringe benefits.
    d. a specific insurance benefit that must be taken by the employee.

13. The most common type perk avialable from American corporations is:

    a. deferred compensation.
    b. employmemnt contracts.
    c. severance pay for execs.
    d. company car allowances.

QUESTIONS AND PROBLEMS

1. Should performance measures be correlated with an organization's goals? Why?

2. Why should worker age influence performance incentives?

3. Are there any disadvantages to group type incentive rewards?

4. What major trends in terms of management and ownership of corporations are occuring in the U.S. today?

5. Who are expatricate employees. What major factors must be regarded regarding their employment.

6. The golden parachute is a benefit given to displaced corporate officers. Comment on the positive and negative aspects of this practice.

COMMUNICATION PROJECT

In your class group, discuss how employee performance and rewards can be used in your university. Discuss what is the basis for salary and bonuses or perks in the university. Concentrate on the college you are majoring in. As a group, find out what basis is used to establish the pay and other rewards for the departments faculty and department heads. How does the system used in your school compare with for profit firms' approach to pay and rewards.

Chapter 23: Rewarding Performance

Be prepared to present in class your findings and discuss this over with your group members.

This project enables you to communicate with superiors issues that concern them but will expand your understanding of how the university setting works. Secondly you will develop confidence in presenting information you are familiar with to colleagues.

SELF TEST SOLUTIONS

TRUE/FALSE

1. F   3. F   5. T   7. T   9. F
2. F   4. F   6. F   8. T

MULTIPLE CHOICE

1. D   6. A   11. D
2. E   7. D   12. C
3. E   8. D   13. D
4. E   9. A
5. D   10. A

QUESTIONS AND PROBLEMS

1. Yes, the performance measu;res should be correlated with the firm's operational targets. Otherwise, workers may get incentive pay even though the organization's goals aren't being met.

2. Older employees are nearing retirement. Much younger employees have many years to work. Incentives for older employees should be based on factors that promote short term results. More recently employed employees should have incentives based on longer range impact on the firm.

3. Yes. As the group get large, some of the group can become free-loaders, people who take the benefits awarded the group but don't personally aid much value to the group.

4. Professional managers are taking over the reins of larger companies. Will these managers have the same stockholder interests that owners-managerrs do? Stock ownership in many firms is being widely dispered. Will these small company share owners have an intense interest in the daily operations of the firm? Institutional ownership of corporations is growing dramatically. Billions of dollars are flowing into the stock market from mutual funds and pension funds. These funds exert little influence in the operations of their investments.

5. Expatriates are employees of the parent company that are working in a foreign country. The differences in living standards and cost of living factors should be considered in the compensation. The tax differences between the home country and the host country should also be affected in the compensation package.

6. Golden parachutes free up the managers' time to devote to company interests in face of a takeover and financial protection that will keep them unbiased towards the suiter. Opponents to parachutes say it protects the ousted managers even if they mismanged the acquired company.